ON THE DORMITION OF MARY

ST VLADIMIR'S SEMINARY PRESS
Popular Patristics Series
Number 18

The Popular Patristics Series published by St Vladimir's Seminary Press provides readable and accurate translations of a wide range of early Christian literature to a wide audience—students of Christian history to lay Christians reading for spiritual benefit. Recognized scholars in their fields provide short but comprehensive and clear introductions to the material. The texts include classics of Christian literature, thematic volumes, collections of homilies, letters on spiritual counsel, and poetical works from a variety of geographical contexts and historical backgrounds. The mission of the series is to mine the riches of the early Church and to make these treasures available to all.

Series Editor
JOHN BEHR

On the Dormition of Mary

Early Patristic Homilies

Translation and Introduction by

BRIAN E. DALEY, S.J.

ST VLADIMIR'S SEMINARY PRESS
CRESTWOOD, NEW YORK

Library of Congress Cataloging-in-Publication Data

On the dormition of Mary: early patristic homilies / translated by Brian E. Daley.

    p.   cm.
   Includes index.
   ISBN 0–88141–177–9
   ISBN: 978–0-88141–177–5
   ISSN 1555–5755
   1. Mary, Blessed Virgin, Saint—Assumption—Sermons. 2. Orthodox Eastern
Church Sermons. 3. Sermons, Greek. I. Daley, Brian E.

BT608.A106 1997
232.91'4—dc21

97–36467
CIP

TRANSLATION COPYRIGHT © 1998
ST VLADIMIR'S SEMINARY PRESS
575 Scarsdale Rd., Crestwood, NY 10707
1-800-204-2665
www.svspress.com

ISBN 0–88141–177–9
ISBN 978–0–88141–177–5
ISSN 1555–5755

PRINTED IN THE UNITED STATES OF AMERICA

Contents

For my Orthodox Brothers and Sisters.

Sumens illud ave
Gabrielis ore
Funda nos in pace
Mutans Evae nomen.
(10th cent.)

INTRODUCTION

This collection brings together, in English translation, the earliest extant theological interpretations of the story and the liturgical celebration of Mary's Dormition: her serene and holy death, and her entry, in the fullness of her humanity, into the divine glory of her risen Son. None of these works has been translated completely into English before, as far as I know. Yet they are important for contemporary Christians in a number of ways: as clues to the original understanding of a feast whose origins are obscure, but which has been solemnly celebrated by the Eastern and Western Churches since the end of the Patristic era; as theological reflections on the meaning, for Christian faith and hope, of Mary and her death; and as works of moving piety and high rhetorical art, representing both the peculiarly poetic character of ancient Christian literature on Mary, and the particular solemnity and importance of the Dormition festival.

I. *Early Christian Literature on Mary*. Most of us would probably agree that listening to speeches is not a prized form of entertainment. For citizens of the ancient Mediterranean world, however, the opposite was often true; in the age of the "Second Sophistic" movement, especially, from the second century of our era onward, epideictic or "show" oratory took the place of epic, lyric and tragic poetry as the Greek world's dominant form of performed and living literature. And as Christian writers—especially after the mid-fourth century, in the face of the Emperor Julian's challenge to their standing as heirs of Hellenic culture—became more concerned to make the public forms of artistic culture their own, the techniques of oratory became more and more evident in their liturgical homilies, and even in their didactic and polemical works.

1

This cultivated, self-consciously artistic character of much Patristic writing from the fourth century on is particularly evident in ancient Greek homilies in praise of the Virgin Mary. The roots of that branch of early Christian literature seem to lie not only in early references to Mary's role in the Christian Mystery by such writers as Justin and Irenaeus, or in popular early narratives of the pre-history of Jesus' life, such as the *Protevangelium of James*, but also—more immediately—in the rich theological rhetoric of St. Ephrem's Syriac hymns and verse homilies on Mary, from the mid-fourth century, and in the corpus of Greek works attributed to Ephrem.[1] As Greek preachers in the cities of the Byzantine Empire began more and more to make Mary the subject of their reflections, in the early decades of the fifth century, their style came to show a celebratory, poetic character rarely met with in earlier homiletics, even in the most highly-wrought festal orations of St. Gregory of Nazianzus or St. Gregory of Nyssa. Most strikingly, perhaps, early fifth-century preachers on Mary tended to invite their hearers not just to think about her, but to participate in celebrating the glories of her person and her role in the story of salvation, both by direct exhortation and by evoking lists of striking Biblical epithets and Old Testament images, in a kind of poetic catalogue directly applied to her.

A classic example is the beginning of the famous sermon on Mary delivered by Proclus of Constantinople, then the young bishop of Cyzicus, in the presence of Patriarch Nestorius, during the Christmas season of 428 or early 429:

> The celebration in honor of the virgin, my brothers and sisters, calls our tongue to speak well today. This present festival is a harbinger of future well-being for all who have met together here—and rightly so! For it shows us the reasons for purity, and offers us womanhood's most exalted boast. Holy Mary has called us together, the immaculate treasure of virginity, the spiritual paradise of

the second Adam, the workshop where natures were united; the festival of our saving covenant, the chamber in which the Word made flesh his bride; the living thorn-bush of our nature, which the fire of a divine childbirth did not burn up; the truly radiant cloud, which bore in a body him who thrones above the Cherubim; the fleece made pure by heavenly dew, in which the shepherd dressed as the sheep; servant and mother, virgin and heaven, only bridge between God and the human race; awe-inspiring loom of God's saving plan, on which the garment of unity was indescribably woven, whose weaver is the Holy Spirit, and whose spinner is the over-shadowing power from on high, whose wool is the old sheepskin of Adam; the warp is the immaculate flesh of the Virgin, the shuttle the measureless grace of her who bore him, and the designer is the Word, who entered her by hearing.[2]

By the mid-fifth century, this style of oratory in praise of Mary, with its richly decorative litany of metaphors and its urgent call on hearers to become participants in a festival, had become a convention; not only Proclus but Hesychius and Chrysippus of Jerusalem, Basil of Seleucia, Cyril of Alexandria, and other preachers now only known through pseudepigraphic attribution, left us examples of this new Marian genre.[3] The poetic style of Ephrem, with its bold images and thick clusters of Old Testament allusions, as well as Ephrem's intense and lyrical devotion to the Mother of God, had suddenly began to echo from the pulpits of Greek cathedral churches.

II. *The Feast of Mary's Dormition.* In the aftermath of the controversy between Nestorius and Cyril of Alexandria over the appropriateness of Mary's title, "Mother of God" (*Theotokos*), which reached a resolution in 433, public veneration of the Theotokos, in virtually all the Churches of East and West, suddenly took on a new liturgical, artistic and architectural importance. In Constantinople, the Empress Pulcheria—long

known for her personal identification with Mary—sponsored
the building of at least three major Churches in the Virgin's
honor, all completed by about 475.[4] In Jerusalem, a basilica in
honor of the Theotokos was apparently built in the Jewish ne-
cropolis at the foot of the Mount of Olives, near Gethsemane,
as early as the 440s, under the patronage of Bishop Juvenal
and the exiled Princess Eudokia.[5] When that building apparently became the theatre for rabid opposition to the Council of
Chalcedon's two-nature Christology and its supporters, including Juvenal, shortly after 451, the embattled bishop and a
wealthy patron, Hikelia, restored a Church and monastery
halfway between Jerusalem and Bethlehem, at the site associated with the ancient story in the *Protevangelium of James* of
Mary's "sitting down to rest" (*kathisma*) on the way to give
birth to the Savior. This basilica may well have become the
center of the cult of the Virgin for sympathizers with Chalcedon in Jerusalem in the decades after the Council.[6] And
while the rest of the Empire, east and west, probably since the
late fourth century, celebrated the memory of Mary, Mother of
God, in the liturgy on a day just before or just after Christmas,[7]
the ancient Armenian lectionary from Jerusalem—a translation of a Greek service book compiled between 412 and
439—lists the commemoration of the Theotokos as taking
place at the Church of the Kathisma on August 15.[8] By the end
of the sixth century, this Jerusalem feast, in late summer, was
to become focussed on the climax of Mary's life on earth and
celebrated throughout the eastern Empire.

The steps by which that transformation took place, however, are vague, and the massive tangle of evidence concerning the origins of the cult and story of Mary's Dormition has
been interpreted in a variety of ways.[9] It seems clear that an interest in the death of Mary, possibly connected with the tradition surrounding her tomb in the Kedron valley, was already

current in the Palestinian Church by the late fourth century. Our first witness to such an interest is the heresy-hunting Cypriot bishop Epiphanius of Salamis, who spent most of his industrious and strident career in the neighborhood of Jerusalem. In chapter 78 of his heresiological handbook, the *Panarion*, completed around the year 377, Epiphanius is arguing against a group he calls the *Antidikomarianitai* or "opponents of Mary," who deny her perpetual virginity. He makes the point that Jesus would not have confided his Mother to the care of the Beloved Disciple, as we read he did in John 19, if she had a house and family of her own. He then goes on to deny that John took Mary with him on his missionary journeys—apparently to prevent clerics of his own day from offering this as a precedent for keeping house with their own female companions—and suggests that she was not living with him at the end of her life. He adds that if one searches the Scripture carefully,

> one will find neither the death of Mary, nor whether she died or did not die, nor whether she was buried or was not buried... Scripture is simply silent, because of the exceeding greatness of the Mystery, so as not to overpower people's minds with wonder.[10]

Referring then to the passage in Apocalypse of John 12, where a woman who bears a child is carried away to the desert to escape the attacks of the dragon who wars against God's people, Epiphanius adds:

> It is possible that this was fulfilled in Mary. I do not assert this definitively, however, nor do I say that she remained immortal; but I also will not say definitively that she died. For the Scripture goes far beyond the human mind, and has left this point undecided because of the surpassing dignity of that vessel [of God]...[11]

Later on in the chapter, while combating the theories of another heretical group, whose failing seems to have been an excess, rather than a defect, of reverence for the Virgin—the

"Collyridians," a women's sect who, Epiphanius says, regarded her as a goddess and celebrated a quasi-Eucharistic liturgy in her honor—the Cypriot bishop makes the same self-consciously inconclusive point:

> If the holy Virgin died and was buried, her falling-asleep was honorable and her end holy; her crown consisted in her virginity. Or if she was put to death, according to the Scripture, 'A sword shall pierce her soul,' her fame is among the martyrs and her holy body should be an object of our veneration, since through it light came into the world. Or else she remained alive; for it is not impossible for God to do whatever he wills. In fact, no one knows her end.[12]

Epiphanius's very caution here—his refusal to decide whether Mary died a holy death and was buried, or in some mysterious way has remained alive, perhaps in the same way as Enoch and Elijah in the Old Testament, who were said to be taken up to heaven—suggests at least that the question had become an open one in late fourth-century Palestine, and that the strong devotion to Mary that characterized the Syrian and Palestinian Churches had already begun to lead believers there to wonder whether her end was not in some way more wonderful and more glorious than that of other Christians.[13]

In the half-century that followed the Council of Chalcedon, the figure of Mary emerged like a comet in Christian devotion and liturgical celebration throughout the world. Spurred on, perhaps, by the powerful role of royal women in the fifth-century Byzantine court and drawn inevitably by the Christological controversies of the age to consider Mary's role in the story of salvation, Byzantine writers began to focus on Mary now not simply as the one who gave flesh to God's Word, but as an object of veneration in her own right: as queen and patroness, and as a participant in the glory and the heavenly mediatorship of her risen Son.[14] Contemporary with this new relationship to Mary came a growing interest in the wonderful character of her life's end, which seems to have found its first written narrative expression among those communities of Syria and Palestine, in the late fifth century, which opposed as irreligious the Council of Chalcedon's description of Christ as a single individual existing in two unmingled and functioning natures, the human and the divine—a point to which we shall shortly return.

This story of Mary's glorious end, which was to become common coin by the end of the sixth century, appears in a variety of earlier forms that are difficult to date with certainty.[15] Most scholars agree that the oldest extant witness to the story is provided by a group of Syriac fragments in the British Library (the documents Michel van Esbroeck labels S 1) describing the burial of Mary, the reception of her soul by Jesus, and the transferral of her body to Paradise, where it is buried under the tree of life—a narrative usually dated to the second half of the fifth century.[16] The earliest Greek accounts—and the earliest known full narrative of Mary's death—are the well-known *Transitus Mariae* attributed to John the Evangelist (van Esbroeck's G 1)[17] and a somewhat different text discovered by Antoine Wenger in a Paris manuscript and first published in 1965 (van Esbroeck's G 2).[18] Both these versions of the story, usually dated to the late fifth or early sixth century,[19] provide a greatly expanded version of the Syriac narrative we have mentioned. Here Mary, living in or near Jerusalem, is informed by an angel that her death is near. She is then joined by the twelve Apostles, who are miraculously gathered from the ends of the earth. After a number of speeches by herself and her companions, she commits her soul into the hands of Jesus and dies. As the Apostles set about burying her body in a new tomb near Gethsemane, a Jew named Jephoniah tries to hinder the procession, and is temporarily deprived of the use of his hands.

The apostles keep watch at her tomb for three days, and then realize that her body, as well as her soul, has been conveyed by angels to Paradise. In the text published by Wenger ("R" or G 2), Jesus actually joins the apostles at her tomb, and he and they accompany the angelic escort carrying her body to Paradise, where it is reunited with her soul.

Versions of this story abound in all the ancient Christian languages, some of them probably of the same antiquity as the texts we have mentioned.[20] There are also versions of it in the works of two major theologians from late-fifth-century Syria, both of whom are usually identified with the moderate wing of the anti-Chalcedonian movement: Jacob of Serug and the Pseudo-Dionysius. The latter's work *On the Divine Names* contains a famous, if somewhat enigmatic passage alluding to the occasion when the supposed author, his "divine guide" Hierotheos, and the other "inspired hierarchs" of the Apostolic Church, including Peter and James, had gathered "to gaze at the body that was the source of our life, the vessel of God," and joined together in an ecstatic outpouring of divinely-inspired hymnody.[21] Jacob of Serug's vast corpus of verse-homilies includes a sermon of 110 lines on the subject of Mary's death and glorious reception into heaven, which was delivered—according to its Syriac title—at a synod of non-Chalcedonian bishops at Nisibis in 489.[22] Jacob, too, depicts Mary's elaborate burial on the Mount of Olives by Jesus and the Twelve; he evokes the jubilation of all nature at her entry into glory, describes her visit to Hades, where she summons all the patriarchs and prophets to share eternal life with her, and portrays the solemn reception of her soul by Christ, who crowns her as queen before all "the celestial assemblies." It is interesting to note that neither Ps.-Dionysius nor Jacob of Serug suggests that Mary's body shared in her glorification; in Jacob's homily, her body apparently joins those of her ancestors in the realms of the dead, to await resurrection. Nevertheless, for both these authors her death is a moment of mystery, parallel in some ways to the death of Jesus, and a time of unique recognition of her holiness by her Son and the heavenly powers. For Jacob, it even means the beginning of a new role for Mary, similar to that of Jesus, as cosmic ruler and herald of renewed life for all the faithful.

By the second half of the sixth century, it is clear that the story of Mary's transition from earth to heaven had come to be accepted as part of Christian tradition in both the Chalcedonian and the non-Chalcedonian Churches of the East. Sixth-century travellers' accounts of Christian Jerusalem now refer to a basilica at the site of her tomb.[23] We know that the basilica near Gethsemane was venerated as the place of Mary's death by the time of the "Piacenza Pilgrim," around 570.[24] The oldest extant Coptic homily (C 5) celebrating the feast of her assumption into heaven, on August 15, by the anti-Chalcedonian Patriarch Theodosius of Alexandria, dates from 566-67 and explicitly locates the wonderful event at Gethsemane.[25] The Georgian lectionary of Jerusalem, based on a Greek original compiled sometime between the end of the fifth and the end of the eighth century, clearly identifies the old *memoria* of the Theotokos on August 15 as the feast of her "migration" to heaven, and specifies that it is celebrated at "the building of the emperor Maurice at Gethsemane":[26] presumably at the fifth-century basilica, restored during the reign of Maurice (582-602), which by then was recognized as the spot where both her burial and her assumption took place. Most important, perhaps, is the laconic testimony of the fourteenth-century historian Nikephoros Kallistos Xanthopoulos that the same Emperor Maurice fixed August 15 as the date for the Churches of the whole Empire to celebrate Mary's Dormition.[27] By the last two decades of the sixth century, the story of her glorious passage from earth to heaven had clearly become the central theme of this important Marian feast, and its celebration in Jerusalem was just as clearly localized at the restored Church at Gethsemane. By this time, too, the supposed site of her residence and of her actual death seems to have been shifted to the fourth-century basilica on Mount Sion, and part of the Dormition festival may have taken place there as well.[28]

From all the extant narrative material, as well as from the earliest homilies for the feast of the Dormition, it is also clear that by the time of Maurice's decree, the mystery being celebrated on August 15 was universally understood as including both Mary's death and her resurrection. The stages by which this understanding of the event evolved, if it was an organic evolution at all, are far from clear; questions about the possibility of her bodily translation, as we have seen, haunted Epiphanius in the fourth century, and the absence of bones in the tomb venerated as hers must have fueled such speculation. Simon Claude Mimouni has recently suggested that the late-sixth-century understanding of Mary's end may reflect a compromise between two wings of the anti-Chalcedonian movement, in which both the celebration and its narrative core had their original home: compromise between the Julianists or "aphthartists," who seem to have held that the pristine purity of the flesh Jesus took from Mary exempted that flesh—in him at least, and perhaps in her as well—from the necessity of dying, and the more moderate Severans, who held that Jesus' humanity—and thus Mary's, too—shared all our natural qualities, including mortality.[29] In Mimouni's view, as the Emperor Justinian continued to push all parties in the Christological disputes to work towards a common position, Severans and Julianists may have come to agree that Mary did indeed die, but was almost immediately raised in body and taken to heaven, because of her unique dignity as mother of the Son of

God. The Chalcedonian Justinian—who himself is reported to have adopted the "aphthartist" view of Jesus' humanity at the end of his life,[30] and who was an enthusiastic promoter of Mary's cult[31]—may well have been responsible for securing the universal acceptance of this understanding of her final glorification.

In any case, it is striking that precisely in the period in which the ancient Church was most engaged in reflection and debate about the person of Christ—between the First Council of Constantinople, in 381, and the Second, in 553—both doctrine and devotion concerning his Mother seem to have evolved most fully. The formulation of the Mystery of Christ's person ratified at the Council of Chalcedon in 451 represented a compromise between the Antiochene and Western approaches, on the one hand, with their insistence that the unity of the divine and the human in the one person of the Son of God involved no diminution in him of the active reality of either of those "natures," and the approach of Alexandrian writers, shared by most Eastern monks and faithful, on the other, which emphasized the overpowering and transforming effect of the Son of God's personal presence in Jesus, even while they affirmed the completeness of his humanity. Love of Mary, attentive focus on her in private and liturgical prayer, recognition of her divine prerogatives as mediator and queen, ultimately even the attribution to her of a full share in her Son's triumph over death and bodily entry into the glory of God, all seem to have grown rapidly during the fifth and sixth centuries as a kind of by-product of the Alexandrian emphasis on the divine identity of Christ's person and the divinization of his humanity by its assumption into the inner life of the Triune God, as the Son's own body and soul. The strongly unitive, God-centered picture of Christ so widely shared in the Eastern Churches of the fifth century, which led first to widespread popular rejection of the Chalcedonian formula of faith and later to its careful nuancing and interpretation, at Justinian's urging, by the official Church at the Second Council of Constantinople, was fundamentally an expression of faith, after all, in God's active and transforming presence in the human sphere, and of hope in the ultimate divinization of all humanity. The early Church's veneration of Mary, the sense of her unique immersion into the Mystery of salvation because of her unique nearness to Christ, beginning in litanies of fulsome praise and ending in the feast of the Dormition, is really part of this growth in understanding of Christ himself, and in drawing out its spiritual and liturgical implications.

III. *The Homilies and their Authors*. The story of Mary's Dormition, as we have seen, began to be told perhaps as early as the late fourth century, and a few Syriac and Coptic homilies on the theme, from Churches that rejected the Christology of Chalcedon, survive from the mid-sixth century. It was only in the early seventh century, however, after the official acceptance of the feast into the calendar of the imperial "Great" Church, that Greek preachers and theologians, as far as the extant literature shows, began the challenging process of interpreting the significance for Christians of the feast of Mary's dormition, and the non-Biblical story it celebrates, within the context of the whole tradition of orthodox faith and worship.[32]

1) The oldest extant Greek homily for the feast is probably that of **John of Thessalonica**, who seems to have been metropolitan of that city for at least some of the years between 610 and 649.[33] John is apparently the same person as the author of the first book of the *Acts* of Saint Demetrius, the soldier-martyr of Thessalonica;[34] he also appears to have composed a sermon showing the agreement between the differing Gospel accounts of Jesus' resurrection, and another on the exaltation of the cross, neither of which is yet published.[35] John's best

known work, however, is this homily on the Dormition of
Mary. Largely taken up with recounting the apocryphal narrative, it was widely read later on in the Byzantine monastic office, and for that reason the text seems to have been adapted to
a variety of interpretations of the feast's real import; the sermon appears in the manuscript tradition, in fact, in two quite
different editions and with at least eleven endings, most of
which vary significantly from the rest in the picture they offer
of Mary's entry into glory. The bishop says he has composed
the homily in order to introduce the celebration of Mary's Dormition on a sound traditional footing in his own Church, since
at the time of its delivery Thessalonica was one of the few
Eastern cities where the feast had not yet become an established part of the liturgical year (1).[36] The reason for this omis-
sion, he insists in his introductory paragraphs, was not the
carelessness of his predecessors, but their realization that the
narratives of Mary's death hitherto in circulation were unreli-
able, and corrupted by heretical additions (1); his purpose here
is to offer what he considers to be a reliable version of the Dormition narrative—one that in fact shows close dependence on
sixth-century Greek and Syriac forms of the story[37]—and to
stress the connection between this climactic event in Mary's
life and the individual Christian's preparation for death. His
homily is a lively work of great emotional intensity and of
straightforwardly pastoral intent, though it lacks the depth and
refinement of theological reflection found in most of the later
Patristic homilies for the feast.

2) Roughly contemporary with John of Thessalonica's
homily, it seems, is a shorter sermon attributed to an otherwise
unknown Palestinian bishop, **Theoteknos of Livias**.[38] Livias,
a small city across the Jordan from Jericho, at the foot of Mt.
Nebo (today Tel er-Ramah), is mentioned by the fourth-
century pilgrim Egeria (*Itinerarium* 10.4-8) and is counted

among the Churches represented by bishops at the Councils of
Ephesus (431) and Chalcedon (451); it disappears from the extant lists of Christian sees after the Muslim invasions of the
630s. Theoteknos's homily, which has the early seventh-
century feature of locating Mary's house and the place of her
death on Mount Sion,[39] clearly attests to belief in her bodily
resurrection. Unlike later Greek homilists, in fact, the author
refers both to the mystery of her glorification and to its liturgical celebration as Mary's "assumption" (ἀνάληψις) (5, 9), a
term more often favored by the Western tradition but rare in
Greek, perhaps because it is used in Luke 9:51 for Jesus' "ascent" to the Father.[40] The work is a general expression of
praise for Mary, in whom the destructive power of the Evil
One—first manifested in Eve's disobedience—has itself been
destroyed (1); it also affirms Mary's continuing role as intercessor for humanity, because of her "free access" to God (7,
9f.). Theoteknos seems to presuppose the apocryphal narratives of Mary's death and glorification, but repeats few of the
details here (5). He prefers to show, by numerous Biblical cita-
tions, how her entry into glory is prefigured in the Old Testament (6-8), and explained in the New (9f.) by her providential
role as Mother of God. This sermon, not mentioned in other
ancient sources and known to us only from one badly damaged
manuscript at St. Catherine's monastery on Mt. Sinai, may
well be our oldest witness to the Palestinian Church's understanding of this feast, whose original home was Jerusalem.

3) In some ways, the most ornate and elaborate of the extant ancient homilies on Mary's death and glorification is that
attributed to Patriarch **Modestus of Jerusalem**, who died in or
shortly before 634.[41] The author refers to his work as a "modest written essay" in explanation of the Dormition festival,
suggesting perhaps that it was not originally delivered orally
in a liturgical context, but was composed as a theological trea-

tise. A clear reference in this homily (10) to the doctrine of Jesus' two naturally distinct wills,[42] canonized at the Third Council of Constantinople (680-681), places its composition after that Council and rules out Modestus as its actual author. On the other hand, the author's claim (1) that he himself knows of no earlier explanations of Mary's Dormition[43] suggests that he may have been writing just prior to the great flowering of homiletic reflections on the feast in the first half of the eighth century. Although the author makes no clear allusions to the Dormition narratives or to the tradition handed on by earlier "prophetic" voices, as other ancient homilies do, he presupposes the accepted story (7-9) and describes Mary's death in some detail (11-13). His presentation of the "mystery" of Mary is centered in the overarching Mystery of Christ, to which he alludes in terms of the classical Christology of the early Councils (7-8); as *Theotokos,* she is the "bridge" between the transcendent God and the humanity he made his own, the human basis of Christ's role as mediator (1, 9), the first realization of the Church as Bride of Christ (3, 6). The mystery of Mary's Dormition, in the author's view, is that of her sharing in the incomprehensible Mystery of human transformation in and through the risen Christ (14): as the "place" of the Word on earth, she has now come to be in his "place" (3), "transferred" to his divine state of being (6), made "one body" with him in his glorious incorruption (10). The Mystery of Easter has now come to fulfilment in her, as Christians hope it will someday be fulfilled in us all.

4) The first half of the eighth century was the period in which the celebration of Mary's Dormition, now firmly established throughout both the Greek- and the Latin-speaking worlds as a major feast in the liturgical cycle, gave rise to the most extended and serious attempts at theological reflection. Probably the first example of this new flowering is a set of three

sermons by **St. Andrew of Crete**, the great homilist and liturgical poet, which almost certainly form a single trilogy, delivered
in sequence during an all-night vigil that ended in a solemn liturgy on the morning of the feast.[44] According to his ninth-
century biography, St. Andrew was born in Damascus, probably around 660, and received his early education in Jerusalem,
at the monastery of the Holy Sepulchre, where he eventually became a notary. Sent on a mission to Constantinople in 685, Andrew appears to have remained in the capital, was ordained a
deacon there, and worked for some time as the administrator of
an orphanage and a shelter for the poor. He probably also had
begun by this time to develop his considerable literary gifts;
some fifty of his homilies exist, many of them still unpublished,
and he seems to have been the inventor of the *canon*, a long and
highly elaborate form of liturgical hymn that took the place of
the earlier *kontakion* as the preferred vehicle for theological poetry. At some point between 692 and 713, Andrew was elected
bishop of Gortyna on Crete, and metropolitan of that island.
During the usurpation of the imperial throne by the monothelete
Philippicus Bardanes (711-713), Andrew seems to have bowed,
as metropolitan, to bureaucratic pressure and taken a publicly
permissive stand towards that heresy, perhaps even signing a
monothelete profession of faith himself; he later wrote an iam-
bic poem about his return to orthodoxy, and may have written
his famed "great canon" as a penance for his lapse in professing
the faith of the Great Councils. He is recorded to have died on
the island of Lesbos on July 4, 740.

Andrew's trilogy of homilies for the feast of the Dormition
are marked by restrained but powerful rhetorical beauty, as
well as new theological depth in articulating the significance
of Mary's death and glorification for the whole Christian community. The date of their composition is unknown, but Andrew's reference to himself in the first homily as "a stranger and

a newcomer" (I, 7) suggests they were delivered either shortly after his enthronement as metropolitan of Gortyna or—less likely—during the early days of his work as a deacon in the capital.[45] The mood of the homilies is one of reverent awe; in the first, especially, the speaker invites his hearers to join him as participants in celebrating a great supernatural mystery, a "feast of light" at Wisdom's table, where Christ is the host and Mary the presiding figure (I, 1, 7-8). Mary's death, like her whole life, can be characterized as a "mystery," according to Andrew (I, 1; II, 2; III, 5); in the second homily, he makes it clear that the heart of that mystery is triumph over death, and that Mary's mystery is in fact rooted in the one Mystery of Christ her Son, God incarnate, dead and risen (II, 1-3). For that reason, her passage through death into life is but a distinctively glorious instance of the mystery of salvation that all of us are called to share: for every Christian who lives in faith, death is a "dormition," a sleep that transforms, rather than a destruction (II, 2; III, 5).

In the third homily, Andrew continues to develop this integration of Mary's death and glorification into the wider Christian context of faith in the saving death and resurrection of Christ, on the one hand, and of hope for our own resurrection, on the other. Here her victory over death, through Christ, is presented as the fulfilment of the long Biblical story of redemption (III, 6-8, 11-13), the goal of which is always the creature's communion with the God who has created us to share his life (III, 4). It was Mary's obedience to the invitation of God, he observes here, that made the Mystery of Christ possible in its concrete historical form; given this closeness to the work of salvation, her life cannot simply end in death and burial (III, 8). Andrew is noticeably reluctant, however, to portray the transferral of Mary from death to heavenly glory in concrete detail; he avoides alluding to the apocryphal Dormition story in any of its extended forms, and draws his portrayal of her burial scene, at the end of the second homily, exclusively from the passage in the Pseudo-Dionysius's *On the Divine Names* which we have mentioned above.

In fact, Andrew skillfully uses this enigmatic allusion of Ps.-Dionysius to Mary's death and burial, surrounded by the Apostles and prophetic leaders of the infant Church, to compensate for the fact that the Scriptures are silent about the end of the life of the Mother of God. For Andrew, Ps.-Dionysius is, in any case, a witness as old as the New Testament, and the triumph of Mary over death, through the victorious power of her Son, is for him clearly to be seen as fulfilling the wider Biblical promise of salvation. So the second homily ends with a litany-like evocation of Biblical images, applied typologically to Mary in the style of Proclus and his contemporaries (II, 15), and the third reaches its climax in Andrew's evocation of a grand procession in Mary's honor, involving all the saints of both Testaments, which the faithful before him are invited imaginatively to join (III, 10-12). The effect of the whole trilogy, in fact, is above all to suggest that participation in the liturgical feast of the Dormition, with its rich array of Biblical texts, its singing, its use of icons and its Eucharistic conclusion, is itself an opportunity for the faithful to share more deeply in the saving gift of life that Mary's "transferral" to heavenly glory so powerfully reveals.

5) A second group of Dormition homilies from the imperial Church of the early eighth century are two apparently unrelated sermons for the feast by **St. Germanus of Constantinople**.[46] Both the dates of his birth and death and the exact extent of his literary work are uncertain; it is known that Germanus was Patriarch of Constantinople from August 11, 715 until January 17, 730, when he was forced to resign by the iconoclast Emperor Leo III because of his outspoken defense of the veneration of icons. Born in the capital sometime between 630 and

650, the son of a prominent courtier and a relative of the Emperor Heraclius (610-641), Germanus became a cleric of the Hagia Sophia as a young man and was appointed bishop of Cyzicus, in Asia Minor near Constantinople, about 703. Like St. Andrew of Crete, he gave brief support to the monothelete policy of the usurper Philippicus (711-713), but returned to the classical Christology of the Councils after Philippicus's fall and was made Patriarch on the accession of Leo III in 715. After initially supporting Leo, Germanus came more and more into conflict with the emperor over the issue of the veneration of icons, until he was replaced by the iconoclast Patriarch Anastasius early in 730; he retired to his family estate at Platanion, in the outskirts of Constantinople, where he died sometime before 742. A man of extensive rhetorical training, Germanus wrote a number of sermons and liturgical poems, as well as dogmatic works on Christology and a controversial tract against the theory of universal salvation (*apokatastasis*). He is probably also the author of a dialogue on the providential limits of human life, although his authorship of other works attributed to him is less certain.

The first of his sermons for the feast of the Dormition, which we have translated here, appears in some manuscripts, and in Migne's *Patrologia*, as two separate homilies; an analysis of the text, however, suggests conclusively that it is a single work, and that it was probably divided by later scribes in order to form, with his other, quite different Dormition homily, a trilogy modelled on those of Andrew of Crete and John of Damascus.[47] The central theme of this first sermon is praise and gratitude for the benefits Mary has conferred on the human race (I, 10), first by becoming the willing instrument of the Incarnation of the Word (I, 2-3), and then through her continuing intercession on behalf of her brothers and sisters (I, 5-6). In both respects, Mary has proved herself to be the central channel of God's saving grace for all humanity (I, 8-9); the rest of our race is blessed because we are related to her by our common nature, and even after her death and exaltation to heavenly glory she remains our companion and patron (I, 12). The purpose of this homily, in fact, seems to be to offer the theological grounds for the continuing cult of Mary in the Church of Constantinople, and the traditional narrative of the Dormition is only briefly alluded to at the beginning and end.

Germanus's other homily for the feast, by contrast, is almost entirely taken up with a dramatic recounting of that story, and seems to make use of several versions of the tradition, including the narrative of John of Thessalonica. Here Jesus appears to his mother before her death (II, 1-2), promising her a share in his glory that is rooted in her lifelong union with him, and offering her the opportunity to be, in heaven, the constant intercessor for her fellow human beings (II, 3). Germanus then describes Mary's careful and joyful preparation for death (II, 4-5), the gathering of the apostles for the event from the distant corners of the earth (II, 6), and the speeches and prayers of Peter and Paul expressing their joy at her coming entry into glory (II, 7-8). In alluding to the actual events of her death, the sermon shows a curious inconsistency: its early pages, like Germanus's first homily, clearly suggest her body was in the tomb—and her shade in the underworld—for some time before entering into the glory of her risen Son, yet the final scene of the narrative depicts her shroud suddenly being lifted out of the hands of Peter and Paul, as they are about to lay her in the tomb, and disappearing upwards only to reappear shortly afterwards, lying empty on the ground (II, 9-10).[48] In any case, the point of this second homily is to remind the congregation of the traditional account of the event celebrated on August 15, and to link it with the veneration of Mary—and her icons and relics—in their own Churches.

6) The most celebrated of all the ancient homilies for the feast of the Dormition, however, are those forming the trilogy for the feast composed by **St. John of Damascus**.[49] One of the great synthetic thinkers of the early Church, and one of the Fathers who had the greatest influence on later theology in both East and West, John—like Andrew of Crete—was born in Damascus, of the influential Syrian Christian family of Mansour, in the early years of Islamic rule there, probably around 675 or a little earlier. His father, Sergius, was one of the chief financial administrators for the caliphate, and John seems to have received an excellent early education in classical rhetoric and philosophy. According to later biographers, he began a career as a public servant himself, but around 700 he went to Palestine with his adoptive brother, Cosmas, and both there became monks at the Great Lavra of St. Sabas, in the Judaean desert. John was ordained a priest by Patriarch John V of Jerusalem (705-735), and seems to have spent the rest of his life either in Jerusalem or in his desert community, studying, preaching and writing; he died there either in 749 or 753. In addition to his great systematic work, *The Fount of Knowledge*, John composed a number of shorter polemical treatises against various contemporary heresies (including Islam, which he regarded as a Judaeo-Christian sect), sermons, and elaborate liturgical poems. His three homilies on the Dormition, distinguished both by their clear exposition of classical doctrine and their devotional warmth, are clearly intended as a single cohesive series. Since John says they are the work of his old age (II,1), and since he alludes in them frequently to the presence of his hearers at the very spot where the mystery occurred, we can assume they were delivered during an all-night vigil for the feast, at some time in the 730s or 740s, in the Church near Gethsemane traditionally identified as the site of Mary's tomb.

The first homily in the trilogy begins with a long prologue on the Mystery of the Incarnation, stressing Mary's role in the divine work of our salvation (I, 1-4)—the theological starting-point for all celebration of Mary herself. John then offers a sketch of Mary's life (I, 4-7), largely dependent on the second-century *Protevangelium of James*; in the manner of classical funeral-orations, his praise of her in the moment of death must begin with an account of the virtues of her parents and the wonderful details of her childhood. After linking her with the great figures of the Old Testament (I, 8-9), John concludes with a brief narrative of her death and entry into glory (I, 9-12), and with the remark that her tomb—presumably within the view of the preacher and his congregation—has remained a place of grace and healing for others (I, 13). The second homily, much longer than the first, returns in great detail to the story of Mary's death, burial and glorification (II, 6-14), all as exemplifying the principle that death itself could not keep the source of life in its power. John draws here on the traditional story known from the apocryphal *acta* and earlier homilists such as John of Thessalonica, though he makes it clear that he does not guarantee the reliability of all the details. Near the end of the sermon, he invites his hearers to imagine Mary's tomb itself telling them what it can of the glorious mystery that took place within its confines (II, 17). The third homily, much briefer than its predecessor, also seems clearly to have been delivered at the traditional site of Mary's burial; here John proclaims in lyrical terms that Mary has been taken from her tomb to share the risen life of her Son, because he wishes to make a new covenant of life with her, and through her with all humanity. Because her Son has personally united our mortal human nature with the eternal, life-giving Word of God, Mary is inseparably involved in the Biblical story of life's triumph over death, and even the tomb before them has become the "bridal chamber" (III, 2) from which divine life issues forth. John concludes by inviting his hearers to join Mary in her holy way of living and dying (III, 5), that they might enter with her into the glory of the risen Lord.

Throughout these homilies, John interprets the events celebrated in the Dormition feast in a squarely Christocentric way; the Incarnation is the central event in all human salvation, the ground of all human hope for life beyond death, and the story of Mary's transformation is no exception to that theological rule. So he explains the traditional Dormition narrative theologically by pointing to the "fittingness" that Mary be allowed to anticipate the fulfilment of all humanity's hope for resurrection in Christ; having been so closely associated with the coming of the Word into the world as a human being, with the way of Jesus and with his death on Calvary, John argues that it is unthinkable she should be separated from him in his glory after her death, even for a limited time (II, 14). As the first human to share directly in the life and grace of the Incarnate Word on earth, she must be understood to be the first to share his eternal life. Freedom from corruption and from domination by the power of death forms an inseparable part of the trajectory of her whole life, as one freed by grace from the passions and burdens normally associated with conception and childbirth (I, 10; II, 14). Her association with the risen Jesus, in whom the Kingdom of God has now come in its fulness, seems also to be the reason John so frequently refers to Mary with titles of royal prerogative, as "mistress" (I, 2, 12, 14), "lady" (I, 12) and "queen" (I, 12; II, 11; III, 4), and identifies her with the royal bride of Psalm 44 (45) (I, 11). Because of her exalted position, Christ desires to "submit all creation to her" (II, 14), and establishes her permanently as humanity's intercessor and patron, its human intermediary with the risen Lord (I, 8).

In addition to John of Damascus's trilogy of homilies on the Dormition, we include here a translation of the liturgical *canon* which he also composed for the festival.[50] The canon was a highly complex form of hymn developed for the Byzantine morning office of *orthros* in the early eighth century, to replace—on major feasts—the eight Biblical "odes" or canticles (nine during Great Lent) traditionally sung at that office.[51] Traditionally identified with Andrew of Crete, as we have already mentioned, the canon was also a form of poetic composition practiced by Germanus of Constantinople and John of Damascus, as well as a number of later writers. In the canon, eight (or nine) units of verse are designed to take the place of the Biblical odes, and usually allude to the odes they are replacing by various phrases and images while celebrating, in more explicit and solemn terms, the particular mystery or saint of the day. Each section of the canon, itself made up of several strophes or stanzas, has its own melody and its own distinctive metrical pattern, expressed in lines of varying length and varying arrangements of stressed and unstressed syllables; the pattern and tune for each section is set in the opening *heirmos* or model-stanza, usually of five to eight lines, and is repeated exactly in the three or four stanzas (*troparia*) that follow within the same section. John of Damascus's canon for the Dormition of Mary, designated to be sung in the fourth mode, is a poetic distillation of the main themes of his three homilies for the feast. The poet summons believers to join in wonder and praise at the great mystery of Mary's triumph over death (III, VI, IX), inviting them to come to Sion and to her sepulchre—at least in prayerful imagination—as to signs of the heavenly Jerusalem (IX). The ultimate reason Mary has already come to glory is that she has given birth to Christ, the Savior (VI, VIII); because of her closeness to him, she has become configured to him in both death and resurrection (IV) and realizes in her own person the Biblical figure of the Bride of Christ (I). In translating John's canon here, I have tried to reproduce in English not only the elaborate thought and imagery of his hymn, but the metrical arrangement of stresses, lines and strophes that give this ancient poetic form its distinctive character. A schematic diagram of the metrical pattern of each section of the canon, in terms of its arrangement of stressed (/) and unstressed (x) syllables, is added as an appendix.

7) The final homily included in this collection is by the great monastic reformer and writer of eighth-and ninth-century Constantinople, **St. Theodore the Studite**. Theodore was born in 759, like St. Germanus a member of an influential Christian family of the capital, many of whom were court officials. Under the influence of his maternal uncle, Abbot Plato of Symbola—a strong defender of the veneration of icons during the early struggle with iconoclasm—Theodore and his brothers and sisters all entered monastic life around 780, turning the family estate in Sakkudion, in Bithynia not far from the capital, into a monastic community. Theodore himself was ordained a priest around 787, and succeeded Plato as abbot of the family monastery about 794. Always an outspoken defender of Christian moral and doctrinal norms, Theodore frequently was critical of the misbehavior of Emperors and Patriarchs and was exiled three times—the third time for opposing the new outbreak of the iconoclastic movement under Emperor Leo V in 815. Under the threat of Arab raids, he and his community moved from Sakkudion to the city of Constantinople in 798, and there took over the abandoned monastery of Studios, turning it into a thriving center of monastic life known both for its orthodoxy and for its liturgical and ascetical observance. Within a few years of its transferral, the community had swelled to a population of some 700 monks, and became

highly influential, under Theodore's leadership, both in the religious politics of the empire and in the shaping of later Byzantine
monastic life. Theodore was recalled from his third exile by Emperor Michael II in 821, but continued to move around the area of
the capital, and died on one of the Princes' Islands in the Sea of
Marmora, the place of his first two exiles, in 826. On January 26,
844, after the solemn revocation of the iconoclastic decrees and
the restoration of Orthodox faith and practice by an imperial
synod of the previous March, Theodore's body was solemnly
brought back to the capital for reburial, along with that of his
brother John, who had been archbishop of Thessalonica—a recognition of their determined and heroic struggle for the tradition
of faith in God's incarnate presence in the world.

In addition to ascetical writings and letters, some twelve
homilies of Theodore are still extant, along with a number of
canons and other liturgical poems. His homily for the feast of
the Dormition[52] distills much of the theology and rhetorical
style of the earlier preachers who had dealt with the subject
into a concise and moving piece—a witness that the creative
endeavors of the eighth-century preachers to integrate the
celebration of the Dormition into the wider context of orthodox theology had, by the later iconoclastic period, become a
convention. Theodore includes a brief narrative of the traditional account of Mary's death, drawn from earlier homiletic
and apocryphal sources and conveyed mainly through short
speeches attributed to Mary and the apostles (3). He presents
Mary's entry into glory as the final stage of her lifelong mission to reverse the defeat of Eve (2). In sharing the risen life of
her Son before the general resurrection of humanity, she is
clearly "different from all the rest" (2); but the roots of this distinction lie in her unique role as Mother of God, and its conse-
quence is that she now acts as intercessor and patron for the
rest of humanity (6). Theodore emphasizes the importance of

the veneration of icons (2), even in this festival, as a way of sharing in the unseen reality of the heavenly liturgy; this may be a sign that the homily was delivered during the final period of the iconoclastic controversy, after his return from his third exile in 821.

IV. *The Thought and Language of the Dormition Homilies.* We have mentioned several times the elaborate literary character of Marian homilies in the ancient Church, and the rhetorical distinction and theological depth of some of the works we have translated here. Although it is impossible to do more than scratch the surface of the art of these rich and sophisticated sermons, let us at least point out some of the distinctive literary and theological features of this late flowering of Patristic Marian oratory.

1) A first characteristic of this whole body of homilies is what might be called their *cultivated vagueness* about the event being celebrated. As I have mentioned, it is clear that from the late sixth century until the tenth (when a certain sceptical reaction against belief in her bodily assumption emerged in certain ecclesiastical quarters, east and west), virtually all treatments of the end of Mary's life accept the belief that she died, was buried, and was raised from the tomb to heavenly glory within a few days of her burial. Nevertheless, it is striking that the authors of these homilies, like the broad ecclesiastical tradition since their time, consistently avoid the language of death and resurrection in speaking of Mary's end. Instead, we repeatedly encounter hallowed euphemisms: Mary's death is almost always referred to as a "falling asleep" (κοίμησις, *dormitio*),[53] her passage into glory as a "transferral" (μετάθεσις)[54] or a "change of state" (μετάστασις),[55] a "crossing over" (μετάβασις, διάβασις)[56] or a "change of dwelling" (μετῳκίσθη).[57] John of Damascus boldly stresses that Mary has been "lifted up" (ἦρται, μεμετεώρισται) (III, 5; cf. 1f.), and Theoteknos of Livias repeat-

edly refers to her entry into glory as an "assumption" (ἀνάληψις) (5, 9)—a word otherwise rare in Greek language for this feast, as we have mentioned. All of our authors clearly believe that Mary's death was real, natural and complete; Andrew of Crete, for instance, refers to "the separation of her soul from her body, her putting-off of flesh, the end of her incarnate existence, the separation of her parts, their dissolution,"[58] and alludes to her entering the "foreign," "unknown regions" of the underworld,[59] while Germanus even suggests—alone of these homilists—that her body had undergone some corruption in the tomb.[60] Yet only Theoteknos, who stands near the beginning of the tradition of the feast, uses the strong metaphor of "assumption" to depict Mary's entry into glory as a kind of heavenly journey.[61] And none of these preachers speaks directly of Mary's final fulfilment, as one might have expected, as a "resurrection from the dead": perhaps because of the inherent conservatism of liturgical tradition, going back to a time when consensus on the details of her end was less clear, or perhaps because it seemed more appropriate to reserve the term "resurrection" for what happened to Jesus, and for the eschatological hope of all Christians for the end of time. So our homilists, especially Andrew of Crete, repeatedly emphasize the mysterious, ineffable character of what Christians discern as Mary's end, and suggest that if the liturgy itself did not call for some attempt at explanation, it might be more reverent, as well as more practicable, to "choose silence over words."[62]

2) This leads us to a second characteristic of these early homilies on Mary's Dormition: their pervasive tendency, despite any doctrinal or apologetic intent they may have, to refer primarily to the *liturgical context* in which they are given. Andrew of Crete expresses what seems to be the self-understanding of all these preachers when he writes, near the

beginning of the first of his sermons:

> If only we, illumined by this present feast of light, could
> be found worthy of the supernal glory of that light above
> all light, and could see the mystery clearly for ourselves!
> These are unknowable realities. But at least we can
> learn, as far as possible, the meaning of the rites we at-
> tend today. Come, then, dear initiates of the Word, fel-
> low lovers of and gazers after Beauty! I appeal to you
> with a great, exalted cry: let me spread out its meaning,
> still hidden in symbolic wrappings, for your contempla-
> tion! Let me show you all its inner loveliness, surpassing
> the rays of the sun in its splendor![63]

One of the conventions of these homilies, in fact, is for the
preacher to invite his hearers, in language recalling both Wisdom literature and the pagan mysteries, to join with him in a
"perfect spiritual banquet of minds," in which the food is heavenly Wisdom and Christ, or Mary herself, the welcoming host.[64]
There are clear allusions, too, in these homilies to the ceremonies that, by the eighth century, surrounded the preacher's efforts: to processions,[65] to the veneration of Mary's tomb (in the
homilies of John of Damascus, preaching at Gethsemane)[66] or
of an icon of the scene of her burial,[67] all as part of the imaginative and celebratory process by which the congregation is
called to witness the events of Mary's "passage" for itself.[68]
Several of the homilies make it clear that the significance of
Mary's entry into glory is not simply the privilege it bestows on
her, but the fact that it makes possible her continuing role within
the community of believers as royal patron and gracious intercessor,[69] a "bridge" between Christ and his people,[70] an instrument of God's providence and grace.[71] The meaning of this li-
turgically celebrated Mystery, in fact, in the view of several of
these preachers, is that it justifies the Church's wider cult of
Mary as a living means of access to God.[72]

   3) In content, these homilies generally take a *cautious ap-*

proach to the narrative tradition surrounding the Dormition festival. The earlier homilies of John of Thessalonica and Ps.-Modestus suggest, in their opening paragraphs, that the details of the story underlying the liturgical celebration are not well known—a reflection, probably, of the fact that neither of these works was composed in Syria or Palestine. Andrew of Crete puzzles over the question of why the New Testament has nothing to say of Mary's end, if it is so important for Christians,[73] and he relies exclusively on Ps.-Dionysius—for him, virtually an Apostolic witness—for the details of the story.[74] John of Damascus is more generous in narrative detail than his contemporaries, Andrew and Germanus, but still tells the story cautiously, in terms of what "might" or "must have been," and gives as his source simply "what we have learned from of old, at our mothers' knees."[75] John is also noticeably diffident about including the detail of the attack by a Jew on Mary's funeral procession, with the resulting severance and healing of his hands, and only does so, he says, to add "spice" to his story.[76] Except for John of Thessalonica, in fact, none of these homilies makes the simple recounting of the apocryphal dormition narrative its central focus, but rather treats the story both as the reason and model for the present liturgical celebration and as the starting-point for theological reflection.

4) It is that *theological reflection* which is, in various ways, the central project of all these Marian sermons. A number of themes appear, in very similar images and phrases, in virtually all the works translated here: Mary's glory and beauty, as the highest embodiment of an idealized humanity, reaching its divine destiny; Mary's enthronement as lady and queen, and her share in Jesus' Messianic rule over all creation; Mary's continuing role in the everyday life of the Church, as intercessor, kindly patron, even mediator between Christians on earth and her glorified Son; the direct link between this new and glorious

status for Mary and the purity of her earthly life—her obedience and fidelity, her total dedication to God, expressed in her virginity, and her freedom from the "corruption" of passion and self-interest; her role as the one who fulfills and epitomizes the hopeful imagery of the whole Bible, realizing the ancient promise of a transforming human intimacy with the God of life—as Ark of the Covenant, Mother Sion, Bride of the heavenly Bridegroom. For all these preachers, the heart of the "mystery" being celebrated in Mary's name is the Mystery of redemption through and in Christ. Just as Mary's title *Theotokos* had come to be recognized as a touchstone of orthodox faith, it now provides the key to understanding her entry into glory:

> For to you [John of Damascus says to the Virgin in his first oration], the beginning, middle and end of all these good things that are beyond our minds, their security and true confirmation, was your conceiving without male seed, God's dwelling in you, your childbearing without damage to your virginity.[77]

Earlier in the same sermon, John sums up the logic of belief in Mary's glorification at death in a single sentence:

> If her childbearing was remarkable, if her conceiving was beyond all nature and understanding and was of saving worth for the world, surely her falling-asleep was glorious, too—truly sacred and wholly worthy of praise.[78]

The reason is not simply that extraordinary honor is appropriate for one who has played such a central role in the Christian story of salvation—though the appeal to what is "fitting" certainly plays an important role in these preachers' theological argument.[79] At a more profound level, all of them see the reason for Mary's present glorification in the eschatological inclusivity of Christ's Paschal Mystery itself. Because her humanity stands closest to the humanity of Jesus, which has passed through death to a new, indestructible life suffused with his own divinity, because she is still "one body (σύσσωμος)"[80] with Jesus, Mary is the first to experience the full transformation of body and spirit—the "divinization" of what is human—that is promised to everyone who becomes "one body" with him in faith and baptism.

In his second oration, Andrew of Crete lets Mary herself explain the central meaning of the festival in simple terms:

> I broke none of the laws of human nature, but having accomplished all in a new, yet fully appropriate way, I 'magnify the Lord in my soul, and rejoice in my spirit' (cf. Lk 1.46), while in my body I am changed and take on a new form, sharing by grace in God's own being. And the source and final form of that transformation into God, I confess, is the form taken by him who is God above all, and who became flesh in an indescribable way in my womb, when he remade his own humanity into something divine.[81]

Because she gave to Jesus the human flesh he has now transformed, Mary's flesh is the first to experience the overflow of that transforming power for itself.[82] But what the faithful now confess as realized in her, as well as in the humanity of Jesus, this "Mystery of the Virgin, now being accomplished," is "our lot, too," Andrew insists," set aside for human nature from the beginning."[83] "This is our frame that we celebrate today," he writes in another place, "our formation, our dissolution."[84] So for every Christian who hopes in Christ, death becomes a "falling-asleep" rather than an experience of terror and demonic subjugation.[85] Even Mary's continuing patronage and intercession, her benign presence in the Church, so strongly emphasized by Germanus as the result of her glorification, is an expression both of the full reality of her salvation in Christ and of her active solidarity with those who hope for the same salvation.[86]

5) It is this theological framework for integrating the Dor-

mition celebration into the wider context of faith, in turn, which explains—almost requires—the *high rhetorical style* and self-conscious craftsmanship of these homilies.[87] Far from being Scriptural commentaries, theological tracts or moral exhortations, all of the works we have been discussing are festal pieces, examples of Christian epideictic or "show" oratory, whose whole purpose is to delight and to engage a devout public. In a little-known monograph of 1939,[88] Johannes List analyzed a number of eighth-century Marian homilies—most of them by Patriarch Germanus I, but none of them, curiously, homilies for the feast of the Dormition—to reveal the high degree of rhetorical art employed in celebrating the events of Mary's life. List's conclusion, that the closest literary model for these sermons is the Greek "prose hymn," as developed in the period of the Second Sophistic, applies virtually without exception to the homilies on the Dormition we have been considering here. Although these orations are variously styled in the texts themselves as *encomia*[89] or funeral orations (*epitaphioi logoi*),[90] their content is simply celebration; even the classical treatises on rhetoric suggest that funeral oratory, when commemorating someone long dead, normally consists of "pure praise," and that the praise of someone with divine characteristics is the defining element of a *hymn*.[91] Hymnic features, all well known from the ancient handbooks on rhetoric, abound in these Dormition orations: *prooemia*, or prologues, inviting the hearers to join in praising Mary's divine qualities and emphasizing the speaker's own inability to utter such praise adequately;[92] narratives of Mary's early life (usually drawn from the *Protevangelium*), as well as the story of her death and burial;[93] evocations of the splendor of the present festival;[94] litany-like lists of Biblical images for Mary;[95] formulas of greeting or blessing (*chairetismoi*) addressed to Mary, hailing her central role in the Mystery of Christian salvation;[96] even the usual final prayer for Mary's continuing intercession on behalf of the community[97]—all of these features find their parallel in such standard late antique models of celebratory religious speeches as the outline of a prose hymn to "Sminthiac Apollo" in the second treatise on rhetoric attributed to Menander.[98] Like all *encomia* in earlier classical oratory, the purpose of an ancient hymn was to bestow glory by the artistic use of words: more specifically, to bestow glory on a divine figure, in the context of a ritual celebration, and so to draw the hearers into the attitude of joy, wonder and dependent trust that is at the heart of worship. So here the preachers frequently allude to their homiletic activity as "making an offering of words"[99] or as "chanting a hymn" to Mary and to Christ.[100] Speaking with self-conscious humility, but with intense emotion,[101] calling on their audience to join them in entering a process of purification,[102] they repeatedly try to capture the mystical, ecstatic level of speech characteristic of ancient mystery cults and attributed to the original witnesses of Mary's death.[103] Their stated purpose is to allow their audiences to join imaginatively in that same sense of self-transcending wonder that characterizes the apostles and other witnesses in the apocryphal dormition narratives.[104] These homilies are not simply narrations or meditations, in other words, but appeals to their hearers to participate in the Dormition feast, as a new and culminating manifestation of the glory of the Mother of God.

It seems significant that it was in homilies for Marian festivals, most especially in homilies for the all-night vigils celebrating Mary's death and entry into glory, rather than in homilies on the main events of the life of Christ or on the other Christian mysteries, that ancient preachers were most inclined to use the exuberant rhetorical form of the classical prose hymn. More than any other body of ancient Christian oratory, these sermons are invitations to personal and corporate involvement in a religious act. Perhaps the reason this particular feast called forth such distinctive homiletic efforts was that the speakers saw their task at the Dormition festival as itself distinctive: perhaps they realized that what was being celebrated there was not so much a particular aspect of Biblical teaching or Church dogma, as a wider, more comprehensive sense of the implications of Christian salvation; perhaps they saw that the admittedly mythic traditional story of Mary's Dormition was really a statement of the Church's impassioned hope for humanity itself, as called in Christ to share, beyond death, the glorious fullness of the life of God.

This collection of translations has been more than ten years in the making. It began as a modest private effort: since none of this rich material was available for the modern English reader, I translated a few of the present homilies for use in my course on Mary and the Christian Tradition, at the Weston Jesuit School of Theology, in Cambridge, Massachusetts. My friend Prof. John Erickson of St. Vladimir's Seminary, a colleague for many years in the Orthodox-Catholic Consultation for the United States, enthusiastically encouraged me to translate the whole collection and and to publish them, and made first contact for me with St. Vladimir's Seminary Press; his constant interest and warm, unobtrusive support for the project through the years is perhaps the principal reason the translations have finally come into print, and I am very grateful to him. Mr. Ted Bazil, of SVS Press, has also been a model of the "encouragement in Christ" St. Paul speaks of (Phil 2:1), as well as of Christian patience; his professional expertise and sympathetic understanding of what such a project might be has made the relationship between translator and publisher extraordinarily pleasant and easy. I am also grateful to Mr. Bruce

A. Bradley, a former student at Weston, for his intelligent and generous help in correcting the manuscript and preparing it for publication. Finally and more broadly, I am deeply grateful to all my Orthodox friends for helping me, as a Roman Catholic, to come to a deeper understanding, through the years, of the full dimensions of the Mystery of our salvation in Christ. I offer these translations to them, in the hope that the glorious Mother of God may make all of us, Christians of West and East, more conscious of our common faith and hope, and freer to live it together. To borrow a phrase from the familiar Latin hymn, *Ave, maris stella*: may she who changed the ingrained, sinful ways of our fallen humanity, by her faith in God's human coming, "establish us in peace".

Brian E. Daley, S.J.
University of Notre Dame
June, 1997

1   For translations of poems and homilies on Mary by Ephrem and the later
    Syriac tradition, see Sebastian Brock, *Bride of Light. Hymns on Mary
    from the Syriac Churches* (St. Ephrem Ecumenical Research Institute;
    Kottayam, India, 1994). See also E. Beck, "Die Mariologie der echten
    Schriften Ephräms," *Oriens Christianus* 44 (1956) 22-39; S. P. Brock,
    "Mary in Syriac Tradition," in A. Stacpoole (ed.), *Mary's Place in
    Christian Dialogue* (Morehouse-Barlow; Wilton, CT, 1982) 182-191; I.
    Ortiz de Urbina, "La Vergine nella teologia di S. Efrem," *Symposium
    Syriacum* (Orientalia Christiana Analecta 197; Rome, 1974) 65-104.
    For the influence of *Ephrem Graecus* on seventh- and eighth-century
    Greek Marian homiletics, see L. Hammersberger, *Die Mariologie der
    ephremischen Schriften* (Innsbruck, 1938); Johannes List, *Studien zur
    Homiletik Germanos' I. von Konstantinopel und seiner Zeit* (Athens,
    1939) vi-vii. For the whole problem of the Greek corpus attributed to
    Ephrem, see D. Hemmerdinger-Iliadou and J. Kirchmeyer, "Ephrem,
    les versions," *Dictionnaire de spiritualité* 4.800-822.

2   *Acta conciliorum oecumenicorum* (ed. E. Schwartz) I, 1.1.103. For an
    outstanding recent discussion of this homily and of Proclus's Mariol-
    ogy, see Nicholas P. Constas, "Weaving the Body of God: Proclus of
    Constantinople, the Theotokos and the Loom of the Flesh," *Journal of
    Early Christian Studies* 3 (1995) 169-194, esp. 176-179. On the origins
    of the liturgical commemoration of Mary, see P. Jounel, "Le culte de
    Marie," in A. G. Martimort (ed.), *L'église en prière* IV (Paris, 1983)
    144-166; M. van Esbroeck, "Le culte de la Vierge, de Jérusalem à Con-
    stantinople, aux VIe-VIIe siècles," *Revue des études byzantines* 46
    (1988) 181-190.

3   For references, see my article, "The 'Closed Garden' and the 'Sealed
    Fountain': Song of Songs 4:12 in the Late Medieval Iconography of
    Mary," *Medieval Gardens* (Dumbarton Oaks; Washington, 1986) 261
    and n. 16; Constas 177f.; and now Simon Claude Mimouni, *Dormition et
    assomption de Marie. Histoire des traditions anciennes* (Beauchesne:
    Paris, 1995) 390-413, and the sources there cited.

4   These were the churches of Blachernai (where Mary's robe or funeral
    shroud was honored) and the Chalkoprateia (where her girdle was ven-
    erated), and the monastery and church of the Hodegon (later known for
    its characteristic icon of Mary holding the infant Jesus and pointing to
    him).

5   For a list and discussion of the sources, see Mimouni 489-512; see also
    the admittedly later and somewhat unreliable fragment of the
    "Euthymiac History," given in the mansucripts of John of Damascus's
    second homily on the Dormition (translated below, 227-229). Some of
    these accounts refer to the Church at Gethsemane being constructed on
    the site of Mary's *house*; the fact, however, that it is surrounded by a
    large necropolis dating back to pre-Christian times, and that the tomb
    beneath it venerated as Mary's is of first-century construction (see Mi-

mouni 571-578 and the literature cited there), suggests that the connection of the Church there with Mary's house may be secondary.

6   See Mimouni 532.

7   In Constantinople and Cappadocia, as later in the West, this commemoration seems to have been celebrated either on the Sunday before Christmas, on December 24, or in the days between Christmas and the older Eastern feast of the manifestation or "Epiphany" of the Son of God on January 5 (see Jounel [above, n. 2]). Homiletic evidence for this Marian celebration in Cappadocia in the last quarter of the fourth century includes a sermon attributed to Gregory of Nyssa (*Clavis Patrum Graecorum* [CPG] 3194: *Patrologia Graeca* [PG] 46.1128-1149) and a homily falsely ascribed to John Chrysostom (CPG 4677: PG 62.763-770), which may also be by Gregory or by Amphilochius of Iconium. On the authorship of this last homily see J. Daniélou's comments in his "Bulletin d'histoire des origines chrétiennes," *Recherches de science religieuse* 55 (1967) 151, and the literature cited there.

8   Ed. A. Renoux, *Patrologia Orientalis* [PO] 35/1, 163, and 36/2, 168.; see also L. Perrone, "Vie religieuse et théologie en Palestine durant la première phase des controverses christologiques," *Proche-orient chrétien* 27 (1977) 226ff. The reason for the date of this festival are unclear, although there is is some evidence in the early Syriac Dormition narratiave in "Six Books" that it may have been associated with the grape harvest: see Mimouni 98f., 381; cf. B. Capelle, "La fête de la Vierge à Jérusalem au Ve siècle," *Le Muséon* 56 (1943) 1-33.

9   Although a great deal has been written on the origins of the Dormition narrative and festival, a few synthetic works remain standard: M. Jugie, *La mort et l'assomption de la Sainte Vierge. Étude historico-doctrinale* (Vatican, 1944); A. Wenger, *L'assomption de la T. S. Vierge dans la tradition byzantine du VIe au Xe siècle. Études et documents* (Paris, 1955); É. Cothenet, "Marie dans les apocryphes," in H. du Manoir, *Maria* 6 (Paris, 1961) 71-156; and now the massive study of Mimouni [above, n.3], which is valuable for the unparalleled collection of material it provides, despite its confusing style and its rather arbitrary assumptions about the development of Marian doctrine.

10 *Panarion* 78.11 (*Griechische christliche Schriftsteller* [GCS], Epiphanius 3.462).

11 *Ibid.*

12 *Ibid.* (GCS, Epiphanius 3.474).

13 There may be a hint that word of these speculations had reached Cappadocia by the last quarter of the fourth century, in a homily (CPG 4677) attributed variously to John Chrysostom, Gregory of Nyssa, and Amphilochius of Iconium (see above, n. 7). Apparently preaching on the occasion of a liturgical commemoration of Mary, the speaker insists that Mary is to be regarded as supremely exalted, "beautiful above all creation"; yet "she has not been lifted up to heaven," but has instead "drawn

the Lord down to earth"! Can this graceful conceit, in the midst of the kind of lavish praise that soon was to become typical of Marian homiletics, also conceal a demurrer on the suggestion of Mary's possible apotheosis?

14 See A. Cameron, "Images of Authority: Élites and Icons in Late Sixth-Century Byzantium," in M. Mullett and R. Scott (eds.), *Byzantium and the Classical Tradition* (Birmingham, 1981) 205-234; V. Limberis, *Divine Heiress. The Virgin Mary and the Creation of Christian Constantinople* (Routledge: London/New York, 1994). For an account of the early development of Marian iconography, see J. Pelikan, *Imago Dei. The Byzantine Apologia for Icons* (Princeton University Press: Princeton, 1990) 121-151.

15 For a list of all known ancient versions of the dormition narrative, and an attempt—somewhat arbitrary, but still useful—to classify them, across the variety of language groups, by narrative detail and possible liturgical and theological origin, see M. van Esbroeck, "Les textes littéraires sur l'assomption avant le Xe siècle," *Les Actes apocryphes des Apôtres: Christianisme et monde païen* (Labor et Fides: Geneva, 1981) 265-288 (repr. M. van Esbroeck, *Aux origines de la Dormition de la Vierge* [Variorum: London, 1995] I).

16 These fragments are found in BL Add 14484, ff. 1r-5v; Add 14669, f. 39; Add 14484, ff. 6-8; Add 14665, ff. 21.24 (palimpsest); Add 17137, ff. 6-11 (palimpsest); and Add 17216, f. 17 (palimpsest). W. Wright, who first described these fragments as a group, dated the text in BL Add 14484, on palaeographical grounds, to the second half of the fifth century (*Contributions to Apocryphal Literature of the New Testament* [London, 1865] 11). This early date was accepted by M. Jugie (*La mort et l'assomption de la Vierge* 108f.) and A. Wenger (*L'assomption de la T. S. Vierge* 53); S. Mimouni (*Dormition et assomption de Marie* 79), for "essentially doctrinal reasons" that are not entirely clear, says that the fragments cannot be earlier than the sixth century. These important texts present a variety of problems for interpretation, and need to be studied further.

17 The best available edition of this apocryphon, which appears in a large number of manuscripts, is still that of K. von Tischendorf, *Apocalypses Apocryphae* (Leipzig, 1866) 95-112.

18 *L'assomption de la T. S. Vierge* 210-240. Since this form of the apocryphon is known, to date, only from one Vatican manuscript (Vat. gr. 1982, ff. 181r-189v), Wenger entitles it "R" (for "Romanus").

19 For a summary of the arguments offered for this dating of G 1, see Mimouni, *Dormition et assomption de Marie* 124. Wenger argues for a similar date for G 2 (*L'assomption de la T. S. Vierge* 61-67), but Mimouni—in accord with his own schema of the development of a doctrine of Mary's assumption—suggests the second half of the sixth century (*op. cit.* 134).

20 Most important among these, perhaps, is the elaborate Syriac apocry-

phon attributed to James, "brother of the Lord," which is composed in six books (S 3); it has been edited by W. Wright, "The Departure of my Lady Mary from this World," *Journal of Sacred Literature and Biblical Record* 6 (1865) 417-448; 7 (1866) 108-160. The earliest extant manuscripts of this work probably date from the second half of the sixth century, but van Esbroeck argues, from hints of liturgical and doctrinal themes in the text, that it comes from the period of the Henotikon or the "Acacian schism" (484-519). For a list of the known manuscripts, see Mimouni, *Dormition et assomption de Marie* 91f.

21 *De div. nom.* 3.2. The sixth-century scholia on this text by John of Skythopolis, as well as the seventh- and eighth-century Greek homilists on the Dormition feast, as we shall see, assert without hesitation that Ps.-Dionysius is referring to Mary's burial, as narrated in the Dormition apocryphon.

22 The only available edition of the Syriac text of this homily is that of Paul Bedjan, *Sancti Martyrii, qui et Sahdona, quae supersunt omnia* (Paris-Leipzig, 1902) 709-719. Anton Baumstark also published a Latin translation based on a different manuscript, with some variations: "Zwei syrische Dichtungen auf das Entschlafen der allerseligsten Jungfrau," *Oriens christianus* 5 (1905) 91-99. An Italian translation of Bedjan's text, with introduction and commentary, has been published by C. Vona: *Omelie mariologiche di S. Giacomo di Sarug* (Rome, 1953) 187-194; and there is a thoughtful analysis of the homily in English, including translations of extensive passages, by Thomas R. Hurst, "The 'Transitus' of Mary in a Homily of Jacob of Sarug," *Marianum* 52 (1990) 86-100. For a full English translation of Jacob's homily, see *The True Vine* 5 (1993) 2-28.

23 *Breviarius de Hierosolyma*, in P. Geyer (ed.), *Itineraria et alia geographica*, CCL 175 (Turnhout, 1965) 112. For a discussion of the dating of this text, which seems not to be earlier than 530, see Mimouni, *Dormition et assomption* 565f. The pilgrims' guide by Theodosius, written between 518 and 538, speaks of a "Church of the Lady Mary, mother of the Lord" in the valley of Josaphat near Gethsemane, but does not identify it as the place of her tomb; see Geyer, *Itineraria* 119.

24 Geyer, *Itineraria* 137. Other, apparently later, recensions of this work identify this site also as the place of Mary's tomb and of her being taken up into heaven. For a discussion of the relative priority and possible dating of these versions of the work, see Mimouni, *Dormition et assomption de Marie* 508ff.

25 The most complete edition of the Bohairic text of this homily is by M. Chaine, "Sermon de Théodose, Patriarche d'Alexandrie, sur la Dormition et l'Assomption de la Vierge," *Revue de l'orient Chrétien* 29 (1933-34) 272-314. For a discussion of its contents, see Mimouni, *Dormition et Assomption de Marie* 202-205.

26 CSCO 204.27. This same lectionary also attests a *synaxis* or liturgical

gathering at the Church of the Kathisma, near Bethlehem, on August 13: perhaps a vestige of the older, simple commemoration of Mary as Mother of God, which had been held there. It is interesting to note that specific veneration of Mary's tomb, in a place distinct from that where she was supposed to have lived and died, is attested only in the period at which the story of her resurrection had become accepted doctrine. Before this, when celebration was focussed more generally on the glorious end of her life, Gethsemane seems to have been venerated as the site of her house, her death and her tomb; see above, n. 5.

27 *Hist. Eccl.* 17.28 (PG 147.292).

28 The first clear witness to this Sion-tradition is the twentieth anacreontic hymn of the future patriarch, St. Sophronius of Jerusalem, datable between 603 and 614: see M. Gigante, *Sophronii Anacreontica* (Rome, 1957) 125f.; PG 87.3821 A). Mimouni suggests that the celebration of Mary's death—in her own house—by Chalcedonian Christians may have been moved to Sion from the Church of the Kathisma, south of the city, for safety reasons, at the time of the Persian conquest of Jerusalem in 614 (*Dormition et Assomption de Marie* 639).

29 There is no direct evidence, as far as I know, that the Julianists held Mary's body was naturally incorruptible. Leontius of Byzantium, however, in his dialogue directed against their orthodox counterparts, the "aphthartist" wing of the Chalcedonian Church, suggests that his opponents were flirting with the notion: see *Contra Incorrupticolas* (PG 86.1328-1330). This dialogue probably dates from the late 530s.

30 So Evagrius Scholasticus, *Hist. Eccl.* 4.39-41 (ed. J. Bidez and L. Parmentier [London, 1898] 190-192); Eustratius, *Vita Eutychii* 33-41 (PG 86.2313ff.); Nikephoros Kallistos Xanthopoulos, *Hist. Eccl.* 17.29-31 (PG 147.291ff.). Modern historians tend to be puzzled by this late heretical turn of an emperor noted for his commitment to theological orthodoxy, but the evidence, contemporary and later, is unambiguous. See F. Loofs, "Die 'Ketzerei' Justinians," *Harnack-Ehrung* (Leipzig, 1921) 232ff.; M. Jugie, "L'empereur Justinien a-t-il été aphthartodocète?" *Echos d'Orient* 31 (1932) 399-402.

31 Justinian was responsible for establishing the feasts of the Annunciation and Presentation of the Lord, and those of the Conception and Nativity of Mary, in the liturgical calendar of all the Eastern Churches, and sponsored the building of a number of major churches in her honor, including the "New" basilica (*Nea*) on Mt. Sion, the monastery of the "Life-giving Spring" (*Zoodochos Pege*) outside Constantinople, and others in North Africa and elsewhere. For the attitude of the historian Procopius to Justinian's building program in Mary's honor, see Averil Cameron, *Procopius and the Sixth Century* (Berkeley: University of California Press, 1985) 89-94, 97, 100, 123f., 181-188.

32 In addition to the comprehensive studies of M. Jugie and S. C. Mimouni which we have already mentioned, the only comprehensive analysis of

these Greek Dormition homilies—their literary structure, historical context and theological content—is L. Carli, *La morte e l'assunzione di Maria santissima nelle omelie greche dei secoli VII-VIII* (Rome, 1941).

33 The text, in both its longer and its shorter recension, is edited by M. Jugie, PO 19 (1925) 375-436. Only the earlier, non-interpolated version of the homily (375-405) concerns us here.

34 See *Acta Sanctorum* October IV, 164-198; PG 116.1081-1324.

35 For details of these sermons, and a full discussion of what is known of the life and work of John of Thessalonica, see M. Jugie, *Patrologia Orientalis* 19 (1925) 226-231.

36 For a discussion of the possible reason for this delay in celebrating the feast at Thessalonica, see below, p. 68, n. 1.

37 Scholars have suggested different sources for John's account of the Dormition: for references to the literature, see Mimouni 142f., n.89. Dom B. Capelle argued for its closeness to an ancient Latin *Transitus Mariae* apocryphon, published by Wilmart (L 4); A. Wenger suggested, more recently, that its closest relative may be the Syriac account of the Dormition in five books (S 3b).

38 This was first published by A. Wenger in *L'assomption de la T. S. Vierge* 272-291. Since Wenger's edition contains no pargraph numbers, I have numbered in square brackets what seem to be the main thought-units of the homily.

39 See above, n. 28.

40 The term also appears in apocryphal sources to designate the heavenly "journey" of a seer: see *Testament of Levi* 18.3; *Ascension of Moses* 10.12; and cf. *Preaching of Peter* 4.15.35. For further references, see Walter Bauer, *Griechisch-Deutsches Wörterbuch zu den Schriften des Neuen Testaments* (Berlin: Töpelmann, 1958) 113.

41 The Greek text of this homily, edited from a single Paris manuscript by Michelangelo Giacomelli, appears in PG 86.3277-3312. The homily appears to be the same one that the Patriarch Photius mentions, along with two others attributed to Modestus of Jerusalem, as part of his report on his library (*Bibliotheca*, cod. 275). Photius there cites what he considers to be significant passages in Modestus's homilies for the feasts of the Myrrh-bearing Women and the Hypapante, or Presentation of the Lord. Between the two extracts, he adds the following notice: "I read a work ascribed to the same author, entitled, 'Encomium for the Dormition of the most holy Mother of God'. It is a long oration, but reveals nothing important (ἀναγκαῖον), or directly related to the oration that precedes it." (PG 104.244 C1-5) Photius seems to have had his own doubts about the authenticity of the homily, and is clearly unimpressed by its exalted style.

42 PG 86.3304 C2-7.

43 PG 86.3280 B6-8. This comment, plus the absence of any reference in the homily to sites connected with Mary's life or death, have led most

scholars who have studied it to conclude that its author was not living in or near Jerusalem; see M. Jugie, *La mort et l'assomption* 214-233; cf. *id.*, "Deux homélies patristiques pseudépigraphes: Saint Athanase sur l'Annonciation; Saint Modeste de Jérusalem sur la Dormition," *Échos d'Orient* 39 (1940-1942) 285-289; Mimouni 157.

44 PG 97.1045-1109. I have also added numbers, in square brackets, to the main sections of these three homilies.

45 Andrew's claim to be dealing with a theme few have attempted before (III, 1) suggests that his homilies on the Dormition antedate those of his contemporaries Germanus and John of Damascus.

46 PG 98.340-372. I have also added numbers, in square brackets, to signify the main sections of these homilies.

47 See M. Jugie, "Les homélies de Saint Germain de Constantinople sur la dormition de la Sainte Vierge," *Échos d'Orient* 16 (1913) 219-221; *La mort et l'assomption de la Sainte Vierge* 227, n.1; C. Chevalier, "Les trilogies homilétiques dans l'élaboration des fêtes mariales, 650-850," *Gregorianum* 18 (1937) 361-378, esp. 372-375; L. Carli, *La morte e l'assunzione* 46f.; Mimouni 168f.

48 This element may have been included by Germanus to explain the origins of the relic of Mary's shroud, venerated in his time at the Church of Blachernai inConstantinople. A similar purpose lies no doubt behind the inclusion in all the manuscripts of a passage from an otherwise unknown life of St. Euthymius, narrating the discovery of Mary's empty tomb and funeral garments, towards the end of John of Damascus's second homily on the Dormition (see the appendix to our translation below, pp. 227-229).

49 The best edition of these homilies is now the critical edition of B. Kotter, *Die Schriften des Johannes von Damaskus* 5 (De Gruyter: Berlin/New York, 1988) 461-555. The older text of Michel Lequien, O.P. (Paris, 1712), which appears in PG 96.700-761, was republished in corrected form, with a French translation and notes, by P. Voulet, S.J., in *Sources chrétiennes* 80 (Paris, 1961).

50 The best edition of the Greek text of John of Damascus's canon, which we have used in making this translation, is that of W. Christ and M. Paranikas, *Anthologia Graeca Carminum Christianorum* (Leipzig: Teubner, 1871) 229-232.

51 These nine "odes," which appear together in most manuscripts of the Greek Septuagint translation of the Old Testament, are as follows:
   1. The Song of Moses at the Red Sea (Ex 15.1-19);
   2. The Song of Moses in Deuteronomy (Deut 32.1-43)—used only in Great Lent;
   3. The Song of Anna, mother of Samuel (I Sam [LXX: I Kg] 2.1-10);
   4. The Song of Habakkuk (Hab 3.2-19);
   5. The Song of Isaiah (Is 26-9-20);
   6. The Song of Jonah (Jon 2.3-10);

7. The Song of Azariah (Dan 3.26-45);
8. The Song of the Three Young Men (Dan 3.52-88);
9. The Songs of Mary and Zacariah at the Coming of Christ (Lk 1.46-55 and 68-79).

They continue to be used regularly, in addition to the Psalms, in the divine office of both the Eastern and Western Churches.

52 Greek text: PG 99.720-730.
53 See, for example, Ps.-Modestus 7; John of Damascus I, 12; II, 3; Theodore 5.
54 E.g., Andrew I, 6; II, 2; John III, 2.
55 E.g., Ps.-Modestus 6; Andrew II, 2; Germanus I, 1; John III, 1; Theodore, 2, 3, 5; cf. *Catechesis chronica monasterii Studii* 5 (PG 99.1696C).
56 Theodore 1, 6.
57 Ps.-Modestus 3.
58 Andrew I, 6; cf. II, 4.
59 Andrew II, 4.
60 Germanus II, 1. In general, these preachers strenuously deny that her body had undergone any corruption: see Ps.-Modestus 7; John I, 10.
61 See above, p. 14 and n. 40.
62 Andrew I, 1, 2, 9; II, 5, 8; III, 1, 3, 15; John III, 2.
63 Andrew I, 3; cf. Ps.-Modestus 1.
64 Andrew I, 7; cf. *ibid*. 4 (Christ as host).
65 Andrew III, 10-12; John III, 5.
66 John I, 13; II, 17; III, 2, 5.
67 Andrew II, 7; Theodore 2.
68 See, e.g., John III, 5.
69 So Theoteknos, conclusion; Ps.-Modestus 13; Andrew III, 9, 14f; Germanus I, 4f; II, 3; Theodore 2, 6.
70 Ps.-Modestus 9.
71 Germanus I, 10; II, 2, 7, 11. Germanus even compares Mary's role to that of the Holy Spirit in II, 6.
72 Ps.-Modestus 10f; Germanus I, 6; Theodore 3, 6. On Mary's present "access" to God, see Theoteknos 7, 9; Ps.-Modestus 14; Andrew II, 6.
73 Andrew II, 8.
74 Andrew II, 9-10; cf. John III, 4.
75 John II, 4, 7, 10-12.
76 John II, 13.
77 John I, 12; cf. Andrew II, 6: "What, after all, is greater than to be called—and to be—Mother of God?"
78 John I, 3.
79 E.g., John II, 14.
80 Ps.-Modestus 10.
81 Andrew II, 6; the "form" taken on by Christ, to which Andrew refers in the last

sentence, is of course the form of Christ's risen body. Cf. Ps.-Modestus
2.

82 See Andrew II, 13-14.

83 Andrew III, 5; cf. Theodore 2.

84 Andrew I, 9; cf. III, 5.

85 Andrew III, 5.

86 Germanus I, 5-6, 9-10; II, 11; cf. Ps.-Modestus 10; Theodore 6.

87 Elements of classical rhetorical techniques used by the homilists in-
    clude frequent speeches put into the mouths of various figures in the
    story (Mary, the Apostles, Jesus, the tomb); the re-creation of the ec-
    static song sung by the first witnesses of Mary's glorification; addresses
    to inanimate objects, such as Mary's bier (Ps.-Modestus 13) or her tomb
    (John Dam. II, 17); anaphora, or emphatic repetition at the beginning of
    clauses, of phrases and words, such as "today" or "O blessed dormition
    of the Mother of God!"; as well as the formal elements proper to the
    prose hymn which we mention below.

88 *Studien zur Homiletik Germanos' I. von Konstantinopel und seiner Zeit*
    (Athens, 1939).

89 So the titles of the homilies of Theoteknos, Ps.-Modestus, and Theodore
    of Studios.

90 So Andrew I, 1, 9; II, 11; III, pp.10, 14; John Dam I, 4; II, 15.

91 See esp. Menander Rhetor (ed., with translation and commentary, D. A.
    Russell and N. G. Wilson [Oxford: Clarendon Press, 1981]) II, 418f.,
    440; Theon of Alexandria (ed. L. Spiegel, *Rhetores graeci* II [Leipzig,
    1854] 109.22-28).

92 Ps.-Modestus 1; Andrew I, 1; II, 1; III, 1, 10; John Dam I, 1-3; II, 1;
    III,1.

93 Andrew I, 2; John Dam I, 5-6.

94 Andrew I, 1, 7; II, 1; John Dam II, 1, 15-16; III, 1.

95 Ps.-Modestus 4-6; Andrew II, 15; III, 6, 13; John Dam I, 8-9; III, 2, 5.

96 John Dam III, 5; Theodore the Studite 4.

97 Andrew III, 15; Germanos II, 11.

98 437-446 (ed. Russell and Wilson 206-225).

99 Andrew III, 14-15; John Dam I, 14.

100 Andrew III, 3, 10, 14; Germanos II, 11.

101 E.g., John Dam II, 5.

102 Andrew I, 3.

103 Ps.-Modestus 9; Andrew I, 12, 16; III, 2-3; John Dam I, 9, 11; II, 6-7.

104 Andrew I, 4-5; III, 10, 12; John Dam III, 4-5.

THE DORMITION OF OUR LADY, THE MOTHER OF GOD AND EVER-VIRGIN MARY

By John, Archbishop of Thessalonica

1. A fitting hymn of honor, praise and glory is always due, from every creature under heaven, to that remarkable, all-glorious and truly great mistress of all the world, the ever-virgin Mother of our savior and God Jesus Christ. She is truly the God-bearer, and through her all creation has received, by God's saving plan, the great gift of the presence in the flesh of the only Son and Word of God the Father. After God the Word, who truly took flesh from her for our sakes and became human, had suffered in that flesh by his own will and had been raised from the dead and ascended into heaven, she herself continued to live, for no small period of time, with the holy Apostles in the region of Judaea and Jerusalem; she remained mainly in the household of that virgin-disciple beloved of the Lord, as holy Scripture makes clear, while each of the others went out, at the command of the Holy Spirit, to proclaim the Gospel in all the world. When some time had gone by, this glorious virgin, the Mother of God, left the earth by a natural death.

Not only this, but some people committed to writing the wonderful things that happened in her regard at that time. Practically every place under heaven celebrates every year the memory of her going to her rest, with the exception of only a few, including the region around this divinely protected city of Thessalonica. Why is this? Shall we condemn the carelessness or laziness of those who have gone before us? Surely we must not say or even think anything of the sort, since they and no one else left this excellent principle as a kind of law for their homeland: that we should celebrate in the Spirit the memory

not only of our local saints, but of practically all who struggled
for Christ, anywhere in the world, so that in these intercessory
gatherings we might grow closer to God. Our forebears, then,
were neither heedless nor lazy; yet although those who were
present then [at Mary's death] described her end truthfully, we
are told, mischievous heretics later corrupted their accounts by
adding words of their own, and for this reason our ancestors
distanced themselves from these accounts as not in accord
with the catholic Church.[1] For this reason, the feast [of her
Dormition] passed, among them, into oblivion.

Do not be surprised at hearing that heretics have corrupted
writings, since they have been caught doing similar things,
from time to time, to the epistles of the divine Apostle and
even to the holy Gospels! Yet we do not reject writings that
contain the truth because of that fraud of theirs, so hateful to
God; rather, we purify them of the bad seed that has been
sown, and embrace what has truly been achieved for the glory
of God by his saints, and commemorate these things in a way
that pleases him and profits our souls. So, we find, our recent
predecessors have done, as did the holy fathers who lived long
before them—the latter when dealing with the so-called "individual travels" of the holy apostles Peter and Paul and Andrew
and John, the former in the case of most of the acts of the
Christ-bearing martyrs.[2] For one must truly "remove the
stones from the path," as Scripture says (Jer 50:20), so that the
flock chosen by God may not stumble.

2. Since, then, it is very necessary for the good of this
Christ-loving metropolis, in order that it lack no blessing, that
the world's benefactress and lady, the ever-virgin Mary,
Mother of God, receive our sincere praise as we celebrate with
spiritual joy the memory of her entry into divine rest, we have
ourselves spent no small effort preparing to set before your devout ears—to awaken and to build up your souls—not every-

thing we have found written, in different ways in different books, about that event, but only what truly happened, what is remembered as having taken place, and what is witnessed until today by the existence of actual sites.[3] We have gathered these testimonies together in love of truth and in fear of God, taking no account of fabricated stories,[4] since they have been interpolated into the traditions by the malice of those who fabricated them. But having listened with beneficial compunction to the truly awe-inspiring and great wonders that took place, in a way really worthy of God's mother, at the time of her entering into holy rest, we shall offer to that spotless Lady, Mary Mother of God, thanks second only to God, and the praise that befits her, and we shall show ourselves worthy of her gifts by our good works.[5] And if you receive from us this little token of love and are favorably impressed by the enthusiasm of the exhortation towards better things implied by our present writing, show us your affection as brothers and sisters and as beloved children in the Lord, and secure for me from God, by your unceasing prayer, the constant support I need. His, after all, is the glory, the honor and the power, for the ages of ages! Amen.

3. When the holy Mother of God, Mary, was about to lay aside her body, the great angel came to her and said, "Rise, Mary, take this branch of palm,[6] which he who planted Paradise gave to me, and give it to the Apostles, so that they may carry it as they sing before you, for after three days you will lay aside your body. For behold, I am sending all the Apostles to you, and they will take care of you and will behold your glory when they carry you to your resting place." "Why have you brought this palm branch only," Mary replied to the angel, "and not one for each of them—lest if it be given only to one, the others will complain? And what do you wish me to do? What is your name, that I may tell them if they ask?" And the angel said to her, "Why do you ask my name? For it is too

wonderful for human ears. And do not be concerned about the palm branch; for by it many shall be healed, and it shall be a norm of testing for all who live in Jerusalem.[7] For revelation shall be given to the one who believes, but shall be hidden from the unbeliever. Come, then—make your way towards the mountain."[8]

Then Mary set out and climbed up the Mount of Olives, while the angel's light shone ahead of her; she had the palm branch in her hand. When she came to the mountain, it rejoiced—the whole mountain, with all its trees, so that the foliage bowed its head in veneration. When Mary saw this, she became agitated, thinking that it was Jesus, and said, "Are you not the Lord? For such a great sign has come to pass through you: so many trees bowing before you! I say that no one can cause such a great sign except the Lord of glory, who entrusted himself to me."

Then the angel said, "No one can perform miracles apart from his hands. For he provides power to everything that is. But I am the one who receives the souls of those who humble themselves before God; I bring them to the place of the just, on that day when they depart from the body.[9] And when you, too, lay aside your body, I will come to you in person."

Then Mary said to him, "My Lord, in what shape do you come to your chosen ones? Tell me what I must do—tell me, so that I may do it, and you may come and lead me on high." "What are your thinking, my Lady?" he replied. "When God sends a mission to you, I will not come alone, but all the armies of angels will come and sing before you. Hold fast, then, to the palm branch." Saying this to her, the angel became as light, and went up into heaven.

4. Mary returned to her home. Immediately, the room was shaken because of the glorious radiance of the palm branch in her hand. After the tremor, she went into her inner chamber and laid

the branch away in a linen cloth. Then she prayed to the Lord, saying, "Lord, listen to the petition of your mother Mary, who cries out to you; send down your favor upon me. Let no power come against me in that hour when I depart from the body, but fulfill what you said when I called out to you in tears, asking, 'What shall I do to escape the powers that will confront my soul?' You gave me a promise then, saying, 'Do not weep—neither angels nor archangels will come against you, nor cherubim nor seraphim, nor any other power, but I myself will come to meet your soul.' For now the pains of childbirth are upon me again.[10] And she prayed, "I bless the eternal light in which you dwell; I bless every living thing planted by your hands, each of which will remain for all ages. O Holy One, who dwell among the holy ones, 'hear the voice of my supplication' (Ps 27:2)."

5. When she had said this, she went out and said to her house-maid, "Hear me: go and call my relatives and acquaintances; say to them, 'Mary calls you'." Her maid went out and called them all, as she had commanded; and when they had come to her, Mary said to them, "Fathers and brothers, help me! For I am about to depart from the body for my eternal rest. Arise, then, and show me a great act of generosity. I do not ask you for gold or silver, because all those things are vain and corruptible. But I ask you for the generosity of remaining with me these next two nights; let each of you take a lamp, and do not let it go out for three days, and I will bless you before I depart.[11]

They did as she told them. The report was passed on to all Mary's acquaintances and to her relatives, and they all gathered around her. Mary turned and saw them all standing around, and raised her voice, saying: "Fathers and brothers, let us help each other; let us light our lamps and stay awake, for 'we do not know in what hour the thief is coming' (Mt 24:43)." It has been revealed to me, my brothers, when I shall depart; I have learned this and am certain of it, and I am not afraid, for it is a

universal thing. I am only afraid of the enemy who makes war
on everyone. He can do nothing, of course, against the righteous and faithful; but he defeats the unbelieving and sinners,
and those who do their own will—he does in them whatever he
desires! But he does not overcome the righteous, because the
angel of wickedness finds nothing in them, but draws back
from them in shame. For two angels come to meet each human
being: one an angel of righteousness and one of wickedness,
and they encounter him at the moment of death. And when
death besieges the soul with anguish, the two angels come and
grasp his body. If he is someone who has done works of righteousness, the angel of righteousness rejoices over him, because
the wicked one has nothing in that person. Then several angels
come to the soul, singing before him all the way to the place of
the just. Then the angel of wickedness is grieved, because he has
no share in him. But if the person is found to be one who has
done evil deeds, that angel rejoices, and brings with him other
wicked spirits, and they lay hold of the soul and pluck it out for
themselves. Then the angel of righteousness grieves deeply.
So now, fathers and brothers, help each other, that nothing evil
may be found in our company."

When Mary had said this, the women said to her, "Sister,
you who have become Mother of God and mistress of all the
world, even if all of us are afraid, what do you have to fear?
You, after all, are Mother of the Lord! Woe to us, if you say
this—where can we flee? You are the hope of us all. We little
ones—what shall we do, or where shall we escape? If the shepherd fears the wolf, where are the sheep to run?"

All who stood near began to weep. And Mary said to them,
"Be silent, my brothers and sisters, and do not weep, but give
glory to her who is at this moment in your midst. If beg you,
make no lament here for God's Virgin, but let your song be
praise instead of lamentation, such that it may pass to all gen-

erations on the earth and to everyone who belongs to God.
Sing praise instead of mourning, so that in place of mourning
you may receive a blessing."

6. Saying this, Mary called to those who were nearest to her
and said to them: "Arise, let us pray!" And when they had
prayed, they all sat down and began to discuss with each other
the great things God had done, and the signs he had worked. As
they spoke, the Apostle John arrived and knocked on Mary's
door, then opened it and went in. When Mary saw him, she
was disturbed in spirit; she groaned and shed tears, and cried
out in a loud voice, "John, my son, do not forget the words
your Master addressed to you on my behalf, when I wept for
him on the cross and said, 'You are going away, my Son, and
to whom do you leave me? With whom shall I live?[12] And he
said to me, as you stood and listened, 'John is the one who will
look after you.' Now, then, my son, do not forget what you have
been commanded on my account. Remember that he loved you
above all the Apostles; remember that you, rather than any of
the others, leaned on his breast. Remember that it was to you
alone, as you reclined on his breast, that he spoke the mystery
that no one knows except me and you, since you are the chosen
virgin, and since he did not wish me to grieve, for I was his
dwelling place. For I said to him, 'Tell me what you have said
to John,' and he gave you a command and shared it also with
me.[13] Now, then, son John, do not abandon me."

When she had said this, Mary wept quietly. But John could
not bear it; his spirit was troubled, and he did not understand
what she had been saying to him, for he did not realize that she
was about to depart from her body. Then he said to her, "Mary,
Mother of the Lord, what do you want me to do for you? After
all, I have left my servant with you, to provide you with food.
Surely you do not wish me to transgress the command of my
Lord, which he laid upon me when he said, 'Travel around the

whole world, until sin is abolished!' (cf. Mt 28:19) Now, then, tell me what burdens your soul. Do you lack anything?" And Mary said to him, "John, my son, I do not need any of this world's goods; but when, on the day after tomorrow, I depart from the body, I beg you to show me a kindness: keep my body safe, and lay it only in a sepulcher. Guard it, with your brother Apostles, on account of the high priests. For with my own ears I heard them saying, 'When we find her body we will commit it to the fire, because that deceiver came forth from her!'"

When John heard her saying, "I shall depart from the body," he fell on his knees and said with tears, "O Lord, who are we, that you let us see such tribulations? For we have still not forgotten our earlier troubles, and now see—we must endure further tribulation! Why, O Mary, do I not depart from the body, that you might keep watch over me?"

When Mary heard John say this, weeping, she begged those standing nearby to be silent—for they, too, were in tears—and she restrained John, saying, "Child, be patient with me and cease your weeping!" Then John rose and wiped away his tears. And Mary said to him, "Come along with me, and ask the people to sing psalms, while I speak with you." And while they sang, she led John into her inner chamber, and showed him her funeral garments and all the things she had made ready for her corpse; she said, "John, my child, you know that I have nothing on earth except my funeral dress and two tunics. There are two widows in this place; when I depart from the body, give each of them one." And after this, she led him to where the palm branch was, which had been given her by the angel, and she said to him, "John, my child, take this branch, that you may carry it before my bier; for so I was commanded." Then he said to her, "I cannot take it without my fellow Apostles being present, lest when they come, discussion and resentment should arise among us. For there is one greater than I among them, who has been set over us.[14] But if we consider it together, they will approve."

7. As soon as they came out of her private chamber, there was a great clap of thunder, so that those who were in the place were terrified. And after the sound of the thunder, the Apostles descended, like hail from the clouds, at Mary's door: eleven of them, each sitting on a cloud! First there was Peter, second Paul—he, too, borne by a cloud and counted along with the Apostles, for he, too, was an original source of faith in Christ. After them, the other Apostles were also gathered, on clouds, at Mary's door. They greeted each other, gazing in astonishment at one another and marveling at how they had come together in the same place. And Peter said, "Brothers, let us pray to God who has gathered us together, especially since our brother Paul is with us." When Peter had said this, they stood still in prayer, and made this petition with one voice: "We pray that it may be made known to us why God has brought us together." Then each deferred to the other, that he might lead the rest in prayer.

So Peter said to Paul, "My brother Paul, stand up and pray before me; for I rejoice with an inexpressible joy that you have come to live in the faith of Christ." And Paul said to him, "Pardon me, father Peter, for I am a neophyte and am not worthy to follow in the footsteps of all of you. How, then, shall I pray before you? For you are the pillar of light, and all the brothers standing around are more worthy than I! You, Father, pray for me and for us all, that the grace of the Lord may remain with us."

Then the Apostles rejoiced at Paul's humility and said, "Father Peter, you have been set over us—you pray for us!" So Peter prayed, saying, "God our Father and the Lord Jesus Christ will glorify you, just as the service which I perform is touched with glory; for I am the least of the brethren and your servant. As I have been chosen, so you will be also—one call has been given to all of us! So everyone who gives glory to an-

other gives glory to Jesus and not to a human being. For this is
the command of the Teacher, that we should love one another
(Jn 15:12; cf. 1 Jn 3:11, 23)."

At that, Peter stretched out his hands and gave thanks, saying, "Almighty Lord, 'who are seated upon the cherubim' on
high (2 Sam 19:15) and 'look upon the lowly' (Ps 112:6
[LXX]), 'who dwell in unapproachable light' (2 Tim 6:16),
you 'loosen what is hardened' (Dan 5:12), you 'reveal hidden
treasures' (Is 45:3), and you have planted your kindness within
us. Which of the gods is as gracious as you to those who pray?
'And you do not remove your mercy from us' (2 Macc 6:16),
for you save from evil all who hope in you; you live, and have
conquered death, from this time and for the ages of ages.
Amen." And once again they embraced each other.[15]

8. Just then John came into the midst of them and said,
"Give me a blessing, too!" Then they also embraced him, each
in the proper order. And after the embrace, Peter said to him,
"John, beloved of the Lord, how have you come here and how
many days have you been here?" And John said, "It happened
when I was in the city of Sardis[16] teaching at about the ninth
hour, that a cloud came down upon the place where we were
gathered. And it took me up, in the sight of all who were with
me, and brought me to this place. I knocked on the door and they
opened for me, and I found a crowd around our mother Mary,
and she said to me, 'I am about to leave the body.' I did not remain in the midst of those who stood around her, but grief
weighed down upon me. So now, brothers, if you go in to her
early in the morning, do not weep or be agitated, lest the crowd
around her, seeing us in tears, should waver in their faith concerning the resurrection, and say, 'They, too, fear death!' But let
us encourage each other with the sayings of our good Teacher."

Then the Apostles, going early in the morning into Mary's
house, said with a single voice: "Blessed Mary, mother of all

the saved, grace be with you!" And Mary said to them, "Why have you come here? Who announced to you that I am to depart from the body? And how have you been gathered here? For I see you gathered together, and I rejoice." And each recounted the place from which he had been transported, and said, "We were taken up by the clouds and brought together here." Then all of them praised her and said, "May the Lord, the savior of all, bless you!" And Mary rejoiced in the Spirit and said, "I praise you, who give all a share in your blessing! I bless the place where your glory dwells! I bless you, giver of light, who came to dwell for a time in my womb! I bless all the works of your hands, which obey you with full submission! I bless you, who bless us! I bless the words of life that come forth from your mouth, and which have been given to us in the form of truth! For I believe that what you have said will come true for me. You said, 'I will send all the Apostles to you, when you go forth from the body'; and behold, they are gathered together, and I am in the midst of them, like a vine bearing fruit, just as in the days when I was with you. I bless you with every kind of blessing! Let the rest of the things said to me by you come to their fulfillment! For you said, 'You will be able to see me, when you depart from the body.'"

Saying this, she called Peter and all the Apostles and led them into her private chamber, and showed them her funeral apparel. And after this, she went out and sat in the midst of everyone, as the lamps remained lighted; for they did not allow them to be extinguished, according to Mary's orders.

9. When the sun set, on the second day of Mary's departure from her body,[17] Peter said to all the Apostles, "Brothers, let one who has the literary training speak, addressing the crowd through this whole night.[18] And the Apostles said to him, "Who is wiser than you? We shall be especially delighted to hear something of your educated words!"

Then Peter began to speak: "Brothers, and all who have come to this place at this hour of our mother Mary's departure, you have done well to light lamps that shine with the fire of this visible earth. But I wish that each of you will also take hold of his immaterial lamp in the age that has no end; this is the threefold lamp of the inner person, which is body and soul and spirit.[19] For if these three shine forth with the true fire, for which you are now struggling, you will not be ashamed when you enter into the marriage-feast to rest with the bridegroom. So it is with our mother Mary. For the light of her lamp fills the world, and will not be quenched until the end of the ages, so that all who wish to be saved may take courage from her. Do not think, then, that Mary's death is death! It is not death, but eternal life, because 'the death of the just will be proclaimed glorious before the Lord' (Ps 115:15). This, then, is glory, and the second death will have no power to do them harm."

While Peter was still speaking, a great light shone in the house in the midst of them all, so that the light of their lamps seemed dark by contrast. And a voice was heard, saying, "Peter, speak to them of a kind of knowledge which they can bear. For the best doctor cares for the pains of those who suffer, and the nurse adapts her care to the age of the child." Peter raised his voice and said, "We bless you, O Christ, the rudder of our souls!"

10. Then Peter said to the virgins who were present there: "Hear about your grace and your glory and your honor! For blessed are all who guard the form of their holy life. Hear and learn what our teacher said to us, 'The Kingdom of heaven is like virgins' (Mt 25:1). He did not say 'it is like a great length of time,' because time passes, but the name of virginity will not pass away. Nor did he liken it to wealth, since money is spent but the name of virginity remains. That is why I believe you are even now in glory: for that reason, he compared the

Kingdom of heaven to you, since you have no cares. For when death is sent upon you, you do not say, 'Woe to us—where shall we flee, and leave our poor children or our great wealth or our planted fields or our large possessions? You do not worry about any of these things. You have no other concern but that for your own virginity. And when death is sent upon you, you will be found ready, lacking in nothing. Learn, then, that nothing is greater than the name of virtue, and nothing more burdensome than worldly things.

"And listen to this.[20] In a certain city there was a man who lived with an abundance of all things. He happened to have servants, and two of his servants committed the offense of disobeying his orders. The master was angry at them, and sent them off to a distant region for a while, with the intention of calling them back afterwards. One of the exiled servants built a house for himself, and planted a vineyard and built a bakery, and acquired other great possessions. But the other servant, if he was able to earn anything from his labor, saved it in the form of gold. And summoning a goldsmith, he drew a crown and said to the goldsmith, 'I am a servant, and have a master who has a son; form their images in a gold crown.' The goldsmith made use of his skill, and said to the servant, 'Come, put the crown on your head!' But the servant said, 'Take your payment; I have a particular time in mind for wearing the crown.' Then the goldsmith understood what was said by the servant, and went home.

"After this, the time set for the end of their exile drew near. And the master sent a severe underling to them with the command, 'If you do not bring them back to me within seven days, you will be in trouble!' The messenger went with great haste, and coming to that region he searched for the servants night and day. And coming upon the one who had acquired the house and vineyard and other possessions, he said to him, 'Let us go, for your master has sent me to you.' Seeming to comply, the servant first said to him, 'Let us go,' but later said to him, 'Wait for me, until I can sell all the possessions I have acquired here.' Then the messenger said to him, 'I cannot wait; for I have an appointed time of seven days, and since I respect his threat I cannot tarry.' Then the servant wept, saying, 'Woe is me—I have been found unprepared!' And the messenger said to him, 'O wicked servant, you forgot that you are a servant and have been sent into exile, and that when the master wished he would send for you! Why did you plant vineyards, from which you will not be able to take anything away? You have been found unprepared! Before I came to you, you should have made yourself ready.' Then the servant wept and said, 'Woe is me! I thought I would always be in exile, and I did not believe that my master would seek me out; that is why I acquired all these possessions in this country.' Then the messenger forced him to get going, bringing nothing along with him.

"But when the other servant heard that he had been sent to them, he got up, carrying the crown, and walking along the road on which the messenger was to come, he waited patiently for him. And when he came, the servant said to him, 'My master sent you for me. Let us go off together with joy, for nothing holds me back! What I have is light—for I own nothing but this gold crown. For I had it made, as I waited day by day and prayed that my lord would be merciful to me, and that my master would send for me and take me from this exile, lest anyone should envy me and take away my crown. Now I have received the answer to my prayer. Let us get up, then, and be on our way!'

"Then both servants went off with the messenger. When their master saw them, he said to the one who had nothing, 'Where is the product of all this time of your exile?' And the servant answered, 'Master, you sent to me a harsh soldier, and

I begged him to allow me to sell my goods and take their value into my hands. And he said to me, "I have no permission to do so." Then his master said to him, 'O wicked servant, now you thought of selling, when I sent a messenger to you! Why did you not consider your exile, or reckon that those possessions would be of no value to you?' In anger, he commanded that he be bound hand and foot and sent off to other, still more wretched places. Then summoning the one who had brought the crown, he said to him, 'Well done, good and trustworthy servant! You desired liberation, as is obvious from the crown you acquired, for a crown is the mark of free people! But you did not dare to wear it without the permission of your master. For a servant cannot be set free except by his own master. As then you desired freedom, receive it from me!' That day he was set free, and was put in command of many."

11. After saying this to the virgins with Mary, Peter turned to the crowd and said, "Let us also hear, my brothers, the things that will come upon us. For truly we are the virgins of the true Bridegroom, the Son of the God and Father of all creation—we, the human race; being angry with our race at the beginning, God cast Adam into this world. Under his displeasure, then, and in a kind of exile, we live in it, but we will not be allowed to remain in it. For the day of each of us is coming, and it will bring us to where our fathers and ancestors are, Abraham and Isaac and Jacob. And when the end of each of us comes, the stern messenger will be sent to us—namely, death. When he comes to the soul of a sick sinner, who has piled up for himself many sins and iniquities, and harasses him severely, then the sinner will plead, 'Have patience with me this one time, until I redeem the sins which I have sown in my body.' But death will accept no excuses. For how will he make any concession when a person's allotted time is fulfilled? So, having no store of righteousness, he will be borne away to the

place of torment. But if anyone does the works of righteousness, he will rejoice and say, 'Nothing holds me back—for I
have nothing now to bring with me, except the name of virginity.' He will then beseech death, saying, 'Do not leave me behind on this earth, lest some envy me and take away the name
of my virginity.' Then his soul will go forth from his body and
be brought to the immortal bridegroom with hymns, and they
will establish it in a place of repose. As for now, then, my
brothers, struggle on in the knowledge that we shall not remain
here forever!"

12. After Peter had said these things and exhorted the
crowd until dawn, the sun rose. And Mary got up and went outside, and raised her hands and prayed to the Lord. After her
prayer, she went in and lay down on her bed. Peter sat at her
head and John by her feet, while the rest of the Apostles stood
in a circle around her pallet. And about the third hour of the
day, there was a great clap of thunder from the heavens, and a
sweet fragrance, which caused all those present to be overpowered by sleep, except for the Apostles alone, and three virgins, whom the Lord appointed to stay awake so that they
might be witnesses of Mary's funeral rites and her glory. And
behold, the Lord came on the clouds, with a multitude of angels beyond number.[21] And Jesus himself and Michael entered
the inner chamber where Mary was, while the angels sang
hymns and remained standing outside her chamber. And as
soon as the Savior entered, he found the Apostles with holy
Mary, and he embraced them all. After this, he embraced his
own mother. And Mary opened her mouth and blessed him,
saying, "I bless you, for you have not grieved me with regard
to the things you foretold. You foretold that you would not allow angels to come again to seek my soul, but that you would
come for it yourself. It has happened, Lord, according to your
word (cf. Lk 1:38). Who am I, lowly one, that I have been

counted worthy of such glory?" And having said this, she brought the course of her life to its fulfillment, her face turned smilingly towards the Lord. And the Lord took her soul and placed it in the hands of Michael, after wrapping it in veils of some kind, whose splendor it is impossible to describe.

The Apostles looked on as the soul of Mary was given into the hands of Michael, filled out with all the members of a human being, except for the form of female and male, but with nothing else in it except the likeness of the whole body and a brilliance seven times greater than the sun. Peter was filled with joy, and asked the Lord, "Is then the soul of each of us bright, as Mary's is?" The Lord said to him, "O Peter, the souls of all those being born in this world are like this, but when they depart from the body they are not in such a brilliant condition, because they were sent here in one state but are later found in another.[22] For 'they loved the darkness' (Jn 3:19) of many sins. But if someone guards himself from the iniquities of this world's darkness, and so leaves the body, his soul will be found to be as bright as this." Again, the Savior said to Peter, "Take care to keep Mary's body, my dwelling place, safe. Go out of the left side of the city[23] and you will find a new tomb; place the body in it, and remain there, just as she commanded you."

After the Savior said this, the very body of the holy Mother of God cried out before everyone and said, "Remember me, King of glory! Remember me, that I am your creation; remember me, that I guarded the treasure entrusted me." Then Jesus said to her body, "Surely I will not abandon you, the treasury of my pearl! Surely I will not abandon you, the guardian of the treasure entrusted to you, who were found trustworthy! Far be it from me to abandon you, the ark who steered the way for your own steersman! Far be it from me to abandon you, the treasury who remained sealed until you were sought!" And saying this, the Savior disappeared.

13. Peter and the other Apostles, and the three virgins, prepared Mary's body for burial and laid it on a bier. After this, all
those sleeping awoke. Then Peter picked up the palm branch,
and said to John, "You are the virgin [Apostle]; it is your duty
to sing hymns before the bier, holding this." Then John said to
him, "You are our father and bishop; it is your duty to be before the bier until we bring it to the place [of burial]." And Peter said to him, "So that none of us may grieve, let us crown her
bier with it [i.e., the palm branch]."

Then the Apostles rose and lifted Mary's bier. And Peter
began the hymn, "Israel went out from the land of Egypt, alle-
luia" (Ps 113:1 [LXX])[24] And the Lord and the angels were
walking along on the clouds, singing hymns and blessing God,
without being seen; only the voice of the angels could be
heard. The sound of a mighty crowd filled all of Jerusalem,
and when the chief priests heard the tumult and the sound of
people singing hymns, they were distressed and said, "What is
this tumult?" Someone told them that Mary had departed from
the body, and that the Apostles were gathered around her,
singing hymns. Immediately Satan entered into them (cf. Jn
13, 27), and they were filled with anger and said, "Come, let us
go out and kill the Apostles, and let us burn the body that bore
that sorcerer!" And they rose up and went out with swords and
shields (cf. Mt 27:46, 55 par.), to put them to death. But immediately the angels on the clouds struck them with the inability
to see and caused them to bump their heads against the city
walls, since they could not see where they were going—except
for one single chief priest, who found a way to go out from
within the walls to see what was happening. And when he
drew near the Apostles and saw the bier, crowned with the
palm, and the Apostles singing hymns, he was filled with a
mighty burst of anger and said: "Here is the dwelling of the
one who despoiled our people; what tremendous glory she

has!" And he went up to the bier in his great anger, and wishing to upset it, he laid hold of it where the palm branch was, and pulling on it, attempted to dash it on the ground. But immediately his hands adhered to the bier and were severed from his elbows, and remained hanging from the bier.

Then the man cried out in pain before all the Apostles, beseeching them, "Do not abandon me in such an urgent condition!" Then Peter said to him, "The action of coming to your rescue does not belong to me, or to any of these men. If you believe that Jesus is the Son of God, whom you rose up against, imprisoned and put to death, surely you will be released from this predicament." And the man said, "Did we not realize that he is the Son of God? But what shall we do, when avarice darkens our eyes? For our ancestors, when they were about to die, summoned us and said, 'Children, see that God has chosen you from all the tribes, that you might have a position of power before all this people, and might not have to work in the mud of this earth. This is your work: to build up this people, and to receive from all of them tithes and first-fruits and every first-born coming forth from the womb. But be careful, sons, lest your holy places become too prosperous and you rise up and go into business for yourselves, and anger God.[25] Give, rather, your surplus to the poor, and to the orphans and widows of your people, and do not ignore the soul in distress. But we did not listen to the traditions of our ancestors, but when we saw that the place abounded greatly, we put the first-born of our flocks and our cattle and all our beasts on the tables of those who sell and buy. When the Son of God came, he cast them all, even the money-changers, out of the holy place, and said, 'Take all of this out of this place, and do not make my Father's house a house of business' (Jn 2:16). But we, looking only at our customs that had been condemned by him, thought up evil plans in our hearts and rebelled against him and put him to death, knowing in fact that he is the Son of God. But do not hold on to the memory of our wickedness, but have mercy on me; for that is what has happened to me on the part of God—he has loved me, that I might live!"

Then Peter ordered the bier to be put down, and said to the chief priest, "If now you believe with your whole heart, go and kiss the body of Mary, and say 'I believe in you and in the God who was born of you.' Then the chief priest blessed holy Mary, in the Hebrew language, for three hours, and did not allow anyone to touch her, offering witness-texts from the holy books of Moses and the other prophets that it is written about her that she would be the temple of the God of glory. Those who heard were struck with wonder at hearing these traditions, which they had not heard before. And Peter said to him, "Go now, and join your hands together." And he did join them, saying, "In the name of our Lord Jesus Christ, the Son of Mary, Mother of God, let these hands of mine be joined to each other." And immediately they became as they had been from the beginning, without any deficiency. And Peter said to him, "Stand up, and take a strand from the branch of palm, and go into the city. And you will discover a blind multitude, who cannot find the way they should walk; tell them what has happened to you. And if anyone believes, lay this strand of plam on his or her eyes, and immediately that person will see."

The chief priest went off as Peter had commanded, and found many blind people—these were the ones whom the angels had struck with blindness—weeping, and saying, "Woe to us, for what happened to the Sodomites has also happened to us! For in ancient times God struck them with blindness, and afterwards he sent fire from heaven and burnt them up. Woe to us! Behold, we have been mutilated already, and it only remains for the fire to come!" Then the man who had taken the strand of palm spoke to them about the faith. And those who believed began to see, while those who did not believe did not see, but remained blind.[26]

14. The Apostles, however, lifted up the precious body of our most glorious lady, Mary, the Mother of God and ever-virgin, and placed it in a new tomb, in the place the Savior had showed them. They remained in that place, awake in unity of spirit, for three days. And after the third day, they opened the sarcophagus to venerate the precious tabernacle of her who deserves all praise, but found only her grave-garments; for she had been taken away by Christ, the God who became flesh from her, to the place of her eternal, living inheritance. And our Lord Jesus Christ himself, who bestowed glory on his immaculate Mother Mary Theotokos, will also bestow glory on those who glorify her. Those who call upon her, celebrating her memorial every year, he will save from every danger, and he will fill their households with good things, like the house of Onesiphorus (cf. 2 Tim 1:16; 4:19). And they will receive the forgiveness of their sins, both here and in the age to come. For he has shown her to be his cherubic throne on earth, an earthly heaven, the hope and refuge and confidence of our race, so that if we celebrate, with the sacred mysteries, the festival of her holy Dormition, we might find mercy and grace in the present age and in the age to come, by the grace and kindliness of our Lord Jesus Christ: to whom be glory and power, with his unbegotten Father and with the all-holy and life-giving Spirit, now and always and for the ages of ages.

Amen.

1   John is referring here to the unwillingness of his own predecessors at
    Thessalonica to accept the circulating accounts of Mary's Dormition as
    authentic. As a result, despite the decree of Emperor Maurice (582-602)
    establishing August 15 as a festival to be celebrated throughout the Em-
    pire, the church at Thessalonica seems to have avoided celebrating it
    until John's time, and the purpose of this homily seems to be both to jus-
    tify and to encourage its adoption. As Martin Jugie, the homily's first
    editor, has observed (PO 19.360f.), the reason for this cautious attitude
    in Thessalonica may have been that see's long-standing connection with
    the Church of Rome, as the metropolitan city of the largely Latin-
    speaking province of Illyricum; until at least the mid-sixth century, the
    metropolitan of Thessalonica was usually designated a "vicar" or papal
    representative in mainland Greece by the bishops of Rome. The Western
    Church did not accept the feast into its calendar until the end of the sev-
    enth century, and a Latin version of the narrative of Mary's Dormition
    had been listed among apocrypha of heretical origin in the *Decretum
    Gelasianum*, an official list of canonical and uncanonical works com-
    posed either during or shortly after the time of Pope Gelasius I (492-
    496): see E. von Dobschütz (ed.), *Das Decretum Gelasianum de libris
    recipiendis et non recipiendis* V, 6 (TU 38/IV [Leipzig, 1912] 12, 53);
    for the date and authorship of this document, see J. Chapman, *Revue Bé-
    nédictine* 30 (1913) 187-207, 315-333.

2   John is referring here to the critical sifting, for liturgical use, of material
    found in the apocryphal acts of the Apostles, apparently by bishops in Thrace
    or Asia in the third or fourth century, as well as to more recent critical analy-
    sis of the acts of the Christian martyrs. It is not clear precisely whom he
    means. As early as Origen, however, Christian scholars were aware of the
    mythical and often Gnostic character of many of the acts of the Apostles.

3   John is alluding to the sites venerated in Jerusalem as connected with
    Mary's death and entry into glory: her house in Sion, as his narrative
    will make clear, and her tomb at the foot of the Mount of Olives. This
    may be an indication that he has visited the sites himself, and perhaps
    that he collected or verified his narrative material in Jerusalem.

4   Greek: αὐτολογία. This word, found in this form only here, seems to
    mean "accounts made up by their authors"; it could, however, also mean
    "(so-called) eye-witness accounts".

5   The moralizing character of this work, especially in the context of urging
    its readers to prepare for a happy death, remains evident throughout, de-
    spite its largely narrative structure.

6   In John's retelling of the Dormition story, the palm branch given to
    Mary by the angel plays an important ceremonial role. This is one of the
    main features of the earlier Greek tradition, represented by the Dormi-
    tion narrative attributed to John the Evangelist; the text appears in K.
    von Tischendorf, *Apocalypses Apocryphae* (Leipzig, 1866) 95-112;
    Eng. tr. M. R. James, *New Testament Apocrypha* (Oxford, 1975). For a

typology of the various forms of the Dormition story based on such details, see M. van Esbroeck, *art. cit.* (above, p. 39, n. 15).

7 This suggests that John is aware of a tradition according to which the palm branch connected with Mary's death was venerated as a miraculous relic and test of faith. In the subsequent narrative here, it also seems to function as a reassuring mark of God's favor during the trials of death.

8 In John's account, Mary apparently lives on Mount Sion, just outside the walls of Jerusalem. She is directed to climb the Mount of Olives, possibly because of its association with the ascension of Jesus. Her own tomb, however, was venerated at the foot of the Mount, in the Valley of Jehoshaphat, next to the traditional site of the Garden of Gethsemane.

9 Many ancient Eastern Christian works, especially those of a more popular character, stressed the assault of demons on each soul in the agony of death, and the protection of angels afforded to the just in that moment. This belief is in the background of John's sermon, and suggests the importance of the Dormition narrative for him as a model of Christian death. For a typology of Dormition narratives based on their inclusion or transformation of these beliefs, see J. Rivière, "Rôle du démon au jugement particulier: contribution à l'histoire des 'Transitus Mariae'," *Bulletin de littérature ecclésiastique* 48 (1947) 49-56, 98-126; see also the critique of Rivière's classification in Mimouni, 45-47.

10 Literally: "For now travail has come upon her who is giving birth." Mary likens the pangs of death to childbirth, perhaps because it, too, is the painful and laborious passage of a human being to new life.

11 Here again, the shape of the story seems partly determined by deathbed customs, and by the author's desire to present Mary's death as a model for other Christians.

12 John of Thessalonica here offers his own homely interpretation of Jesus' words in Jn 19:26f.

13 John of Thessalonica seems to assume that the secret words spoken by Jesus to the Beloved Disciple at the Last Supper had to do with Mary's future life.

14 John is obviously referring to Peter.

15 Peter's prayer of thanks, laced with Biblical allusions and followed by the kiss of peace, has a decidedly liturgical character, even though it does not reproduce any known ritual text.

16 Martin Jugie, the original editor of this sermon, points out that this is the only ancient narrative which asserts the Apostle John was in Sardis, on the coast of Asia Minor, when he heard of Mary's coming death. Several other traditions place him in nearby Ephesus. This mention of Sardis may be an echo of traditions linking the dormition story with Melito of Sardis, a connection witnessed in the widely-circulated Latin *Transitus Mariae* associated with his name (L 2). For details and bibliography on the Pseudo-Melito, see Mimouni 264-276; for similarities between this work and Pseudo-Melito, see *ibid.* 270.

17 John of Thessalonica presents Mary's death or "departure from the body" as a three-day process, solemnly celebrated by herself and all who have been gathered around her by her own invitation and God's miraculous intervention.

18 John hints here at the expectation that seems to have accompanied the Dormition festival in late antiquity: it was to be an all-night vigil, marked by preaching of the highest rhetorical art.

19 The theme of moral exhortation and consolation in the face of death, so central to John's treatment of the Dormition, is expressed clearly and succinctly in this paragraph spoken by Peter.

20 Peter now proceeds to tell a long parable about readiness for death, whose details suggest several of the Gospel parables, especially that of the talents (Mt 25:14-29) and that of the vinedressers (Mt 21:33-41). This reveals once again the central concern of John's Dormition narrative: to move his hearers to prepare for death properly. The figure of the "severe soldier" sent to bring the two servants home, although later identified with death itself, also resembles the angels believed to act as instruments of testing and punishment at the hour of death (see above, n. 8). The story-line of Peter's parable here—servants sent into distant exile to prove themselves, after an initial fall from grace—also bears some resemblance to the Origenist myth of the fall of souls. John may have inherited this image from the same sixth-century Palestinian sources that furnished him with the story of Mary's death.

21 This detail suggests the image of Jesus' final coming in judgment in the Synoptic Gospels: e.g., Mk 13:26f.

22 Here again, John of Thessalonica seems to assume that souls exist in a condition of innocence before being "sent" into their bodies.

23 This might suggest Mary's tomb was west of Jerusalem; actually, the traditional site is directly to the east.

24 Mention of this psalm here probably reflects the liturgical practice for burials in the early sixth century.

25 John may be including here a word of warning for his confreres in Jerusalem on the spiritual danger of being responsible for places of pilgrimage.

26 At least five different versions exist of the final paragraph, on Mary's burial, in the various manuscripts studied by its editor, Martin Jugie; two other manuscripts simply break off at this point without a conclusion. Among the extant forms of the homily's ending, some speak simply of Mary's burial; others speak of the translation of her body to paradise, where it is buried beneath the tree of life, "and now she lives for all ages"; others, like the version given here, affirm more clearly her bodily resurrection and entry into glory. The version I have translated, from the manuscript Vaticanus Graecus 2072, ff. 178r-v, is judged by Jugie to be, in all probability, closest to John of Thessalonica's original ending. For the various alternative versions, see Jugie's edition, PO 19.401-405.

AN ENCOMIUM ON THE ASSUMPTION OF
THE HOLY MOTHER OF GOD

By Theoteknos, Bishop of Livias

[1.] "Sing to the Lord a new song, because he has done wonders." (Ps 97:1) Let us all rejoice greatly in the resurrection of the Lord, our God and Savior Jesus Christ, and let us sing spiritual songs, constantly praising him who arranges all things for our salvation. After his resurrection from the dead and his ascension into heaven, after he had taken his throne at the right hand of his God and Father—even though he is inseparable from his heart—in the immaculate flesh which he had taken from Mary, the holy Mother of God, he summoned all his holy disciples and apostles to come through the clouds and gather by that spotless, holy one who never knew marital union; he gathered them for a great event, for she who had become wider than the heavens and higher than the cherubim was to receive the palm of reward to which she had been called, and to be taken up into heaven. For if he has blessed his saints with the whole kingdom of heaven, if he opened Paradise to a thief with a single word, how much more [would he have been eager to welcome][1] the one who made him a home in her womb—the one whom he had created, whom he had formed, from whom he became flesh, as [he willed]. His purpose was that the power of the Prince of Evil should be destroyed through her by whom he had deceived us,[2] and that through her all women should find freedom from the curse that bound them; "for she shall be saved through childbearing," as the Apostle says. (1 Tim 2:15)

[He has glorified] her, the holy and all-beautiful one, the venerable one worthy of all joy, mother and virgin, holy and spotless; her, who nourished with her milk the one who

71

brought honey from the rock (Ps 80:16), who nursed in her arms him who needs no nourishment at all, and who was found worthy to bear as her own son, without human seed, her own creator.

[2.] She was begotten like the cherubim, from pure and spotless [clay].[3] For while she was still in the loins of her father Joachim, her mother Anna received a message from a holy angel, who said to her, "Your seed shall be spoken of throughout all the world."[4] Therefore Anna brought her to the temple of the Lord as an offering.[5] And during all her time there, the maiden stood alongside Christ the king, "at his right hand, splendidly clothed in a robe of gold," as the prophet says: "Listen, daughter, and see, and incline your ear; forget your people and your father's house. The king desires your beauty; he is your Lord—pay homage to him." (Ps 44:10-13)

She was found worthy of unspeakable joy, which the prophets had foretold for her; her heart was penetrated both by a sword (Lk 2:35) and by joy. When she considered her conception [of Jesus] without seed, and the divine overshadowing, and [when she thought of] his human career—of how the invisible one had become visible, how the incomprehensible one shared her nature and reclined with publicans, stood before Pilate like a slave and was nailed to a cross and sealed in a tomb—and was in great confusion at the thought, surely a sword did pass through her soul. But joy filled her at his resurrection from the dead... and his ascension... and at the thought that the flesh that had come forth from her own womb, without seed, now sits enthroned with the Father; and this joy is great, and gladness has taken hold of the blameless one.

[3.] For it was right that the holy woman who brought forth the Son should see him on his high and lofty throne, and should see "every knee bend to him, of those in heaven and of those on earth," and [hear] "every tongue confess" his praise

(Phil 2:10), who "is to judge the living and the dead" (Creed of Nicaea, etc.).

It was right that she be surrounded by the holy apostles, as mother of all of them—for the only-begotten Son, the Word of God, called his own disciples brothers; right that her most holy body, which bore God, which had received God and was made like God, that spotless body radiant with divine light and full of glory, should be borne in procession by them and by the angels and confided for a short time to the earth, and then to be taken up in glory to heaven along with her soul, which was so pleasing to God.

For if, when he saw his disciples discouraged by his passion, Jesus said to them, "I go to prepare a place for you" (Jn 14:2), how much more will he have prepared a place for the one who begot him—all the more so, as she had all the more right of access to him! So the immaculate body of the all-holy one, and her pure soul, in which God took delight, were taken up [to heaven] with an escort of angels. For if she had received nourishment from angels in the Lord's temple, while she was still a child,[6] how much more should she be served by the powers on high after she had become herself the Lord's temple!

[4.] The holy one was pleasing to God the Father; the virgin was pleasing to the substantial Word, begotten from the Father before the ages; the virgin was pleasing to the life-giving Spirit, who gives every being light and transforms them into citizens of heaven. For if Enoch, who pleased God, was taken up "that he might never see death" (Gen 5:24; Heb 11:5), how much more would God have taken up the soul of her whom he had made one body with divine grace,[7] to the paradise of delight where the divine light shines without end! And if he commanded that Elijah, who was a prophet, should mount to heaven in a chariot of fire (1 Kg 2:11), how much more she who is foretold and called blessed in the prophets' writings, who shines in an outstanding way among the prophets and the apostles like the moon in the midst of the stars.

The whole heavenly court, the whole assembled choir of angels [now came] to [the service of] the all-holy one...[8] And even though the God-bearing body of that holy one did taste death, it was not corrupted; for it was kept incorrupt and free of decay, and it was lifted up to heaven with her pure and spotless soul by the holy archangels and powers; there it remains, exalted above Enoch and Elijah and all the prophets and apostles, above all the heavens, below God alone—who has been pleased to arrange all things for our salvation. The divine nature, after all, is not circumscribed by any place, since it is beyond measure, unknowable, uncomposed, unlimited. <It was the good pleasure of our Lord, the Word, to become flesh from her, as the prophet had foretold: "The Lord said, 'You are my son, and I have begotten you this day.'(Ps 2:7)" That is: this day he has taught us that he has become human among us, he who came forth from the holy one in a childbirth without human seed. And he says, once again, "From the womb, before the morning star, I have begotten you (Ps. 110.3)." That is: having been born from the Father before the ages, he has manifested by the Holy Spirit what has been since the beginning, and what is so by God's decree.

[5.] The assumption of the body of the holy one, and her ascension to heaven, took place on the fifteenth day of August, which is the sixth day of the month of Mesore. And there was joy in heaven and on earth,>[9] as the angels struck up the hymn, while human beings glorified the mother of the King of Heaven, who had herself glorified the human race: the Mother of God, the pure one, the three-storied ark, the impenetrable rock that gushed forth the stream of life—Christ, who said, "If anyone thirst, let him come to me and drink." (Jn 7:37)

What terms of praise can one use to give adequate voice to the actions of the all-venerable one while she still lived in the flesh? While on earth, she was heaven; she associated with angels, and was the ambassador for the human race before the immaculate King, before him who "cancelled the charges against us" (Col 2:14). For if [God] glorifies those who glorify him, if he honors them with the gift of prophecy and offers them eternal life, how much more will he glorify, in soul and body, his mother according to the flesh. Truly, "he has glorified her and will glorify her again" (Jn 12:28).

[6.] Her all-holy body was being borne in procession by the holy Apostles—in whose number the apostle Paul was also included—and was being carried from Mount Sion to the place called Gethsemane, where the Savior's betrayal occurred, and where the judgment will take place,[10] "and the books shall be opened, and the Ancient of Days shall sit, and a river of fire" will gather sinners together and reproach them in the place where all peoples <will be judged> (Dan 7:10). We await the judgment in which we will give account to the Son of God. For the Ancient of Days has given him the right to judge (cf. Dan 7:13f). There the Lord promised the disciples that they would "sit on twelve thrones, judging the twelve tribes of Israel" (Mt 19:28).

The all-blessed body, then, of the holy one was being carried towards the place I have mentioned, accompanied by angels' songs of praise; and the unbelieving Jews, who had killed the Lord, looking down the valley, saw her remains lying on the bier and went towards it, intending to do violence in that very spot to the body which God had honored: his temple, his lampstand, his vessel containing pure oil, his altar of holocausts, appearing in splendor within the Holy of Holies.

All those who meant to attack her and to burn her body were struck with blindness; and one of them, who touched her bier with his own hands, was deprived of them—they were cut off! So that immaculate flesh was glorified; all of them came to believe and confessed her Mother of God, and the one whom they had vilified as a seductress they now praised in song as God's own Mother. And those who had lost their sight now saw the wonders worked by God towards his mother...[11] For a wonderful thing happened: the hands of the one who had lost them [were restored to him.] And all believed in Christ, who was before her and from her and with her, "the Son of David according to the flesh" (Rom 1:3).

Let no one think that the miracle worked by the all-holy body of the Mother of God was something impossible—for she had remained a virgin incorrupt. It was, after all, fitting for the spiritual ark, which contained the vessel of manna and the blooming rod of Aaron (Num 17:23), for she blossomed and bore the fruit that can never be consumed. The former ark defeated the hostile foreigners, who wanted to do it violence; how much more, then, should the spiritual ark defeat those who from the beginning have fought against God and against the beautiful name "that is invoked over us" (Jer 14:9)?

[7.] For she is ark and vase and throne and heaven. She was judged worthy to be entrusted with ineffable mysteries; she was judged worthy to reveal things hidden and sealed in the Book of Daniel, and through her "all of us, with faces unveiled, will gaze on the glory of the Lord" (2 Cor 3:18). Through her, the veil on Moses' face has been lifted.

Her all-holy body was guarded now by the apostles, who continued to attend her at the Lord's command...[12] Peter, the chief of the apostles, and Paul, who according to the witness of Scripture "bore the Lord's name" (Acts 9:15), rivalled each other in speeches rich in hidden wisdom. Suddenly there was thunder and a great earthquake; and they saw the holy virgin being taken up into heaven, so that there, where a place had been prepared for her by her Son, she might abide in free access to him, joining the choirs of angels and the company of prophets and apostles. She is teacher and prophet, the boast of virgins. She has "sought her beloved and found him," as is written in the Song of Songs (3:1-4); she has run across the mountains "like a gazelle... or a young stag"[13] (*ibid.* 2:17), "like a deer that years for running streams" (Ps 41:1) and is not deprived of her goal. She has found what Eve had lost; she has found what Adam was deprived of, because of his disobedience. She has entered, saying, "Breathe on my garden" (Cant 4:10). God the Word has entered, has dwelt in her, and Paradise is opened. The Advocate has entered, and welcomes the thief: "Amen, I say to you, today you will be with me in Paradise" (Lk 23:43).[14]

[8.] O wonderful mystery—O strange miracle! A thief is in Paradise, and the priests and scribes are outside, and do not dare to draw near. The drawn sword which guarded the way to the tree of life (Gen 3:24) has recognized the thief, because of the one who sent him; but those who read the Law have fallen from grace, because they would not glorify her who was a member of their people. Moved by envy, they rejected the voices of the prophets and ignored Moses, who taught them in the Law, and they remained without grace, the enemies of God. For Moses said, "The Lord God will raise up for you a prophet like me", God and a human being—for Moses was like a god in Pharaoh's eyes (Exod 22:20); "hear him in all the things that he will say to you" (Deut 18:15). "And everyone who will not listen to that prophet will be cut off from the people" (Deut 18:19; Ex 30:33).

Those unbelieving ones! They did not glorify their sister Mary, nor did they receive her son, who had been announced by Moses as God and a human being. But they will see and be amazed, when they look at him coming in glory on the clouds of heaven (Mt 24:30). Then they will be converted, and will beat their breasts and will call her blessed, along with Anna, the bosom that nursed her.[15] Then they will give glory to her who is descended from David, and will say to her, "You are of our race and our flesh. Now we know that you are higher than the heavens, and the bride of the heavenly King. Now we know that all the prophets spoke on your account.[16] One of them said, 'He will descend like dew upon the fleece' (Ps 71:6; cf. Jg 6:36-40); and another, 'Behold, a virgin shall conceive in her womb' (Is 7:14). And another, 'Grace has been poured out on your lips' (Ps 44.2); and Ezekiel, 'A gate looks towards the East' (Ezek 44:10). And another, 'O mountain, from you a holy stone is cut out, and the place of its cutting cannot be found' (Dan 2.34); and another, calling you the moon, has said, 'The sun has risen, and the moon remains in its course' (Hab 3:11)—that is, Christ has come forth from you and your virginity remains in its place.

"Truly, we have made a mistake 'in our foolishness, and have considered her life madness' (Wisdom 5.4); we have not plucked the fruit of righteousness, for we had a veil of smoke [before our eyes]. For when the prophet had seen the Lord, sitting on his throne of glory, and the six-winged ones chanting 'Holy, holy, holy,' he noticed that the house was full of smoke (Is 6:4). We are that house. Now we know what the prophets meant to reveal to us. But what good is it to us to say these things? For if one does not acknowledge Christ before men and women, Christ will not acknowledge him before the Father (Mt 10:32)."

[9.] Let us all confess our faith in Christ, let us praise the Father and the Holy Spirit. Let us rejoice with the Mother of God; let us sing along with the choirs of angels, and let us celebrate, as the festival of festivals, the assumption of the Ever-virgin. On earth she was radiant, as the treasure and teacher of virgins; in heaven she is available to us all as our intercessor. She has free access to God, and so bestows on us spiritual gifts; she gives grace to our words, and teaches us wisdom, for she is the mother of wisdom.[17] "Wisdom cries out in the streets, and moves with assurance in the open squares" (Prov 1:20). She cries out in the streets: "The tree that grows by streams of water bears fruit, and its leaves do not wither" (Ps 1:3). So the Lord Jesus Christ, our God, the incomprehensible Wisdom, the ever-flowing spring, was made flesh of the Virgin, and when her womb bore its fruit, her virginity was not destroyed. She is the mother of Christ, who said, "The one who believes in me, as Scripture says, rivers of living water will frow from his heart" (Jn 7:38). He calls "water" the teaching that comes from the Holy Spirit. Thirsting for this water, the prophet said, "As the deer yearns for streams of water, so my soul yearns for you, O God" (Ps 41:2).

[10.] "In the open squares she moves with assurance." Dwelling in the world and associating with the human race, she bestowed on the world the prize of peace. Christ himself is our peace (Eph 2:14), who said to his disciples, "My peace I give to you" (Jn 14:27). He means by "peace" a love of him and of our neighbor, and the readiness to die for him, in order that we might become sharers in his resurrection. This is real peace.

And the prophet referred to the Mother of God as peace, too, when he said, "Righteousness and peace have embraced. Truth has sprung up from the earth" (Ps 84:11). Mary is peace; Christ is righteousness and Christ is truth. The Mother of God is the earth. The Lord Jesus Christ, our God, has sprung up from her, and has said, "I am the life and the truth" (Jn 14:6). And again, the same prophet said, "The earth will yield its fruit" (Ps 84:13). Our earth is Mary, our sister and our lady; she has given her fruit "in due season" (Ps 1:3), the bread that will never fail us, Christ, who says, "I am the bread of life; the one who eats my flesh and drinks my blood has eternal life. For my flesh is truly food, and my blood is truly drink" (Jn 6:48, 54-55).

This is the fruit our earth has yielded—the ever-virgin Mother of God. While she lived on earth, she watched over us all, and was a kind of universal providence for her subjects. Now that she has been taken up into heaven, she is an unassailable fortification for the human race, and intercedes for us with God the Son, with whom and through whom be glory to the Father with the all-holy Spirit, now and always and for the ages of ages.

Amen.

1 Words printed in square brackets are conjectural translations of defective passages in the original text.

2 Here Theoteknos identifies Mary with Eve, as mother of a renewed human race.

3 "Clay" here is conjectural, reading **phl *d*** for a lost word in the manuscript beginning with **p**.

4 This is a quotation from the *Protevangelium of James* 4.1. The whole paragraph on Mary's birth is inspired, in fact, by the *Protevangelium*.

5 See *Protevangelium* 7.1f.

6 *Protevangelium* 8.1.

7 The text here is uncertain.

8 The text is again defective here.

9 The section in angled brackets here is missing in the Greek manuscript, and is supplied from the Arabic translation; see Wenger, 429 (addendum).

10 The traditional site of the tomb of Mary near Jerusalem is only a few yards away from that of the Garden of Gethsemane, in the Cedron valley at the foot of the Mount of Olives. This valley has also been associated, since at least the fourth century, with the Valley of Jehoshaphat, where the last judgment was expected (see Joel 3:2, 12).

11 There is a lacuna of about two lines in the manuscript at this point.

12 Again the text is defective, and the translation "to attend her" is conjectural.

13 "Or a young stag" is conjectural here, since the manuscript is again defective.

14 Theoteknos plays here and in the following paragraph with the image of "entering the Garden". Mary, as the new Eve, re-enters the Garden of Paradise, and even the Good Thief is welcomed into it, because Christ, the first "Advocate" of humanity (see Jn 14:16), has entered the "garden" of Mary's womb.

15 Cf. *Protevangelium* 6.3.

16 This list of prophetic *testimonia* applied to Mary is part of a repertory famililar from fifth- and sixth-century Greek preaching and poetry.

17 Theoteknos applies to Mary herself the characteristics ascribed to Wisdom in this verse of Proverbs, because of the traditional identification of Jesus, the incarnate Logos, as Wisdom itself.

AN ENCOMIUM ON THE DORMITION OF OUR MOST HOLY LADY, MARY, MOTHER OF GOD AND EVER-VIRGIN

By Our Father the Holy Modestus, Archbishop of Jerusalem

1. Knowing the holy significance of the sacred feasts of The Mother of Christ, our God, is a gift beyond telling. For the mystery itself[1] is full of glory, beyond the grasp of all mortals and all the powers of heaven, and the manifold revelation of Wisdom, rich though it is, is at a loss to offer worthy praise of this miracle that exceeds all the intellectual power of rational, conscious creation. She who is truly and literally the Mother of God has been sanctified by God himself, and is holier and more glorious than cherubim and seraphim. And in order to address this boundless dignity of hers, exalted beyond all the heavenly powers by the glory of the ineffable divine mystery which engulfs her—a glory impenetrable to both thoughts and contemplation—those who were chosen to be teachers in the Church of Christ our God, by the divine grace of the all-holy Spirit, and who were given strength by him, have risen up valiantly to their task, and have loved to dwell on it in pious contemplation, as in the sun's fiery chariot, as long as they could. For her sake, because of our Savior Christ, who issued forth from her and "in whom lie hidden the treasures of wisdom and knowledge" (Col 2:3), these inspired prophets have been judged worthy to discover sacred writings and to expound them for each holy festival of the Mother of God, and so to escort the devout people towards riches that can never be taken away, towards the Spirit's most splendid array of honors, towards the divinely designed edification of the orthodox Churches, for the glory of God our Savior.

But for some reason they have revealed nothing about her glorious falling-asleep, nor have those who came after them explained it to us. Therefore on the day of the falling-asleep of the Mother of God, most people who are eager for knowledge, most disciples of Christ and wise persons who love to listen to divine things, intensely yearn to know something of this unspoken mystery that surrounds her. And because of this eager interest of theirs, so pleasing to God, I have most gladly made this holy and welcome project my own: moved by deeply reverent longing, and by confidence in the Mother of God, who brought our life and salvation into the world, even I—poor wretch that I am—have found strength to attempt to compose a little essay about her. So I turn my voice now to God, like the thief crucified at the right of Christ our Savior; and from him, through his all-holy Mother, I beg to experience his great mercy. For the glory, then, of his Father and the Spirit, let us begin as follows.[2]

2. How amazing, my brothers and sisters in the love of Christ! Today she who gave birth to the life of all people has moved on to be a sharer in that life. The life which was begotten before the ages from the Father, which is God and the Word of God, which she bore in the flesh and nursed from her own breasts, the life that built all things from nothing and generated life in them—this life she has inherited, and has come as its mother to share in it above all the holy ranks of heaven and earth. The life that is the fountainhead of the universe she received from God and made a spring for this world, the light of mortal beings; for it is written, "The life was the light of men and women" (Jn 1:3f.). She has gone to dwell with this light, the true and substantial light, "the shining-forth of the glory of God the Father" (Heb 1:3), which lightens the world, which has become flesh through her by the Holy Spirit, "enlightening every man and woman who comes into the world" (Jn 1:9). And when Christ our God, co-eternal with his Father and the

Spirit, chose by decree to take her to himself, to share in his glory—his most-blessed mother, who is, after him, the greatest of all beings—all the angels and archangels rushed through the air to gather in a joyful visit to this world, sent from heaven by God to be the celebrants of her holy falling-asleep.

All the holy powers of heaven, too, rejoice to learn of the mystery; they praise the kind Savior Christ, who was born of her and who calls her to himself, and give abounding glory, as Scripture says, to him who formed the stars (Gen 1:16; cf. Ps 147:4), for revealing her as more glorious than the heavens. She is heaven for his divinity, and through her rational beings on earth now shine like heavenly bodies with the radiance of his divine grace, above the sun and moon and stars; for he says to them, "You are the light of the world" (Mt 5:14). From all of rational and intelligible creation, he has chosen her to be his all-holy Mother, and has endowed her with gifts above all others. The cherubim do not dare to look at him, or have the strength to gaze at him; the spirits worship him with his all-holy Father and Spirit, ceaselessly crying out, "Holy, holy, holy Lord, God of hosts" (Is 6:3). Yet he has, through her, set creation free from slavery, and has brought into reality surpassing joy for the whole cosmos; he has said to the powers above, "Rejoice with us" (Lk 15:9)! For through her, the mortal drachma is found, and the good shepherd has put on the skin of his sheep and has saved his intellectual beast from its wandering, laying it across his shoulders (Lk 15:3-10). The Lord of hosts rejoices, who became flesh from her without ceasing to be what he is, who sanctified her as a field ready to receive God, where God the Father graciously willed to be the farmer, and the Holy Spirit the workman who planted the seed. Christ, God's only Son, grew up and bore fruit in her as the true vine, providing joy for the holy powers of heaven and salvation for mortals on earth; for he says in the Gospel, "I am the true vine, and my Father is the farmer" (Jn 15:1). The Mother of God has come to this true vine that she brought forth, to harvest the grapes of incorruption and immortality, rejoicing over her new fruitfulness in the Kingdom of God. She is nourished on the heavenly bread of life, vitalized forever by him who entered our history from her sacred womb and came forth to share our mortal life, strengthening our hearts by right faith in him. Like an olive tree, like God's cultivated field, she has borne for us the fountainhead of mercy: Christ, whose mercy fills all things to overflowing.

3. The radiant cloud that bore the Lord of glory has been lifted up—lifted up to him: she who flashed forth his perfect divinity in her body like lightning, who rained down holy gifts from him on everything under heaven. There the orbit of that spiritual moon above our world, which the prophet spoke of (Hab 3:11), comes to completion: the moon which gave birth to the sun who is one of those three suns that share a single substance—the Trinity, as revealed by the tradition of the Fathers.[3] "And the moon stood still in the tracks" of her virginity (Hab 3:11); [she is] truly the Mother of God, revealing his radiance that all of this creation might come to know its God. She is received with rejoicing and unspeakable delight in the house of God the Father, herself the house which God built for his Son, who dwelt in her without being circumscribed and was made flesh from her by the Holy Spirit; who remained in her nine months and became an infant; yet who was God, inseparable from his Father and the Spirit. She who was made the dwelling-place of the consubstantial Trinity has come to a better dwelling—she who is forever his home, having heard from the archangel Gabriel, "The Holy Spirit will come down upon you, and the power of the Most High will overshadow you; therefore the one born of you will be called holy, the Son of God" (Lk 1:35). So she is glorified above the holy ranks of

heaven and earth; she is transplanted from here, as "from glory to glory" (2 Cor 3.18)—the mortal bush that bore the fire of divinity (see Ex 3:2f.)—to "the land of the living" (Ps 116:9), where she shall join in radiating the light of the face of Christ our God, who was truly and wholly contained in her womb: preserved unburnt by him, as the one who, above all women, is blessed with the name of Virgin Mother.

Beyond this, she has flourished as the stock of Jesse, blooming forever, bringing to fruition the one planted by the Father, whose boundless and inconceivable greatness gives joy to the holy powers of heaven and the choir of the saints by the beauty and the abundance he shares—the joy of seeing his delight freely accessible and abounding above all other pleasures. For the Lord of hosts has called to himself that field which he chose above all the earth; he grew up from her like an unplanted shoot, whose grain can neither be gathered nor thrown away, nourishing all things forever without being consumed, harvested only in the Father's bosom. She who had become the all-glorious bridal chamber of the hypostatic union of the natures of Christ, the true heavenly bridegroom, has entered the bridal suite of heaven, while all the holy powers of heaven long for his supernatural beauty. The immaculate spiritual room, from which the King of the ages came forth in making his descent to us, has been transferred to the Jerusalem on high, since like a soldier the King has put to flight the enemy, with all his armies. Christ our God, in fact, when he grew to manhood, betrothed his orthodox Church to himself, and poured forth for her his precious blood and gave his life; in the words of Paul, that light of the world so rich in divine wisdom: "This is a great mystery: I speak of Christ and of the Church" (Eph 5:32). She who is higher than cherubim and seraphim, being truly designated Mother of their Lord, has now come to live in the Kingdom of heaven.

4. When she had completed her life's voyage happily, that spiritual vessel of God dropped anchor in her new, safe harbor, near to the helmsman of the world, who through her saved the human race from the floods of wickedness and sin and gave it new life. The one who gave the Law on Sinai, and who administered it from Sion, our God, summoned his ark of sanctification to be brought home from Sion to himself, just as David, her ancestor, had said of her in a psalm, "Go up, O Lord, to the place of your rest, you and your ark of sanctification" (Ps 131:8). She is not carried like Moses' ark of old, drawn by oxen, but she is escorted and surrounded by an army, heaven's holy angels. She is not an ark made by hands, not plated with gold, but is God's spiritual handiwork, resplendent all over with the radiance of the holy and life-giving Spirit, who descended upon her. She does not contain the vessel of manna and the tablets of the covenant, but the Lord who provided both the manna and the eternal blessings promised in the Old and the New Covenants, and who was born as her child—he who freed from the curse of the Law those who have faith in him. She does not contain the rod of Aaron, nor is she crowned with glorious cherubim, but rather the incomparably more glorious rod of Jesse, revealed by the prophet and overshadowed by the almighty power of the Father on high (Is 11:1; Lk 1:35). She does not move before the Hebrew people, like that former ark, but follows the God who has appeared on earth in flesh furnished by her; she is called blessed by angels and by men and women, for the glory of the one who magnified her above all ranks of heaven and earth, as she cries out her holy words, "My soul glorifies the Lord, and my spirit rejoices in God my savior." (Lk 1:40).

5. The bright spiritual dawn of the sun of justice, then, has gone to dwell and to shine in his brilliance; she is called there by the one who rose from her, and who gives light to all things. Through her, that overwhelming radiance pours the rays of his

sunshine upon us, in mercy and compassion, rekindling the souls of the faithful to imitate, as far as they can, his divine kindness and goodness. For Christ our God, who put on living and intelligent flesh, which he took from the ever-virgin and the Holy Spirit, has called her to himself and invested her with an incorruptibility touching all her corporeal frame; he has glorified her beyond all measure of glory, so that she, his holy Mother, might share his inheritance, as the Psalmist says: "The queen stands at your right hand, wrapped in a golden robe woven with jewels" (Ps 44:9 [LXX]). That precious, holy vessel, most sacred of all things, she who became Mother of God, has taken up her "pearl of great price" (Mt 13:46); she is glorified with the splendor of his supernatural beauty, to whom "silver and gold belong" (Hag 2:9) and through whom "kings have their royal power" (Prov 8:15)—he who has shone forth from heaven in her, and who received a body from her virgin womb, while she was still being tossed in the great sea of this life; he who came forth [from her], to give himself as the world's ransom from slavery. So as soon she had completed the course of this temporal life, in a way far beyond the ordinary, she arrived at the true joy which lies at the heart of things, for she bore that joy in our nature in a way beyond our telling. This is that joy which is God by nature, begotten of God before the ages, the joy that has appeared on earth at the end of the ages from her, and which fills heaven and earth with its divine gladness, having finally banished the sadness of Eve.

6. But today, the one whom the inspired Prophet called "the cornerstone" (Ps 117:22 [LXX]) has wonderfully accomplished the transferral[4] of his own mountain, which looms over all creation in the height of its glory. From this mountain, Christ our God has been "cut without touch [of human hands]" (Dan 2:45), and has "set the whole universe right" (Ps 95:10 [LXX]); he has constructed in the world communities of right faith, so that

those who reverently take refuge in him by way of that mountain might be saved from all impious heretical belief,[5] just as Holy Scripture says, "Everyone who believes in him will not be put to shame" (Rom 10:11). She who remained a Virgin, the "sealed fountain" (Cant 4:12) of divine gifts, has been led out to meet him; through her, the garden of the orthodox Church is watered, and is tended by the second Adam, born of her, who drank from the virginal fountain of her breasts as from a flowing spring, and who gave life to Adam, God's first creation, as he lay in death. Today, the spiritual tent that supernaturally housed the God and Lord of heaven and earth in the flesh has been folded up and pitched anew by him, ready to share his incorruptible bodily existence forever: "a mighty shield" (Sir 6:14), offering all of us Christians safety and protection.

7. O most blessed dormition of the glorious Mother of God, of her who always remained a virgin, even after giving birth, and who did not experience corruption in that life-sheltering body of hers, even in the tomb! She is preserved [from it] by Christ the Savior, who came forth from her and who is mighty to do all things. O most blessed dormition of the glorious Mother of God, through whom "the spirits and souls of the departed just" (Dan 3:86) are judged worthy of the everlasting divine patronage of Christ! O most blessed dormition of the glorious Mother of God, through whom we have been created anew in mystery, and have become God's temple! O most blessed dormition of the glorious Mother of God, through whom a double healing has come to all the world—healed herself in body and of spirit, she leads the entire universe to complete well-being! O most blessed dormition of the glorious Mother of God, through whom our race, as his undivided body,[6] is glorified and made blessed in Christ our God—is itself praised and reverenced, as it is written, by all things "in heaven, on earth and under the earth" (Phil 2:10)!

O most blessed dormition of the glorious Mother of God, through whom we have received "the remission of our sins" (Eph 1:7) and are redeemed from the tyranny of the Evil One! O most blessed dormition of the glorious Mother of God, through whom all things are renewed, and things on earth are united to those in the heavens, crying out with them in praise, "Glory to God in the heights, and peace on earth, good will among men and women" (Lk 2:14)! O most blessed dormition of the glorious Mother of God, through whom the kindness of the three-personed Godhead, far exceeding all our conjectures, is revealed to us—making the holy powers of the heavens wonder, and rousing us to confession and ceaseless praise of God's unspeakable compassion and unbounded goodness! O most blessed dormition of the glorious Mother of God, about whom prophets and just men made proclamation with their holy trumpets, hoping to have a share in her most welcome day of days, when the Savior came forth from her to redeem them from the inescapable bondage of Hades! O most blessed dormition of the glorious Mother of God, through whom God is on earth and a human person in heaven, remaining the same yet undergoing transition without change or division,[7] through his compassion and his saving will! For she once heard, "You are earth, and to earth you will return" (Gen 3:19), but Christ, who is God, put on her flesh, and sits at the right hand of the Father, above the cherubim and seraphim, the thrones and virtues and principalities and powers, the archangels and angels. O most blessed dormition of the glorious Mother of God, through whom "we have put on Christ, and have been counted worthy to become children of God" (Gal 3:27)! O most blessed dormition of the glorious Mother of God, through whom "the True Vine" has sprung up, and the glorious apostles have grown out from it as branches, reaching to the limits of the earth and filling all the world with the excellent fruit of religion and with

their miracles! O most blessed dormition of the glorious
Mother of God, through whom Christ, the divine light and
light-giver, has shone forth, and the holy martyrs, conformed
to his sufferings, are kindled from him like lamps shining in
the world! Even with their blood, they confess her to be
Mother of God, and receive from him the crown of righteousness. O most blessed dormition of the glorious Mother of God,
for whose sake angels and archangels come down from on
high, and divine apostles gather from the ends of the earth, in a
way known to God alone, who leads them on the way and
gathers them for the holy celebration of her dormition as
Mother of God! In this our Lord, who is good above all others,
fulfills the command which he gave to Moses long ago,
"Honor your parents" (Ex 20:12), since he is by nature one
who gladly shows honor.

8. Think of it! Holy angels were sent from God to his holy
and glorious Mother, to one who is higher than they and all the
powers of heaven, the one who had "found grace with God" (Lk
1:30); they are sent from heaven on high to one who has been
shown by God to be higher and wider than heaven itself—sent
now, not to announce the incomprehensible news that God has
been conceived, as once the archangel Gabriel did, but to lead
her towards the one she conceived, in his heavenly kingdom;
not to proclaim her inconceivable childbirth to all the world by
bringing good tidings to shepherds (Lk 2:9), but to receive her
with everlasting glory and to let her enter into the ineffable joy
of the Lord (Mt 25:21), who was born of her. For since they
knew "the manifold wisdom of their Lord" (Eph 3:10), as it is
written in the Church's Scripture, it was reasonable that they
should also be divinely eager to gaze on his glorious mother, on
her whom they discovered to be most dearly desired and revered by the God who is by nature desirable and lovable, on
her who was chosen from the beginnings of our race, "accord-

ing to his foreknowledge" (Eph 3:10), to become, for the salvation of all the world, the ever-virgin Mother of God. With
prophetic eyes, her ancestor David foresaw that she would
have this role, and said in the Psalms, "Listen, daughter, and
see; incline your ear. Forget your people and your father's
house. The king yearns for your beauty, for he is your Lord;
bow down to him" (Ps 44:11 [LXX]). They were eager to see
and admire her divine beauty, shining with God's glory,
through which Christ our God, God's only Son, made human
nature fair with the loveliness and beauty of his Godhead, di-
vinizing it in himself. They longed to see her form, so "full of
grace" (Lk 1:28), from which he formed himself by the Holy
Spirit and became, in truth, mortal in form while remaining
what he was and "existing in the form of God" (Phil 2:6). They
yearned, too, to see his real, holy, individual [human] substance,[8] more powerful than the powers on high, and to give
praise to the super-substantial, really existent Word of the Father, who made that substance holy and became flesh from her
by his Holy Spirit. And perhaps they were amazed to consider
how this mortal being had come to be mother of the maker of
mortals—to wonder who she might be, and how great are the
personal qualities of the one who nurtured God. She contained
the uncontainable one, she bore the fire of divinity without being singed, she gave birth to the maker of all, she cradled in her
arms him who carries the universe in his hand, she fondled him
"who looks down on the earth and makes it to tremble" (Ps
103:32 [LXX]), she fed him "who gives food to all flesh" (Ps
135:25 [LXX]).[9] So they wondered how they might sing her
praises, and exalt her journey from this earth to the God who is
beyond the universe.

9. So the divine apostles, whom we have mentioned before,
hastened from every corner of the earth, led and assisted by an
impulse from on high, to find that all-holy Mother, through

whose offices they had been found by Christ and had been considered worthy of a mission in the Holy Spirit—the highest dignity by far which the Spirit bestows. She had already attained that honor,[10] and was, at that moment, about to receive in addition Christ's heavenly gifts, "which eye has not seen, nor has ear heard, nor has it yet entered the human heart" (1 Cor 2:9)—gifts given also, through her, to the race of mortals. She was to become, on earth, God's bridge beyond this universe, by the grace of her virginity. That is why his assistance towards us has been so marvelous, and why he can save us while utterly destroying the evil schemes of the enemy: it is not a divine ambassador, not an angel who has come to accomplish it, but the Lord himself. So it is written, "My help comes from the Lord, who made heaven and earth" (Ps 120:2 [LXX]): through her, he has made known to us the way to ascend to him by right faith, and by the good life that leads to heaven.

Not only this, but they walked in a sacred procession, through the gate built on Sion facing eastward and letting in the dawn,[11] which was an inspired anticipation of her transferral—for she was foreseen and revealed in prophecy by the activity of the life-giving Holy Spirit—the gate to which no falsehood draws near; there the one truly life-giving way leads us on, and our Lord and God lifts us, by that way, to his Father, saying in the Gospel, "I am the way and the truth and the life; no one comes to the Father except through me" (Jn 14:6). They gathered at that gate, and like archangels greeted the celebrated Mother of God; and just as they were ready to send on to the Lord that [angelic] escort whom they dispatched with her to the heavens, they announced the good news to her, proclaiming it, in what seemed an appropriate way, in this divinely inspired funeral hymn:

10. "Hail, woman so desired by God, living temple of the Most High, whom no place can contain! In you the personified, uncreated Wisdom of God the Father dwelt, and built the Tem-

ple of his body: Christ our God, who found his resting-place in you for the salvation of all the world, and who is pleased to welcome you into his own eternal, glorious resting-place. Hail, holy Mother of God! The king of glory, the Lord Jesus, chose you to be his spiritual kingdom on earth, and through you he has bestowed on us his heavenly kingdom; there he has ordained that you became one body with him in incorruption, more glorious than all others, to the glory of his Father and the Spirit. Hail, everlasting divine reward of the devout! Christ received our ancestral heritage from you, 'and raised up for us a horn of salvation' (Lk 1:69), so that we might proclaim the word of his truth as good news to all nations. For he truly saves from all tribulation those who confess you to be Mother of God—the God who has initiated you into his mysteries, that you might be with him to intercede for us. Hail, daughter of Joachim and mother of the God who created all things! You are summoned by him to share in blessedness beyond all joy of the holy ranks who are called blessed on earth and in heaven. Hail, spring of healing! You have poured forth Christ, who cures every illness. He bursts on us with the mystical waves of the grace of his life-giving Holy Spirit, bearing us like a rushing river towards life eternal; and he has summoned you, to nourish you 'by the water of his rest' (Ps 22:2 [LXX]). Hail, glorious Mother of everlasting light, which is by nature and in substance the true God! He has shone forth from you in our substance on earth, and has 'let the light of his face shine upon us' (Ps 4:7); now you are gloriously called by him to be, by God's grace, 'before him in the light of the living' (Ps 55:13 [LXX]).

"Hail, refuge of mortals with God! He made us his own through you, and became 'our refuge and our strength' (Ps 45:1 [LXX]), working through us great healing and giving strength to the whole world, in order to give increase to the chosen race of Christians; and he called you, O blessed Mother of God, to be the everlasting memorial of his ineffable kindness and love of humanity, which has touched us through you. Hail, God-given treasury of the heavenly kingdom! In you, 'The lamb of God who takes away the sin of the world' (Jn 1:29) was escorted into our midst, to call together a festival of heaven's holy angels and the mortals on earth. You were foreordained to be the priceless jewel, stored up in the 'Church of our ancestors' (Heb 12:23) on high. Hail, holy Mother of God our Savior, who has come through you to be with us, and we to be in him! He it is who has judged you worthy to be celebrated and venerated by all devout people on earth, and now—even more—to be venerated in heaven by the holy angels as the revered mother of their Lord.

"Hail, most holy virgin Mother, who have brought forth Christ, the Son of God, made flesh from you by the Holy Spirit! He is perfect in divinity and perfect in humanity; in two natures, two wills and two fields of operation, he wills and acts as God and wills and acts as a human being, and as one and the same subject he possesses full power in both realms, without confusion and without division.[12] Since you abide in his presence, with full freedom of access, pray to him for his Church, that it may be preserved forever in this reverent state of mind. Hail, venerable, immaculate Mother of God! The Lord God came from on high to dwell in your womb as his earthly homeland, without being limited and without leaving heaven behind; now he deems you worthy to come from this earthly, temporal homeland into a better land in heaven, a place also given—through your mediation—to the saints as their longed-for goal. Hail, divine altar erected on God's foundation! Through you the atoning and saving sacrifice for the whole world came forth, Christ our God. For from you, holy Mother of God, he put on that vestment of flesh prepared for him by the Holy Spirit, and came forth as 'a priest forever, according to the order of Melchizedek' (Ps 109:4 [LXX]; cf. Heb 5:6), as Scripture says; and he has decreed that he will take you as his partner, in order to provide forever a propitiatory sacrifice for all humanity, as you intercede for them.[13] Hail, Mary, resplendent spiritual Paradise! For you produced, by the Holy Spirit's gift, that fruit of immortal life growing from God the Father, Christ our God. By sharing right faith in him, we have been brought to life; and he has settled you now in Paradise, in the tent of an immortal body, so that through you he might open up for us a means of access to him. Hail, mistress of the mortal race, holy Mother of God! From you the God who is holy and good above all things, our Master, has come forth in the world to share our mortal nature in all things except sin. He has judged us worthy 'to become partakers of his divine nature' (2 Pet 1:4); having bestowed on you the grace of being his spiritual citadel, he calls you now to himself, 'the Lord of hosts in his city' (Ps 47:9 [LXX]). Hail, lovely and splendid harbor! God has revealed you as truly the Mother of God. The human race is tossed by storms on the sea of this life, but it finds safety in you; and it has gained the gifts of the Spirit and eternal blessings through you, from him who has done wonderful things for you in our history, and who glorifies you in a surpassing degree for ages and ages."

11. Those holy angels we have mentioned, sent by God, stood by the side of God's Mother; being spiritual and invisible, they gazed at the sublime glory of the divine grace and power that accompanied her, and stood dumbstruck by the incomprehensible divine mystery that enfolded her. They rejoiced in exaltation to receive her as the Mother of their Lord; but the apostles, who were now left orphans by the Mother of God, as far as her bodily presence was concerned, grieved no less than they had done in that sacred night when they were initiated into the sacraments of the whole world's salvation, and

heard from Christ the Savior, "Grief has filled your heart" (Jn 16:6). Then, as the Mother of God was surrounded by both choirs singing her praises, visibly and invisibly, both heard, it is said, the divine decree for her; Christ, our good God, according to his promise, did not disdain to "be in their midst" (Mt 28:20) and to appear to his Mother, in a way known only to him. And that blessed one, gazing on him and deeply moved, as always, by the holy yearning of her divinely maternal heart, left her holy body behind and "committed into his hands" (Ps 30:6 [LXX]) her blessed, holy soul.

12. What a marvel! She has fallen asleep! She has fallen asleep! She who gave birth to the life and resurrection of the world has fallen asleep! By the grace that came from her, every spiritual and intellectual nature shares eternal life. Her Son is the one who has despoiled the underworld and death,[14] who has "neutralized the devil" (Heb 2:14), who will raise up by his command (cf. 2 Thess 4:16) those who have died since time began and who sleep in him—the one who is Lord, and who says, "I am the resurrection and the life" (Jn 11:24). She follows him as his Mother, the all-holy one, and says to him in a kind of prophetic address, "My heart has not grown tired following after you, and has not longed for the day of men and women" (Jer 17:16).

Today, she who gave rest in her arms to the joy of cherubim and seraphim and all the heavenly powers has fallen asleep. He is the rest of the angels and of all things, and the holy and life-giving Spirit, who proceeds from the Father, rests in him as the Son who shares God's very substance; he is the true rest, who says in the Gospels, "Come to me, all who labor and are heavily burdened, and I will give you rest" (Mt 11:28). She now closes her holy eyes, who once set the light of the world shining, who carried the maker of lights himself in the world like a golden processional torch, untouched by human hands; "he it is who planted the ear and formed the eye" (Ps 93:9 [LXX]), and who summons people from all the ends of the earth "into his marvelous light" (1 Pet 2:9). Her glorious body, the receptacle of life, must be laid to rest by holy hands, for it was the source of immortality and incorruptibility, which flowed from the Holy Spirit within that mortal and corruptible nature that belongs to all of us. She clothed the Lord, who "wraps himself in light as in a robe" (Ps 103:2 [LXX]), in the fleshly garments in which he advanced in age, for he was born of her.

13. Then, in fact, that holy body of the Mother of God—where the single Jesus was formed, where the God who is over all came truly to be called human—was lifted up on a bier. O holy bier, who bear that truly immaculate body, through which he who makes all things holy has come forth! O holy bier, bearing another couch not made by hands, "where the God who laid down the heavens" has "chosen to take his rest" (Pss 17:10; 131:13 [LXX]). O holy bier, bearing the holy dwelling place—greater than all the world—of the God whom no place contains! O holy bier, bearing God's workshop for the salvation of the universe! O holy bier, bearing the palace of heaven's king, built by him as the place of his real yet uncircumscribed presence—the presence of his Incarnation! O holy bier, bearing that wonderful chariot, in which the God "who sits upon the cherubim" (Is 17:16) came forth to ride over the earth! Having fully clothed himself with the purple robe of our nature, "he rules over the nations" (Ps 46:9 [LXX]). About him, the prophet said, "Why are your robes red, as from a winepress when the grapes have been trodden down" (Is 63:2)? O holy bier, bearing the pure, chosen spiritual mine, from which the creator and Lord wrought anew for himself his own creation! O holy bier, bearing the blessed tent that came from Abraham and David—the tabernacle from which the most high and incorporeal God took his living, spiritual body, which did not exist before him, but took up its very existence

in him![15] O holy bier, bearing the spiritual incense that fills the whole world "with the fragrance of Christ, our God" (2 Cor 2:15). O holy bier, bearing the sacred vessel filled with the myrrh of a divinity beyond all divinity! O holy bier, bearing the all-holy body of the most glorious Mother of God, which is carried away amid celebration by the holy angels and the divine apostles, to the praise and glory of her Son and our God!

They placed it in a tomb as in a shrine of life, in the place called Gethsemane—they who had become the eye-witnesses and servants of the Word, and those holy ones who then were in their company. Their desire in doing this was that through her, our kindly and just judge might be rendered merciful towards us—Christ our God, who came forth from her, and who will appear in glory like lightning from heaven, to take his place where the prophets have foretold,[16] to judge the living and the dead with the divine apostles, through the ministry of the holy angels.

14. What mighty feat of the mind, what power of the word can grasp and give worthy voice to the many things that took place then—holy things, things beyond our comprehension, performed and sung by these witnesses to celebrate her glory? God revealed to them ineffable mysteries; a variety of blessings were bestowed on them, and they were initiated, through her power, into gifts of healing beyond number. For this reason, then, and because she is the glorious mother of Christ, our God and Savior, who bestows life and immortality, she was raised to life by him, to share his bodily incorruptibility for all ages. He raised her from the grave and took her to himself, in a way known only to him. So to him be glory and power, with the Father and the Holy Spirit, now and always and for the ages of ages!

Amen.

1 I.e., the Mystery of Mary's divine motherhood. For the author of this oration, this is the fundamental "mystery of faith" associated with Mary, from which all her other privileges flow.

2 This first section of the encomium seems to have been added as a prologue after the completion of the work.

3 For the image of Father, Son and Holy Spirit as three primordial lights, whose light remains one in substance, see Gregory of Nazianzus, Or. 31.3, 32; Or 44.3.

4 Greek: μετάστασις.

5 The oration here introduces the idea that Mary is a kind of personified protection against heresy; cf. *Akathistos Hymn* 17.

6 The "race" (γένος) Ps.-Modestus refers to here seems to be the Church, viewed in its eschatological form of universal unity.

7 Here Ps.-Modestus makes reference to the Christological formula of Chalcedon, implying that Mary's glorified humanity can be conceived of in some of the same terms of personal unity and transformation in which Christ was understood to exist.

8 The author here is using the classic language of post-Chalcedonian orthodox Christology, by which the one divine person or hypostasis of the Son has become "substantial" (ἐνούσιος) in a new, human nature, as well as in the divine nature in which he eternally exists. Mary has provided the Word with that new substance.

9 This passage briefly recalls the tradition of emphasizing the paradoxes of the Incarnation; see, e.g., Origen, *De Principiis* II, 6.2; Gregory of Nazianzus, Or. 38.16f.; Augustine, Serm. 188.2.

10 I.e., the honor of receiving a mission from the Holy Spirit. Mary's mission, presumably, was her role as Mother of God.

11 This somewhat obscure image seems to be alluding to Ezekiel's elaborate vision of the restored Temple and its worship: Ezek 43-47, esp. 43:1-9; 44:4-8; 46:1-10.

12 The author here refers summarily to the Christological definition of the Third Council of Constantinople (Sept. 16, 681), in which the Christological definition of the Council of Chalcedon is elaborated by explicit references to the two natural wills and operations or modes of activity in the one person of the incarnate Word. For the full text of this definition, see G. Alberigo *et al.*, *Decrees of the Ecumenical Councils* (English trans., ed. Norman P. Tanner; London/Washington, 1990) 1.128-130.

13 Here the author assigns to Mary a continuing share in Christ's eternal work of mediation and redemption—a notion that has had continued, if often controverted, support in Western theology.

14 This image of Christ the victor, triumphantly stripping death and Hades, its personification, of his armor, is familiar from earlier Alexandrian and Palestinian authors, especially Cyril of Alexandria (*Comm. on Jonah* 19 [*PG* 71.625 A4]; *Oratio ad Augustas de fide* 41 [ACO I, 1.5.56.22]). Cf. Philo of Carpasia, *Comm. on the Song of Songs* 126 (PG

40.100 B14); Oecumenius, *Comm. on the Apocalypse* 5.6 (ed. H. C. Hoskier; University of Michigan Studies 23 [1928] 79); Eulogius of Alexandria, *Sermon for Palm Sunday* (PG 86.2925 B2).

15 For this small but crucially important point, that the humanity of Christ did not pre-exist the moment of the Incarnation of the Word but was formed precisely by the Word's coming to dwell in Mary's womb, see Leontius of Byzantium, *Epilyseis* (= *Solutio argumentorum Severi*; PG 86.1944 C1-11); cf. Augustine, *Contra sermonem Arianorum* 6.8 (PL 42.683); *Enchiridion* 11.36 (CCL 46.69).

16 I.e., in the valley of Jehoshaphat, where Mary's tomb was located. For the participation of the Twelve in the judgment, see Mt 19:28; for the service of angels in its execution, see Mt 24:31; 25:31; for Jesus' appearance then—"like lightning"—see Mt 24:27.

ON THE DORMITION OF OUR MOST HOLY LADY, THE MOTHER OF GOD

By St. Andrew of Crete

HOMILY I[1]

[1.] The present feast celebrates a mystery that we refer to as "the falling asleep (dormition; κοίμησις) of the Mother of God," a mystery that exceeds the power of speech. It is a mystery that has not, in the past, been celebrated by many people, but that today is honored and welcomed by all. And this is the point of our feast: to reveal, to expound the mystery. Even though this day might choose, if it could, silence over words, it is driven by longing, and so yields to language—in however small a way—the opportunity to speak. Our words, for their part, have little confidence and are not unaware of their weakness, or of how, in all modesty, one ought to avoid saying the unsayable by keeping a deep silence. But the gift must be celebrated, not buried in silence: not because it is some new discovery, but because it has now come to its fitting outward form. For we ought not to consider this mystery worthy of silence today, just because some in the past were unaware of it; rather, it is a holy duty to proclaim it now, because it has not escaped our knowledge altogether. Therefore today let there be one common feast for the dwellers in heaven and on earth, let human beings rejoice along with the angels, and let every tongue join in the chorus and sing "Hail!" to the Mother of God.

Gabriel, after all, did this before us, he proclaimed the preface to this mystery, when the most brilliant moment of God's self-revelation, the divine formation of Jesus as one like us, took place by an unprecedented and indescribable act of God's providence, in the workshop of a virgin's human nature. So we, once again, must offer this gift of thanks and principal honor to the Queen of our race: it is right to say "Hail!" to her, now that she is removed from our midst! She alone has made joy her possession, for all our sakes, and has put to flight the sadness of our first mother.

"Let us blow the trumpet in Sion; let us take up psaltery and harp!" (Ps 80:3 [LXX]) Let us sing to the Mother of God—sing not a bridal song (ἐπιθαλάμιον), but strike up a funeral melody (ἐπιτάφιον). Someone who prides himself on accurate speech will no doubt want to ask, "Why do you recall Sion, you who sing the glory of this holy feast?" Not without purpose, I would say to him. My friend, I recalled holy Sion, for in that mountain we are introduced into the great mystery of the Mother of God.[2] There marble slabs, laid out as a floor, resounded far and wide under the bending knees of the holy body. For this was her dwelling for the whole time of her presence on earth; there she obeyed the laws of nature, and reached the end of life; there she escaped the Prince of Darkness [at death], just as in giving birth she escaped the pains of motherhood. Her name is holy, her title divine; she is above all stain, she has filled heaven and earth with glory and grace by the greatness of her divine journey.

[2.] If I wished to narrate all her glories in order, I would not find sufficient time to tell of her life, her conception, her birth, nor would I find a power of words equal to those realities. It is impossible to compress all her privileges into a single moment:[3] her noble ancestry, renowned on both sides (for her parents were of priestly rank on one side, of royal on the other); her parents' childlessness, her mother's barrenness, their prayers and constant sacrifices for a child, by which they begged and entreated and besought God to release them from the bonds of sterility, to show that the childless can be made fertile and that the barren can bear fruit.[4] Then their release from sterility, the fulfillment of the message—and shortly before that, the visions in dreams, the hearing of voices in the night by her parents, together and singly, in which those saints were enlightened with heavenly knowledge, their prayers answered, in a wisdom that surpassed human sight.[5] And then, after this, her conception, her development until birth, her infancy, her arrival at God's Temple; how she was offered as a sacrifice to God, how she traversed its sanctuaries as if they were bridal chambers of gold, and was fed not on common food, but on ambrosia.[6] Then her return from there, her growing-up, her change from childhood to youth, and all the signs of human perfection with which she approached maturity and which corresponded to her supernatural state. I will not mention the mysteries of her utterly unfathomable conception (of Jesus), which was realized in secrecy, nor the supernatural, indescribable theophany of the birth of Jesus which followed—including its freedom from corruption and the pains of childbirth, the stainless inviolability of her virginal treasure.[7] I will not speak of her strange, miraculous way of nursing,[8] her purification according to the Law, the prophecies given in the Temple, in which the future was foretold by Simeon, a prophet governed both by the Law and by God's Spirit. Then her persecution, her flight into Egypt, her return from Egypt, her long journeys, her life in the open country,[9] her suffering at the insults that preceded the crucifixion, her grief at the foot of the cross, her lamentation after the crucifixion—all that she said and did, in a word, in the course of such a life. It was a life without spot or stain, utterly filled with every pure and holy quality, a life such as the world cannot grasp, since it cannot interpret it with words or bring it to the light—a life that the world had to respect, until the end, as "the King's mystery." Only to those who had been divinely taught to discern divine realities, who had been purified by nearness to the divine, only to them did the Most Holy One make known an offprint, as it were, of this mystery, lifting the intellectual curtain in a silence and an unknowing far above speech, to reveal some portion of the hidden, secret glory within.

[3.] If only we, too, illumined by this present feast of light, could be found worthy of the supernal glory of that light above all light, and could see the mystery clearly for ourselves! If only we could receive at least a modest ray of mystical initiation and express ourselves clearly, even if we are incapable of doing justice to that ineffable life of hers! These are unknowable realities. But at least we can learn, as far as we are able, the meaning of the rites we attend today. Come then, dear initiates of the Word, fellow lovers and gazers after Beauty! I appeal to you, with a great, exalted cry: let me spread out its meaning, still hidden in its symbolic wrappings, for your contemplation! Let me show you all its inner loveliness, surpassing the rays of the sun in its brilliant beauty!

Since I have reached this point in my sermon, I think it would be good to warn some of you here, so that I do not throw holy things, as they say, before unwashed or unholy feet:[10] the choir of the saints is not accessible or receptive to everyone equally. It is only open to those who have moved beyond all material things in purity of mind, who have crossed the boundary of the world of perception; to those whose "setting sail" is favored by the holy tent of God, and whose "coming home" is honorably prepared there[11]; to those on whom the supplies for this spiritual banquet, at which we feast, have been generously bestowed. For if they who dared to approach Mount Sinai on their own, not worthily, were overwhelmed with lightning and thunder and terrible sights and trumpet-blasts and dreadful threats,[12] and if it was unsafe for the ordinary folk to touch the walls of the tabernacle, so that a second, outer ring of walls was necessary;[13] and if one had to go to great lengths to purify oneself before touching sacred objects, and to make lengthy preparations before sacrificing;[14] and if all this was for those who worshipped in shadow, and had symbolic curtains hung around them,[15] then how much more must those who have the light of truth dwelling within them show care in attempting to approach this glorious and surpassingly great tabernacle of God's grace! He came to her in a way beyond knowledge, beyond mind and speech, emptying himself. He who is containable in no place made his dwelling in a virgin's womb without being constricted—a womb that utterly surpassed all mutable nature in purity; and from there, as from the recesses of a temple, he entered the world of flesh. Who did this? He who needs nothing, yet clothed himself with the full wretchedness of human nature. In this tabernacle, formed by God, all the law and the prophets are concretely fulfilled. Here the shadowy forms of things meant only as types fade away, the mirror is dissolved by the truth.

[4.] But we have said enough now by way of preparation. Come, let us put aside figures and run towards truth itself; let us enter the sanctuary! How long, after all, should we tarry in the vestibule of our discourse, admiring the beauty of the entrance, when it is possible to enter with the Mother of the Word, to pull aside the curtain and gaze into the Holy of Holies, to be initiated into greater and more perfect mysteries? If the forecourts of the Temple are so beautiful, the gates so grand and so massive that they dazzle the mind's eye with their surpassing beauty, what must the inner sanctuary itself be like, the recesses that may never be entered or seen—or that can only be seen by those eyes and mentioned by those lips that clearly mirror the Lord's glory, have been purified by the coal in the Seraph's tongs, have attained the highest degree of freedom from passion? If you trust me, as a friendly counselor, you will bid farewell to the lusts of the flesh, you will purge yourself as far as possible from all friendship and commerce with this material world below; you will put on the blessed and holy light which shines from above, and walk with the Mother of God.

Once we have begun to shine with radiance in deed and word, brilliant with the beauty of every kind of virtue, then Christ himself—the pure sacrifice, the ever-living light who shines forth from the Father like a sun from the sun, a ray gleaming out without beginning and without motion in distance[16]—Christ wishes to gather us together as our host. He shows this clearly by taking up his ever-virgin mother from this earth today as Queen of human nature—that mother in whose womb he who is God took our form in a way totally beyond our power to describe. The manner [of her assumption] cannot be told, yet he has not left the meaning of this mystery totally inaccessible to us. For the most holy Virgin did not walk this earth in a way contrary to the laws laid down for us from above; she was not born, nor did she live by rules foreign to those of our nature, even though she received a supernatural pattern of life that *was* different from ours—in its end as in other respects. She lived, after all, and she gave birth, and finally she left this world, in a way superior to our normal way; so she really surpassed, in greatness of nature, all who live in this world of change.

[5.] Come, then, let us celebrate now in a way that befits her: everything conspires to make this feast more beautiful, to increase our joy! For look, all of you who hear my words, look at what is now before our eyes: the Queen of the nations—I mean the Church of the faithful—today leads the solemn procession for the Queen of our race, who today is received royally into the Kingdom of Heaven by God, the King who rules over all. The Church brings in tribute today her most beautiful and festive possessions. She who turned dust into heaven [i.e., Mary] today strips the dust away, lays aside the veil of this world of change, and gives back to the earth what belongs to it. She who bestowed life ascends to the transformation which is rebirth, and enters the place where life begins and never ends, a place far from all the conditions and complications of matter and the passions. Now, finally, her visible frame rises up from the visible world and is joined to the spiritual in a spiritual way: something only he understands who first joined matter and spirit together, then separated them to rejoin them again—if I may speak boldly and touch upon the intangible! Let no one doubt this, who thinks of Elijah or Enoch, who both appeared above the visible world, having put sensation to rest and been released from this world of flesh—the one carried off in a chariot, the other raised up in the air. Their human parts were not separated, did not decay; but the limits of their lives were set in this world, where Providence places them for all of us—that Providence which arranges all things wisely, and by which past and present are together shaped and led in a consistent, fitting way.

If these two men are too modest a parallel to her whom we celebrate today, she herself must suffice as her own criterion and model. Consider, then, if there is any greater miracle on record than what has been accomplished so astonishingly in her. The law of nature has at last grown weak, and slowly falls away. The bitter sentence of death has passed into utter uselessness and is overturned, the power of the curse is destroyed. Yet no one has overturned God's ancient decrees—least of all he who is himself God by nature, and who transforms us and re-creates all things by his own kindly will. It fully befits him to work this new wonder in his Mother; for thus he not only shows her to be his mother by nature, but gives credibility to the saving plan he has realized through her, which we have extolled so much in our more explicitly spiritual discourses. In this plan of salvation, the Word who is the source of our life burst into our world and incomprehensibly entered her womb, took up our human nature, and supported it, for our sakes, in a supernatural way. Therefore what was once accomplished in her, what we now celebrate, even if it seems to be strange and far beyond the bounds of our nature, still has its ready and understandable explanation in her case, because of the supernatural character of her indescribable childbearing. For [that child] was, after all, the Word, who came to be with us, and who by his law put an end to the relentless law of death.[17]

[6.] It is truly a new spectacle, never before conceived of: a woman who surpasses the heavens in purity of nature enters the holy tabernacle of the heavenly sanctuary; a virgin, who surpasses the very nature of the Seraphim by the miracle of giving birth to God, draws near to God, the first of natures and begetter of all things; a mother, who has brought forth life itself, produces an ending of her own life to match that of her Son. It is a miracle worthy both of God and of our faith! For as her womb was not corrupted in giving birth, so her flesh did not perish in dying. What a miracle! The child put corruption to flight, and the tomb did not admit of corruption—for it has no claim on holy things. What proof is there, you want to know? Let no one here ask in ridicule how her tomb could have been empty. For I will ask you in return: how has her body disappeared? Why was there no shroud in her sarcophagus, if what was laid in the tomb did not escape corruption—if the treasure was not carried away? And if these facts are correct, why was her passing over to heaven[18] not genuine, when the rest of the details were: the separation of her soul from her body, her putting-off of flesh, the end of her incarnate existence, the separation of her parts, their dissolution, their rejoining, their rehabilitation, their removal to the invisible realm? For her sepulcher remains empty until today, as a continuing witness to her passing. I do not know if the parts of her body were all immediately joined to form a single, composite whole—for I shall make little philosophical speculation on

these things, since the Creator apparently saw fit, in his inscru-
table mind, to honor his mother this way—of if each part
emerged over the other, one taking its new position on the outside, the other on the inside, after they had all been separated
from each other; of if the sequence [of reconstitution] which
supernaturally ran its course in her was strange and different,
and all happened in a truly new way in her, as she received beyond her own nature a supernatural structure[19] that lies beyond
all words and all knowledge of ours.

[7.] To this perfect spiritual banquet of minds, the fleshly
mother of the eternal Mind invites us. The royal table is ready,
and the subject of our discourse today is enlivened and swelled
by God's mysterious action. All this radiant beauty, shining
beyond the power of words in the faces of the guests at the banquet, suffuses our surroundings today. I, too, am a reveller
here, though a stranger and a newcomer.[20] Unworthy though I
am, I am to lead our exalted contemplation. Let no one refuse
to join this feast, on seeing our shabby wretchedness; the mystic story behind these inspired reflections was not prepared by
us, but by the Mother of God herself. Since, then, the table is
covered with such riches to allure its spiritual guests, let us go,
as befits the Spirit, into the Spirit's depths. Already she, who
begot Wisdom itself in the flesh, has imitated Wisdom in her
own being and has offered herself completely as a mystical,
heavenly banquet-table, prepared for those who are spiritually
initiated in divine realities, and she invites us generously to the
feast. We are not offered slaughtered victims of sacrifices or
drinks from a mixing-bowl—not that blessed sacrifice from
days gone by, nor that cup filled with God's own nectar[21]—but
meditations on *her* mysteries, supernatural and truly divine.
She who presides at the feast, who invites us to share in it,
shows us from her own experience how great the house is which
Wisdom has built. She shows us herself as the holy table, bear-

ing in her womb, through God's dispensation, our Lord and God Jesus Christ, who is nothing other than our life-giving bread—him who is eternal life, holding all creation together, made bread from the leaven of Adam's dough. Those who approach him in a holy way he leads to new life and transforms into divine reality, cleansing them and making them immortal by making them his own, through participation in a totally new kind of fellowship with him. This, surely, is what refreshes those who love him, what constitutes their very life. It is an excellent, indescribable life; nothing we know in this creation is more exalted than this! He who is beyond all theology, by an incomprehensible self-emptying, bent down in pity for the human race, though he was the source of creation, and chose to come down a second time to share in our poverty, to be mixed into the dough of our race, "to share in flesh and blood like us" (Heb 2:14). He who needs nothing, who is full beyond measure, who is rich, did not choose to dwell in this realm of existence by leaving the divinity which is above all essence, but kept unmingled within himself, even after the ineffable union, the natural structures of what had come together, with neither confusion nor separation as the key to the relationship between them.[22] He did not even reveal what he was accomplishing to the angels, nor to the generals of those battalions ranked in the highest heaven—only to one of the chief angels, who served to advance the saving progress of the new mystery. So the Incorporeal One took on a body and joined himself with us in mind and flesh, so that, wholly mingled with our whole substance, he might renew the whole of what he had taken from us.

[8.] This, as far as I can understand it and put it into ready words, is the spiritual table of Wisdom to which God draws us. These are the "orgies"[23] mystically celebrated around her—sacred rites given by God! To these mysteries we must rightfully add the mystery of today, in which the Mother of God, without altering anything of the laws of our nature, obeyed the law laid upon us and completed her life in the flesh under the same conditions as we do, though she entered and left this life in a wonderful way. Let no one be surprised if any privileges above our lot have been given her by the divine nature. Let him simply consider the ineffable, unprecedented mystery realized in her, a mystery infinitely exalted, in an infinite number of ways, beyond all infinity! Certainly all these things are veiled, unspeakable; their rhyme and their reason remain unchanged, but also unuttered. Let us simply celebrate, with shining hearts and splendid rites, the memory of the holy entombment of that tabernacle where our life began. Together with this visible world, let all intelligent creatures, all in heaven and all on earth, who have gathered for the feast, honor the Queen and lead the procession that will involve our whole race. The body which became the altar of propitiation for us all he took from her body, and it became a temple not made by hands, lordly and rich in salvation, sharing in all our natural and spiritual activity except sin alone. O, the wonder of it! She who supernaturally received the infinitely great God, to whom all limit is foreign, into the small space of her womb, today is borne on the small space of a bier, tended by holy hands.[24] She who enthroned in her bosom the one who rides on the backs of Cherubim, is laid in the bosom of a tomb carved from the rock. She at whose child the angels sang in wonder, today is sent on her way, in her earthly tabernacle, accompanied by the solemn chorus of the Apostles. Who can explain, in rational terms, what happened there? Who is worthy to be a match for this mystery? Who can so fit his mind with wings that he can soar up to the miracle and experience communion with it? Who, to speak of more modest things—who, even among those writers second only to the Apostles, could describe for us the ebb and flow of our material composite? Our nature is powerless for this; it is struck dumb by the incomprehensibility of its own structure. When it turns its energy to consider this wonder, it cries out the inspired words of David towards the God of all things: "Your knowledge is too wonderful for me; it is over-powering—I cannot attain it!" (Ps 138:6 [LXX]) Our mind does not only wonder at our own construction, our human composite, or even our dissolution into the elements; now it also speaks out a baffling oracle about this our Queen, his im-maculate and illustrious Mother—reports a miracle that we know is common to us all, yet proper to her,[25] and understood completely, for all ages, only by him who is alone creator of all things and worker of this mystery.

[9.] This is *our* frame that we celebrate today—*our* forma-tion, *our* disintegration. So I gather my forces, I honor the mystery in fear, and I join in the cry of Isaiah, the most outspo-ken of the prophets, as he says: "Woe is me! I am finished! For I am a man of unclean lips!" (Is 6:5) And yet I have dared to speak about the pure and spotless one, who is filled with all ho-liness; I have tried to utter her praise in a funeral oration, though clouds cover her ascent from view, though a spiritual mist swirls around any logical explanation of her mystery and does not allow us to express clearly the understanding which that mystery conceals. God alone can praise her worthily; in ways that he alone understands, he has "done great things to her" (Lk 1:49). This is not in my power—I lie on the ground, and do not fully understand even the earth under my feet, for lack of moral virtue. Shall I not, then, be ashamed to speak of what is beyond my worth, if I cannot even speak of what corre-sponds to it? But since even the little that lies within our power is never wholly contemptible, I have used my speech to shatter the silence, and I offer my discourse to God, to whom be glory and power for all the ages of ages!

Amen.

1   This homily was erroneously published by François Combéfis, its original editor, as Andrew's second homily on the Dormition, an ordering reproduced by Migne.

2   Here Andrew develops a familiar image for Mary: she is for the people of the New Covenant the fulfillment of the type of Sion: the mount on which the Temple stood, the holy place of God's self-revelation, a part of our earth that is both elevated and made sacred by God's presence. For another example of a homily presenting Mary's mysterious holiness in terms of Biblical mountains associated with God's self-revelation, see Severus of Antioch, Homily 67 (*On the Presentation of the Lord*: PO 8/2, 349-367). Andrew also alludes here to the Jerusalem tradition, represented in the apocryphal accounts of the Dormition, that Mary lived there, on Mount Sion, until her death.

3   In the rest of this paragraph, summarizing the tradition on the birth and childhood of Mary, Andrew draws especially from the familiar second-century apocryphon, the so-called *Protevangelium of James*.

4   *Protev.* 1-3.

5   *Protev.* 4-5.

6   *Protev.* 6-7.

7   *Protev.* 11, 17-20.

8   It is unclear what tradition on Mary's nursing Andrew is referring to here; no specific mention is made of this in the *Protevangelium*.

9   Andrew seems here to be suggesting that Mary acccompanied Jesus and his disciples on their missionary journeys.

10 See Mt 7:6: "Do not give dogs what is holy; and do not throw your pearls before swine, lest they trample them under foot and turn to attack you."

11 I.e., to those whose death and entry into heaven are protected by Mary herself.

12 See Ex 19:10-25.

13 See Ex 27:9-19.

14 See Lev 10:6-10; 16:2-14, for regulations concerning the rituals of preparation Jewish priests had to perform before sacrificing.

15 See Ex 26:31-37.

16 Andrew is developing the conception of the generation of the Word expressed in the phrase of the Niceno-Constantinopolitan creed, "light from light".

17 Here Andrew argues clearly that the mystery of Mary's death and resurrection is a logical outgrowth of her role as Mother of the Word made flesh, since the purpose of his incarnation was to overcome death and its oppressive implications for all humanity.

18 Greek: μετάθεσις, literally "transferral."

19 Greek, *logos*, which means first of all "word," then "mind" or "reason," and also "rational structure." Note the play on words here, in suggesting that Mary's new intelligible identity (*logos*) was above both language (*logos*) and reason (*logos*).

20 This may suggest that Andrew is preaching this festal triad of sermons as
a guest speaker—perhaps even at the court liturgy at Constantinople—rather than in his own metropolitan Church of Gortyna in Crete,
where he became bishop sometime between 692 and 713; alternatively, it
may suggest that he delivered them in Gortyna soon after his installation.

21 I.e., the festive gathering to which Andrew now invites his hearers is not
the Eucharist, but a "mystical banquet" of contemplating the fullness of
human salvation as revealed in Mary.

22 Again Andrew alludes to the Christological formula of Chalcedon.

23 This word, in its original Greek sense, refers to a religious ritual, to
which only initiates were admitted; it does not necessarily suggest self-
indulgence and excess, as it does in English.

24 Andrew here begins a series of meditative paradoxes, reflecting the
meaning of the dormition scene, that parallels the paradoxes often invoked by Patristic preachers in describing the scene of Jesus' birth.

25 Here and in the concluding paragraph, Andrew emphasizes that the
"miracle" of Mary's entrance into glory, in the fullness of her humanity,
is essentially no different from the resurrection all of us hope to share;
what is "proper to her" is the full anticipation of what must, for the rest of
her brothers and sisters, only be awaited at the end of history. The eschatological transformation of our human nature, accomplished by Christ
through his incarnation, death and resurrection, is revealed to us already
fulfilled in Mary, as a sign of hope and a promise for our own future.

ON THE DORMITION OF OUR MOST HOLY LADY, THE MOTHER OF GOD

By St. Andrew of Crete

HOMILY II[1]

[1.] All you who have come to this venerable sanctuary of the Mother of God, draw near me, I beg you, and help me today as I struggle to speak, overpowered by the loftiness and the profundity of this wonderful occasion. Let us ascend the summit of the heights, so to speak, and let us hesitantly peer from there into the mysteries of God. Let us listen to a funeral oration!

The saving Word, who is good beyond all goodness, who subsists in himself above all being yet has lived out on earth, in flesh, the whole of God's plan for our sakes—who fulfilled the ancient prophecies about himself by revealing our reality in himself and his whole reality in us—has now filled heaven and earth with glory, and has made all creation rich with his sacred splendor. He has conquered the author of evil, after grappling with him on the cross, and by his own struggle with death he has destroyed its tyranny over us. He has devastated the unspeakable regions of the underworld and all their domination, sealing up hell's voracious belly so that it might never again hold the godlike souls of his holy ones in its power.

It was right, in my judgment, that the lawful claims marked out by the ancient curse should not simply be declared void. For it was God's voice that ordered those once formed from earth to return there, so that human nature might not be freed from its bondage to growth and decay until it had first been made earth again. And it was necessary that "he who was made like his brothers and sisters in all things except sin" (Heb 2:17) should show in himself all the marks of our nature.

Though he was God, he became human out of love for humanity, and tasted our sufferings for one reason only: to show how close he had drawn to us, so that by the passion of the impassible one we might be placed outside passion's power. For this same reason, he accepted even the experience of corruption, he mingled with the dead and entered the cheerless realm of the underworld, so that we might escape the bonds that awaited us there and might pass over to the world of incorruption. Nevertheless, we shall not escape bodily death as a result, since we have received our immortal being and have been created anew not in our nature, but only by the gift of grace.

[2.] Why do I say all this, my brothers and sisters? What has led me to speak of these things? Simply this: if we are to touch on the mysteries of [Mary's] supernatural departure, we must, at least briefly, turn our attention in the direction of our Lord and God Jesus Christ, and then, in proper order, link what we say about him to our subject of today. For since it is the necessary lot of all human beings to die once (cf. Heb 9:27), since this is simply the inescapable fate of our nature—indeed, at the start of our history we received this sentence from our creator, because of our disobedience—for this reason the Lord died once and for all, becoming the ransom for the one death that faces us all, in order to free us all, in a single act, from death's bitter tyranny: to free "those," as the sacred writer says, "who all their lives were held fast in slavery by fear of death" (Heb 2:15). "What?", some may ask; "shall we, then, not die that death?" Indeed, we shall die; but we shall not remain enslaved by death, as once we did when we were bound by it through the legal bond of sin. "If that is true," someone may reply, "then death is not really death!" There are indeed some, in fact, who will escape it; but "they shall be changed," according to divine revelation (1 Cor 15:51). It is death's tyranny, *real* death, when we who die are not to be allowed to return to life again. But if we die and then live again after death—indeed, live a better life—then clearly that is not so much a death as a sleep (κοίμησις; "dormition"), a passage into a second life, which brings us as migrants from here to there and sends us on our way by giving us complete release from earthly cares. The author of Proverbs expressed this more clearly than I when he said, "Death, for a man, is rest" (cf. Sir 38:23). For by death God puts an end to his labor, so that he no longer has to act in the way that his nature requires. What else can we understand death to be, but the separation of soul from body, which calls forth our hope for resurrection by so separating our bodily parts that they must be joined together again? This leads us to believe, in hope, that we will be brought to share in incorruption and enjoy a better lot, since we are no longer enslaved to sin by a life caught up in the desires of the flesh—a life, in other words, directed towards sensible things.

[3.] If, then, he is Lord of life and death, the life of all people and the resurrection of the dead—if he is "the light of the world" (Jn 8:42), who "with his own death annihilated the one who had power over death" (Heb 2:14)—then surely, in the love for humanity that constrained him (cf. 2 Cor 5:14f), he would not have thought it right to bypass even this law of death and leave it unfulfilled. Intending, rather, to be like us in all things, and to prove that he had strictly followed the same path that we do, even down into the earth, he chose to be held by the same bonds that hold us, "walking in the midst of the shadow of death," as Scripture says (Ps 22:4 [LXX]). So he spent three days in the depths of the earth, where the souls of those who died before him lay wrapped in unbreakable chains. He proclaimed the good news to them, as St. Peter tells us: "Going also to the spirits in prison, he preached to them" (1 Pet 3:19). How, then, can it be anything but completely and undeniably clear that the souls of all people, even those of the saints, enter into that place of darkness but are not detained there: none, that is, but those who have brought death on themselves by sinful self-indulgence in this life? (see Lk 16:19, 25) For surely the souls of all who submit to God's law and show, in the Holy Spirit, a heavenly pattern of life while they are still in the flesh, will be taken from there to a place of light that more befits the holy state of the saints—a place over which the Lord keeps watch, and which his eyes and his word guard forever (cf. Zach 4:10 [LXX]). As for the beauty and greatness of that place, its infinite blessedness and its loveliness that exceeds even the mind's power to comprehend, they will doubtless see all these things more clearly and more profoundly who have drawn closer to God than we have; when they have come to the end of this life's course, they will receive the rest that is re- served for them by the Providence that so wisely guides all things.

So the souls of the saints will go through the gates of the underworld, as we have explained, "for the disciple is not above his master" (Mt 10:24). But I do not believe they will be detained there as souls were once, when, as Scripture says, "sin ruled along with death" (Rom 5:21). They shall pass through [those gates]—listen carefully!—not to be destroyed, but to be examined and to be initiated there into the strange mystery of God's plan of salvation: I mean the descent into the underworld which Jesus, the source of our life, willingly ac- complished for our sakes, having undergone death on a cross even though he was himself above both suffering and destruc- tion. In addition, souls will be taught the supernatural meaning of what he accomplished there: how great and wonderful a vic- tory the Savior won in that battle, when he destroyed the ever- lasting gates [of the enemy].

[4.] All of this, then, we recall from sacred Scripture; and what has just been explained to you is not beside the point of what we are about to say. In fact, it now flows most fittingly from this, I think, for us also to try and grasp the hidden, glorious mystery of the dormition of her who was holy from her birth and always remained a virgin: to discourse also of these things before a people who love what is good, and who long to gaze on the good more deeply. Indeed, if I must speak the truth, the death that is natural to the human race even reached as far as Mary: not that it held her captive as it holds us, or that it overcame her—far from it! But it touched her enough to let her experience that sleep that is for us, if I may put it this way, a kind of ecstatic movement towards the things we only hope for during this life, a passage that leads us on towards transformation into a state like that of God. Mary's death was, we might say, a parallel to that first sleep, which fell upon the first human being when his rib was removed to complete the creation of our race, and he received flesh to take the place of what had been taken away. In the same way, I think, she fell into a natural sleep and tasted death, but did not remain held by it; she simply followed the laws of nature and fulfilled God's plan, which the Providence that guides all things laid down for us from the beginning. Her role, surely, was to show us clearly the way she has moved through transformation from a corruptible state to an incorruptible one—something that is only thinkable if a natural dissolution of these elements of our body should take place first, and if then the life that has melted away should be forged anew.

If, as the saying goes, "there is no one who will live and not see death," then she whose praises we sing today is clearly both human and more than human, since she kept the same law of nature that we must keep, yet in a way not like us but beyond us, it seems, and beyond the reason for which we are forced to suffer it. This, then, is how I suggest you understand her descent into the underworld: the period of time for which death and bodily decay held power over her—in my judgment, at least—was only as long as was necessary for her to move, at natural speed, through unknown regions and to come to know them first-hand, regions where she had never set foot before and which she was now crossing as in a journey through foreign, uncharted territory.

[5.] Be gracious towards us, O Virgin, vessel of God and bearer of life; forgive us as we dare to penetrate the unknown, as we search the hidden mysteries of your life, as we struggle to understand what God has determined to accomplish in you, the unsearchable abyss of his judgments. The attempt to gaze at these mysteries with the mind's eye puts fear even into those blessed with the highest intellectual gifts; how much more frightening, then, is it to us who are fleshly in mind, who can only cover the wild beast within us in sheep's clothing! All we have tried to show thus far, with great timidity, is that you shared with us in the laws of nature. But the higher wonders achieved in you, O most blessed one—wonders that you also share by first-hand experience—are too pure and too divine, as you know better than we, to be expressed in our human words. Your only-begotten Son, who brought all the ages into being, has clothed you with fitting glory and radiance before all others, because he was conceived and given human substance in flesh that you provided. Your glory is such that none of us, perhaps not even one of the higher angels, can grasp it with our minds. Let it all remain honorably wrapped in the mysterious obscurity of God, and preserve its reality and its truth unshaken, until the final restoration of all things.[2]

[6.] But that you might not send us away without some share, at least, in the story of the marvels God has worked in you, speak a word to us, as Mother of the Word, and tell us how you finally did depart from this world. For now every hearer of God's word, past and present, stands and turns his ear towards you, hoping to hear your voice, just as once Israel longed to hear the voice of God. And your voice, now sounding from on high more powerfully than any trumpet (cf. Ex 19:9-16), proclaims, "I broke none of the laws of human nature, but having accomplished all in a new, yet fully appropriate way, 'I magnify the Lord in my soul, and rejoice in my spirit' (cf. Lk 1:46), while in my body I am changed and take on a new form, sharing by grace in God's own being. And the source and final form of that transformation into God, I confess, is the form taken by him who is God above all, and who became flesh in an indescribable way in my womb, when he remade his own humanity into something divine. Through a share in the Spirit, he bestowed this grace on us, whom he had never abandoned, when he ascended from earth to heaven along with that body. Moved by his care for the human race, 'he looked upon the lowliness of his handmaiden' (Lk 1:47) and decreed an end to the curse of the first Eve. By his appearing in the flesh, he has overshadowed 'those who dwell in darkness and the shadow of death' (Lk 1:78; cf. 1:35), rising 'like the dawn from on high' (Lk 1:78), and he has 'guided our feet into the way of peace' (*ibid.*). Though he is truly God, he became human in me, in a spiritual way, from a virgin's blood,[3] bringing about a conception and growth that were unknown to our nature. So, by a new relationship of both natures, he destroyed the old order and brought in the new order that will never grow old, so that all things might become new—in truth, a new creation—through this new, most praiseworthy incarnation of the Word.

"When was it ever heard, after all, before our time, that a woman had become Mother of God? Or that God called himself a woman's son? Or that a human form was revealed, by a divine birth, as being above the cherubim and as ruling all things? Who ever taught God's worshippers, both in heaven and on earth, to worship as Lord, in one indivisible act of adoration, clay made divine, earth raised on high? Who ever raised the farthest bounds of humble, earth-bound humanity to heaven, letting it float upwards, by divine gift, past the limits of its nature? Who ever made the inaccessible seem accessible, blazing a new and unknown path for the inhabitants of the earth, so that human beings might be revealed as fellow-citizens with the angels? These were the 'great things' that so clearly came to pass in me; these were the reasons I received such glory and brilliance as my lot. Therefore, with good reason, 'henceforth all generations shall call me blessed; for the Mighty One has done great things for me, and holy is his name' (Lk 1:48f.). What, after all, is greater than to be called—and to be—the Mother of God?

[7.] "As for my departure from human company, you may derive a clearer understanding of it by considering that place from which my material, earthly dwelling—I mean my virgin body, of which God took hold to form, from different elements, the one Jesus[4]—was transported to its new home. Anyone who chooses can confirm what I am saying with his own eyes. For before the gaze of those who look on holy things with faith, there stand here clear images (εἰκόνες), eloquent representations of my passing.[5] This tomb [which you see in the icon] is that one carved out of rock, which stands intact even today, proclaiming with soundless voice the evidence of my burial. The hollows of that rock are incontrovertible witnesses that my body lay within it, showing—in sacred art—the gracious form of my limbs. And this foremost of torrents, Kedron, by which the whole scene is surrounded, trumpets forth these miracles loud and clear: it is the Valley of Weeping (cf. Jg 2:5; 2 Kg 5:23 [LXX]), I tell you, where the tomb of Josaphat, king of Judah, was erected (but cf. 1 Kg 22:57), and where the blessed passion of the impassible one had its beginning. There the Savior often met with his disciples (Jn 18:2); there he prayed on his knees to his Father in heaven, asking that the cup, which in accord with God's ineffable plan he had previously desired, be taken away (Mk 14:36 par). There he was kissed by his betrayer, and became the prisoner of those who murdered God. Those who have visited the place will know all of this more reliably from their own experience.[6] Let anyone who doubts what I say go there himself, and learn my meaning first hand; but let the believer be content with what I say, and learn from images about what he has not seen, so that he may come to marvel at marvelous things!

"This, at any rate, is how my burial took place. As for the manner of my passing over [to heaven], it had its own peculiar dignity, above the lot of every other mortal, even though the change itself will be common to you all. My passing was greater than words can say or ears can hear, even though it resembled the pattern of earlier events. What is this place of my rest? Is it a place perceptible by the sense, or graspable by the mind? Not at all! Who, then, can see it, who shall understand it? No creature, except those who have come here by that freedom from passion that only limitless grace can supply, and who have been found worthy to enjoy in this place the delights of being made like God. As my ancestor David said, '[I will go] into the place of the wonderful tabernacle, as far as the house of God, with cries of rejoicing and praise, and the sound of celebration' (Ps 41:5f. [LXX])."

[8.] So speaks the Mother of God, from whose tongue drips the sweet nectar of the Spirit, for "grace has been poured out upon her lips" (Ps 44:3 [LXX]). What may we say beyond this, brothers and sisters? We can only marvel at the immensity of God's provident care, which guides all things so wisely; we can only say, "O depth of the riches and wisdom and knowledge of God! How inexorable are his judgments, how unsearchable his ways," and all the words that follow (Rom 11:33f.). These things are certainly the work of God's hand, and are above human understanding. Even to turn one's mind to such things brings fear to the most noble and purified heart; how much more, then, to me, whose lowly mind creeps along the ground and can think of nothing but matter and clay and the other things that change and pass away! For this reason, I tremble and reel at the thought that the greatness of this day might be spoiled or made trivial by the sordid efforts of my brazen yet ineffectual oratory.

Someone truly eager for knowledge might well wonder why none of the sacred writers, as far as we know, wrote about the immaculate, supernatural passing of the Mother of God, or left us any account of it at all, in the way they composed the divine book of the Gospels or gave us other revelations of the mystery of God. Our answer is: she whom God took as his own[7] fell asleep much later [then the events of the Gospels]—for it is said that she had reached extreme old age when she departed from this world. Or perhaps the times may not then have favored a full account of these events; it was not appropriate for those sowing the seed of the news of God's saving plan to speak in detail of these things, at the same time they were writing the Gospels, since these events needed another, specific and very deliberate kind of treatment, not possible at that moment. If, on the other hand, the reason for their silence is that the inspired writers were only telling the story of God's plan of salvation up to the end of the Word's presence among us in flesh, and that they simply did not [choose to] reveal anything that happened after Jesus was taken up from the earth, I can accept this as well. But lest some wonder why we have so much to say, while tradition is completely silent about today's mystery, I think it would be good to add to my own words what I have been able to find [in the tradition], to support and confirm what I propose for your reflection. For even if the mystery appears only obscurely in sacred literature, it has not remained completely unmentioned in their pages.

[9.] It was, in fact, referred to by a man learned in sacred doctrine, who, they say, investigated holy things with wisdom and erudition, and to whom hints of the mysterious representations of super-celestial minds were revealed, in a way worthy of the angels. In addition, the indescribable revelations that were made to Saint Paul were passed on to him, because of his outstanding purity: revelations that included the divine names—names more radiant than light, names the very universe cannot contain, because they lie beyond all obscurity and ineffability. "Who was this?" you ask me. Should I omit his name, and let the man be known to you simply by the characteristics that mark him, as the lion is known by his claws? I think the man is not wholly unknown to anyone even somewhat aware of his great gifts; so let us mention his name, in the hope that will make his word more credible.

The man was Dionysius. He knew much about divine realities, heard great secrets about heaven and about the many forms and shapes of the unspeakable names of God. In his holy book *On the Divine Names*, in the third chapter—where he is writing about what power there is in prayer, and about the blessed Hierotheos, and about reverence and the way one should write of God—he digresses to tell us various things about that holy man [Hierotheos]. He writes to Timothy [the addressee of the book] as follows:

> We have observed this rule very carefully, that we would not attempt to paraphrase what the divine guide [i.e., Hierotheos] himself said clearly, or give in explanation the same thing as his own words. Once he was with our inspired hierarchs, a time when, as you know, we and you and many of our holy brethren had come together to gaze at the body that was our source of life, the vessel of God.

James, God's brother, was there, and Peter, our leader, the senior and most outstanding among those who spoke of God. After we had seen her, it seemed right to all the hierarchs, as each was able, to sing the praises of the limitless power and goodness of that weakness that gave birth to God.[8] Hierotheos, as you can imagine, surpassed all the other participants in this sacred event, except for the divine spokesmen [= the Apostles] themselves. He was wholly in ecstasy, rapt completely beyond himself; he experienced a union with the realities he was praising. Because of all he heard and saw, because of what he knew and of what exceeded his knowledge, he was recognized to be an inspired man—a singer of God's praises.[9]

[10.] O truly divine mind and tongue, to be initiated into such mysteries and to utter such sounds! Who will provide my ears even with distant echoes of these heavenly songs of praise? If those who lived on such an exalted plane, whose minds' contemplation was so unmingled with lowly things, admired his hymns so greatly, what must the objects—or more precisely, the object—of that praise be? Dionysius' words continue:

> But what shall I tell you about what they said there of God? Unless my memory deceives me, I know I often heard from your own lips phrases from those inspired songs—such is your care not to approach divine things in a careless way. Let us, then pass over those sacred events, because they cannot be communicated to the masses and because you know about them yourself already.[10]

So writes Dionysius, the exalted interpreter of our knowledge of God, the soaring eagle, the one mind most adept at depicting the divine. It is right, I think, not to rush hastily past what he has written, but to stay with it as long as we can, and to penetrate the depth of his thought;[11] the knowledge we long for will be revealed to us there more vividly, and more clearly, too. And you, my venerable audience—you must consider the meaning of what I am about to say, so that you may grasp the point of these mysteries we are celebrating, and know what a great multitude has gathered here [i.e., in the icon of the Dormition], and who they are. Let the holy seer lead us on, proclaiming this wonder as a prophet proclaims his oracles!

[11.] Come, then, let us descend the steps of unforgettable Sion (cf. Ps 137:1)—for there we had gathered in my discourse, a short while ago, there where the Mother of God had her earthly dwelling. It is time now to accompany her virgin body on its way from there, in a funeral procession. The Mother of God has committed her soul to him in whose hands all our souls rest; she has finished her life in the flesh. So, having begun the solemn cortege, let us join to our opening hymn a commemorative ode fitting for a funeral; in that way our words will flow in abundance, and what we have said already will reach full clarity in explanation. To do this each of you must come with me, dear friends—walk on to that holy place, Gethsemane, and see it with the radiant, joyful eyes of your mind; imagine these marvels clearly for yourself, and join what I have already said with the story's end. If you gaze on the events themselves, you will not need long speeches to lead you to true knowledge;[12] "for all things are clear to those who understand, all paths straight for those who have discovered knowledge" (Prov 8:9 [LXX]).

There [in Gethsemane] you will find a splendidly decorated Church, and rich, shining ornaments will surround you. Beneath this superbly constructed house of God, recognize the bridal chamber, the tomb of the virgin Mother of God. Gaze with eyes of faith at the reclining limbs of that royal lady, as she is painted by the sacred artist. The chamber, hollowed out of the rock by other-than-human hands, has been dug at no great distance from the place of her funeral rites; there her holy tabernacle [i.e., her body] has been carried. You will find there the assembly of holy teachers, all gathered together at the right moment and recognized by the mysterious working of the contemplative mind. The sacred seer tells us that they had arrived at the same time, in God's inexplicable providence—a gathering of holy men beyond easy counting.

[12.] In order to grasp more easily the meaning of what they said, come, let us be drawn into the mysteries by the Holy Spirit, and let us make the Mother of the Word the patroness of our words, too. As giver of good gifts, she is nearby, teaching us and explaining the things that are beyond our comprehension. And come to my aid as well, O teacher initiated into the vision of the incomprehensible, O priest of the true tabernacle![13] Be a guide for one who longs to linger with you; lead my understanding directly to the meaning of what I seek, and let me grasp it in mystical contemplation.

The divine author shows us in his own words that nearly the whole company of holy apostles was gathered for that great and venerable event, that climactic spectacle in the life of the Mother of God. All the disciples, scattered over the whole earth, were brought together then at once; he himself was with them, along with the wise and holy Timothy and Hierotheos. For he writes, "When we, as you know, and you and many of our holy brothers had come together to gaze at the body that was the source of life, the vessel of God..." The "body that was the source of life" we understand as none other than the virginal tabernacle that received God, from which the one who exists beyond all essence took the humanity that he made divine. Coming in truth to [share in our] essence, he made it his own in a super-essential way. The phrase here [of Dionysius] does not refer to the Lord's body, since those who after his passion believed in him were not all present with him before his passion. And by "inspired hierarchs," I understand him to be referring clearly to the members of the company of disciples, as the principal spokesmen of the Word. It is nothing to wonder at, if the Spirit that once raised Elijah and carried him off in heaven's fiery chariot now brought them together all at once, in the Spirit, through the clouds. All things are easy for God, as we know from the story of Habakkuk and Daniel.[14]

[13.] How many do you imagine there were then, dear friend, gathered from all points of the compass to be with her? Dionysius speaks of "many of our holy brethren," so it seems clear that the seventy, those appointed disciples of Christ in second place, were also present in that divinely chosen gathering. For it was right both that [the Twelve], the protagonists and willing witnesses of the mystery [of Christ] should be there, and that some others, too, should be brought together by the Holy Spirit in that moment—others who stood next to them in rank, because they shared after them in the responsibility of speaking divine things. Dionysius makes this clear when he adds, "James, brother of God, was there, and Peter, the leader and first in seniority among those who spoke of God." One is struck with wonder at the thought that all of them arrived at the same time!

What happened then, what events followed when they all had arrived in Jerusalem, accompanied by an immense crowd, Dionysius's next statement makes clear. "After we had seen her," he says, "it seemed right to all the hierarchs, as each was able, to sing the praises of the limitless power and goodness of the weakness that gave birth to God." Let us consider, then, what they had seen—what this beauty was, and what godly language they used to praise the loveliness in which the Lord delights—if the eyes of our minds can conjure up such things! The sight that then appeared so radiant and beautiful to those inspired men would have been, I imagine, the splendid, shining vision of the Virgin's earthly frame: the condition in which the Mother of God's body appeared, radiating life and all light, far above us and yet a body like our own. Jesus, the author of our life, has made available to us, from this body, the source of divine life; he transformed the first springing-forth (ἀπαρχή) of our redemption into a spring of life (ζωῆς ἀρχήν),[15] shaping it anew for his own purpose in a supernatural way, from the Virgin's womb. "If the first-fruits (ἀπαρχή) are holy," the Apostle says, "then the whole mass is so as well; and if the root is holy, then the branches are also" (Rom 11:16).

[14.] The body of the Mother of God, then, is a source of life [for us], because it received into itself the whole life-giving fulness of the Godhead; it is the precious bridal-chamber of virginity, the heaven above us, the earth that brings forth God, the first-fruits of Adam's mass made divine in Christ, exact image of [creation's] original beauty, divinely confirmed guardian of God's unspeakable judgments, dwelling-place of human perfection, spiritual book of God's words of redemption, inexplicable depth of the endless "full-ness that fills all things" (Eph 4:10), impregnable fortress of our hidden hopes, treasury of a purity beyond our understanding, royal robe of the Word who is beyond all beginnings and who became a human being, earthly palace of the heavenly King, celebrated workshop for God's dealings with us, utterly suitable material for the divine embodiment, divine and perfect clay for the sculptor of all creation—from whom he who is above all substance came to share, wholly and truly, in our substance, and took on a substance like ours, for our sake.[16]

[15.] Oh, truly blessed were those eyes, and the lips that praised these things! Who could interpret these mysterious sights with the tongue? Who is the most shining vessel of spiritual light? She was the lamp, by which our nature super-naturally received the sun of justice.[17] She is the spiritual mirror for the ray that shines forth from the Father. By her radiance, we are illuminated with the God who is, before the morning star (cf. Ps 110:3). She is the throne exalted on high, on which the Lord of Hosts is seated, in the vision of that most far-seeing of all the prophets, Isaiah (Is 6:1). She is the standard of royalty for the heavenly race, the sanctuary where all sacred worship and sacrifice takes place, the spiritual altar for the divine holocaust, the tongs for the purging coal (Is 6:6f.), the Levites' staff (cf. Num 17:16-26), the root of Jesse (cf. Is 11:10), the sceptre of David (cf. Ps 89:44?)—mother of him who formed us, nurse of him who nourishes us, gate for the rising Christ, who ascends from the depths of dawn (cf. Lk 1:78), narrow bosom sheltering the one who contains all things, spotless vestment of the lamb who is shepherd (cf. Apoc 7:14-17), unyoked heifer of the fatted calf, pure fleece drenched by the heavenly dew (cf. Jg 6:36-40), virgin earth for Adam's re-creator (cf. Gen 2:7), heaven for him who made earth into heaven, great vision of the prophets: vision which the saints [of old] saw "in many patterns and many modes" (cf. Heb 1:1), when they taught us in symbols of their mystic conceptions of God and prefigured the great mystery of God's plan of redemption. She is the great world in miniature, the world containing him who brought the world from nothingness into being, that it might be the messenger of his own greatness.

[16.] How could they fail to wonder as they saw her, lying on her funeral couch with her bodily powers now at rest—her who had been so honored and graced by the God who creates and contains all things? This, I believe, is what the sacred seer means when he speaks of "the limitless power and goodness of the weakness that gave birth to God." What they all saw surely filled them with fear: the bearer of life, now borne away by death; her who spoke with God, now voiceless; her who bore life in her womb as in an ark, now dead, breathless, lying on a couch. If these things are <not> foreign to our nature, still they are no less wonderful.[18] There are spiritual mysteries here, for one who can see God's work in a spiritual way: childbirth and virginity (cf. Lk 1:34f.); words that speak of divine care and judgment, exaltation and submission, greatness and humility (cf. Lk 1:46f., 52). Here the form of her body obscured the brilliant rays of the sun. Here mortality becomes immortal, blinding the eyes of the beholders. Here are riches that fill all heaven and earth. It is a new spectacle, the most spectacular of all we have witnessed. What is this but the Mother of God, his tabernacle, lying on the ground: she from whom God came forth, manfully bearing our humanity as his trophy—Christ the head, in whom the mass of our nature, formed from the earth, was transformed and made divine?

This was what they saw; this is the story—and greater, in all likelihood, than what we have so poorly narrated here! What was their song? What did they celebrate? May Christ be with us, and give us words to recount this, for he is Word and Wisdom and Power; may he guide our minds on his way, towards the shining splendor of the heavenly anthems.[19] And may our minds always be able to see these things clearly; may we be illumined and strengthened by them in him, Christ our Lord, to whom be glory and power, with the almighty Father and the life-giving Spirit, now and always and for ages of ages.

Amen.

1   This homily is published as the first of Andrew's homilies on the Dormition in the edition of Combéfis, reproduced in Migne.

2   The phrase here is τῶν ὄντων ἀποκατάστασις, but Andrew is presumably using it in the generic sense of "final restoration" (see Acts 3:21), rather than suggesting the doctrine of universal salvation associated with Origen and his followers.

3   Andrew here reflects the general ancient belief that the role of the mother in gestation was to nourish with her own blood the life implanted in her by the paternal seed. See, e.g., Aristotle, *De Gen. Anim.* I, 727b30-33, 729a22-b26; *Wisdom of Solomon* 7:2. See also John of Damascus, Homily 1.3 (below, p. 185).

4   This rather labored phrase (literally: "my virgin body, laid hold of by God, from which the simple Jesus is composed") is an allusion to the classical Christology formulated at the Councils of Chalcedon (451) and Constantinople II (553), according to which Jesus is understood to be one hypostasis subsisting as a single "composite" individual, from and in two distinct natures.

5   Andrew seems to be directing his hearers' attention to an icon of the deposition of Mary's body in the tomb, as a way of helping them enter imaginatively into the events celebrated by the feast. He will return later in the oration to the importance of visual imagination in the contemplation of the mystery.

6   Andrew makes it clear, in these detailed allusions to the surroundings of Mary's tomb, that he has firsthand knowledge of Jerusalem, but implies that most in his audience probably do not.

7   Andrew calls Mary θεόληπτος, a word usually meaning "inspired" but probably intended here in its more etymological sense of "taken up by God."

8   The word used by Ps.-Dionysius here, θεαρχικήν, can simply mean "divine"; Andrew, however, in this oration, seems to take it as specifically denoting Mary's privilege as Mother of God, and so as suggesting more than its usual rather general connotation. See his explanation below, 1068 A—1069 C.

9   Ps.-Dionysius, *On the Divine Names* 3.

10   *Ibid.*

11   The rest of this oration, in fact, is simply Andrew's imaginative meditation on the paragraph from Ps.-Dionysius' *On the Divine Names* which he has quoted above.

12   Andrew again emphasizes the importance of the visual imagination, and apparently also of an actual icon, for a thorough participation in the mystery of the feast.

13   Andrew here invokes the aid of Ps.-Dionysius himself, as the one whose 'mystical vision' is the main source of the narrative background for the feast.

14   This story appears, in the Septuagint and versions dependent on it, in the apocryphal account of "Bel and the Dragon" appended to chapter 12, vv. 33-39.

15 Andrew here plays on the various meanings of the word ἀρχή, "source" or "beginning," in speaking of the humanity of Mary as both the means of God's redemptive presence in Christ and as the first example of redeemed humanity.

16 This lyrical paragraph, a series of epithets aimed at expressing Mary's role in the central event of the Incarnation, follows a long tradition of Marian oratory going back at least to the fourth century, in which striking biblical or poetic images expressing Mary's dignity are simply gathered together in a series or litany, without further explanation. See above, pp. 2f, 33.

17 Andrew here continues the mode of a litany of titles or series of acclamations; now, however, almost all of them are images taken from the Old Testament—part of a tradition of applying these images to Mary as types or figures of the incarnation, which is itself the central object of all prophecy, the fulfilment of God's history of love towards his creation.

18 The sense seems to require that one add to this sentence a "not" absent from the Greek text.

19 Andrew here prepares his audience for his continued discussion of the mystery of Mary's "passage" or assumption into glory, which will be the subject of his third discourse.

On the Dormition of Our Most Holy Lady, the Mother of God

By St. Andrew of Crete

HOMILY III

[1.] The continuity of what we have to say calls us back, once again, to the festival. Indeed, we must add what is still missing to all we have said, so that our discourse may be complete and unbroken, free of all gaps and disjunctions. In the earlier sections we spoke briefly, as best we could, about the [disciples'] vision of that life-giving body, the virginal tabernacle that was the Mother of God. What remains is to describe the hymn that then was sung, and the message that it conveyed. Let no one blame me now for boldness or rashness, if I attempt such a lofty theme; I did not rely on the powers of my own speech when I composed the oration now in my hands, but only on the assurance of your prayers; and I was constantly concerned to keep the tone of what I am about to say, as far as possible, modest and lowly. Even so, my address is not meant to trivialize this mystery, although it is an attempt—rather brash, perhaps—to deal for the first time with an unconventional theme, to speak of what has not been addressed before. So if our present discourse should contain, perhaps, notions few people have reflected on, let no one wonder; we have considered them ourselves, in a speculative way, to the extent that our mind could reach them—but even the angels could hardly grasp them with precision!

[2.] That countless company of inspired human witnesses is gathered together, as we have already said, and all the spiritual orders of heavenly powers, perhaps, are hovering invisibly above, gathered for this wonderful spectacle. The holy

souls of the saints are there, too, I think, drawn together by
God around her bed: these are the ones the Book of Canticles,
in its spiritual meaning, called "the young men" (Cant 1:6). It
is fitting, after all, that the souls of those who have finished
their lives and are now made like God should gather near the
queen of our nature, to go before her on her way—to lead her
and be her escort, and to begin the final hymns in her honor. In
the midst of them, before the gaze of them all, lies the body of
the Mother of God: three cubits in height, radiant with
light—the body that received the complete fullness of God's
Word, who rules all things. You can see it lying on a couch:
that body that has filled all creation with the fragrant myrrh of
holiness.

[3.] What mind, what tongue could find adequate words
for what they see there? Everything exceeds the bounds of our
ignorance, the limitations of our sight, in more than infinite
measure. For this reason, those chosen ones, whom God inspired with a share in his Holy Spirit, found the abundance of
light within them transformed into ecstasy, from the sheer
gladness and joy God gave them to revel in; so they began to
sing—gone in response to the other, as each best was
able—divinely inspired hymns that were poetic evocations of
her falling asleep. These were not hymns such as we ourselves
could understand, or such as one of us might compose; but
they were hymns that the Spirit taught these men to sing, and
enabled them to hear.

This was the hymn, these were the themes sung and heard
by those singers, limitlessly soaring above our lowly human
harmony and concord. It lacked little or nothing by comparison to the song of the angels feasting in heaven, whose height
and depth, whose limitless beauty is not for us rashly to describe; we have, after all, never tasted such sweetness ourselves, and should rather honor it by silence[1] as something

incomprehensible, unutterable. The only subjects safe for us to consider are those "in which success is pleasant and failure is not dangerous,"[2] subjects that neither offend the learned nor bore the ignorant. Still, even though that hymn and what it celebrated were beyond our comprehension, it might yet be possible, within our own limitations, to give an impression of it all by speaking as follows:

[4.] "This is the final goal of the covenants God has made with us; this is the revelation of the hidden depths of God's incomprehensibility. This is the realization intended before all the ages; this is the crown of God's oracles, the inexplicable, supremely unknowable will of him who has cared for humanity since before creation began. This is the first-fruit of God's communion with his creation, of his identification, as maker of all things, with what he has made. This is the concrete, personal pledge of God's reconciliation with humanity, the surpassing beauty of God's own sculpture, the perfectly-drawn portrait of the divine model. This is the first step to all ascent, to all contemplation; the holy tabernacle of him who made the world; the vessel that received the inexhaustible wisdom of God; the inviolate treasury of life. This is the spring of divine radiance, which can never be drunk dry; the impregnable stronghold, raised so high over all of us in its purity that it can never be conquered by passion. Through this woman, the pledge of our salvation has been made and kept, in that this marvelous creature has both reached the limits of our lot and has paid the common debt proper to our nature. And if not all the features of her life were the same as ours, that is due simply to her nearness to God.

[5.] "It is easy to show her supreme freedom from passion. Which of the qualities that we consider truly great did she not acquire, with virtues enough and to spare? What remarkable gift was not hers, in order to reveal God's wonders? She was, quite clearly, the repository of all the miraculous things that have either come to pass before our time or are still being achieved; this present miracle is simply the latest in the series, even though it was decreed before all time—so it is that God's will decides in advance the end of each of our lives. O Providence, whose final purpose no mortal has ever plumbed, whose path none has ever traced! The mystery of the Virgin, now being accomplished, is your work! For it is a mystery, even if we consider our own end: this is our lot, after all, set aside for human nature from the beginning![3] But how has the wall been broken down—the wall built by sin? How have the fetters woven by transgression been loosed? How has death come to be regarded simply as an everyday sleep? Fear is gone, no longer haunting the little ones in Christ. Yet if it were not God's own dwelling-place who died, would the corruption sowed by disobedience be dispelled? Yes—it *has* been dispelled, since Christ died before her! Nature itself has been called forth from the condemnation of corruption, has taken on a new state, rooted in incorruption. What a transformation! What newness! What a divine exchange![4] Nature brought forth a will that produced only thorns (cf. Is 5:1-7); but she, in contrast, has brought forth the one who fulfilled his father's will. Nature gave painful birth to the death we freely chose in our disobedience; but she, instead, has brought forth the one who destroyed death by his obedience. She, she alone has been chosen for the renewal of our nature, beyond nature's powers; she alone subjected herself fully to the one who formed all nature from nothing.[5] The tent of God's presence lies here before us as God's vessel of prophecy,[6] a generous benefactor urging onwards all who love what is right, so that no one may be excluded from the gathering.[7] The gift calls for no labor on our part, except for our free choice. Let each one go forward boldly, then, whose faith is free of doubt: let him go forward to the place of the Virgin's oracle, and learn there by experience where to find his heart's desires. Our common altar of reconciliation is ready: come, all of you, and be reconciled with God! (cf. 2 Cor 5:21)

[6.] "See here the inexhaustible spring of immortality; come, you who are dead, and drink! (cf. Is 55:1) See here the ever-flowing river of life; come, everyone, and be made immortal! O daughter of Adam and Mother of God! O Mother without a husband, and Virgin who bore a child! O creature of him who was created in you—created in time, without leaving his own eternity! All the Spirit's spokesmen bore witness to you in ancient times.[8] Moses was the first, for when seeing the bush he said of you, 'I will go over and look at this wonderful sight' (Ex 3:3). God's ancestor David prayed to Christ on your behalf, saying, 'Arise, Lord, you and the ark of your holiness' (Ps 131:8 [LXX]). He also referred by anticipation to your death when he sang prophetically, 'The rich among the people will make supplication before your face' (Ps 44:13 [LXX]). 'Behold all the glory of the king's daughter within; she is robed and ornamented in cloth fringed with gold' (*ibid.* 14). The holy book of Canticles described you in advance, when it made this hidden allusion: 'Who is this who comes up from the desert like a column of smoke, breathing myrrh and incense made from all the merchant's powders?' (Cant 3:6) the same holy book also foretold you when its author wrote, 'Here is Solomon's resting-place; he has made its posts of silver, its base of gold, its steps of porphyry. Within it is paved with stone, [a gift of] love from the daughters of Jerusalem' (*ibid.* 7, 10). And further: 'Come out, daughters of Sion, [and gaze] on King Solomon. He is wearing the crown with which his mother crowned him on his wedding day, on the day of his heart's delight' (*ibid.* 11). See her, daughters of Sion, and call her blessed; queens and concubines, praise her, for the fragrance of her garments is beyond all perfume. (cf. Cant 3:6; 4:10f.)

"Isaiah foresaw you in the Lord, and cried: 'Behold, a virgin shall conceive' (Is 7:14), and 'The root of Jesse shall survive' (*ibid.* 11:10)—'blessed is the root of Jesse'—and 'A
shoot will spring forth from the root of Jesse, and a flower will
rise from the root' (*ibid.* 11:1). On your account, the great Ezekiel prophesied, 'Behold, the eastern gate; it shall be a locked
gate, and no one shall enter through it. The Lord God, he alone,
will go in and come out; and this gate shall be locked' (Ezek
44:2). And that 'man of desires' [= Daniel: cf Dan 9:23; 10:11,
19] called you, in prophecy, a 'mountain,' when he said: 'A
stone' will be taken from you, 'not cut by any human hand'
(Dan 2:34)—removed, but not divided, in the conception of a
humanity like our own.

[7.] "You are the great achievement of God's awe-
inspiring plan, 'into which the angels long to look' (1 Pet
1:12). You are the 'lovely dwelling-place' (Ps 83:1 [LXX]),
where God has consented to be with us, the truly desirable
land. 'For the King has desired the glory of your beauty; he has
fallen in love' with the riches of your virginity (cf. Ps 44:11
[LXX]; Wisd 8:2). And he has dwelt in you, 'and pitched his
tent among us' (John 1:14); he has reconciled us, through you,
with God the Father. You are the eternal treasure, 'the mystery
hidden for all ages' (Eph 3:9). You are, in truth, the living
book in which the spiritual word has been silently inscribed by
the living pen of the Spirit. You alone are the text of the new
covenant, unerringly written by God, which he promised the
human race in former times (cf. Jer 31:31-33). You are the
manifold 'chariot of God,' leading those 'countless thousands
who life has been transformed' by his incarnation (cf. Ps 67:18
[LXX]). 'You are Mount Sion, the fat mountain, full and solid
as a cheese, where God dwells' (Ps 67:17; Ps 73:1f. [LXX]);
there he who is above our substance took solid flesh from you,
giving body and firmness to a rational soul like ours.

"O divine temple, and woman of earth! O lifeless monument, and life-giving pillar! You did not lead the fleshly Israel on its wandering by your light, but you were enkindled by the divine fire to light the spiritual [Israel] on the way towards unfailing knowledge. O radiant cloud, and 'shaded mountain' (Hab 3:3 [LXX]), overshadowing not the ignorant Jewish people but God's 'chosen people, the holy race' (Ex 19:6; 1 Pet 2:9), leading them through the darkness by the beacon of your maternal light. O woman purer than all gold—purer than all creation, both sensible and immaterial! O virgin earth, from which the second Adam came forth, who was the model for that Adam of old!

[8.] "What tomb shall cover you, what earth receive you, who exceed heaven and the whole heavenly realm in holiness? What kind of shroud can we offer you? What kind of wrappings and robes for burial? What unguents shall anoint your body—that body so fragrant, so spotless, so full of goodness, so rich in forgiveness, so flowing with incorruptible power; that body from which we draw divine life, in which we find our perfection, through which we receive our salvation? You are truly the one who is 'beautiful, and there is no stain in you' (Cant 4:7). Let holy Solomon sing to you yet another verse: 'You are as lovely as Jerusalem, and the fragrance of your garments is as the fragrance of Lebanon' (Cant 6:3; 4:11). You are the new flask of inexhaustible myrrh; you are the gladness in the oil that anoints us (cf. Ps 44:8 [LXX]). You are the incense full of spiritual aromas. You are the flower of immortality, the earth that brings forth perfume, the treasure-chest of life, the shining lamp, the purple garment woven by God, the royal vestment, the robe that God has embroidered, the lined cloak made of gold; beyond all our power of telling, you are the seam of that royal robe that makes the Word intelligible. You are the crown of kingly power, woven by the high priest;

you are the 'throne on high' (cf Is 6:1), the gate that stands
high above the heaven of heavens; you are the queen of all humanity, a title as well deserved as it is commonly used. Aside
from God alone, you are higher than all beings.

"What hands shall lay you to rest? What arms shall carry
you, who carried in your arms the Uncontainable One? What
funeral prayers shall we make at your grave? With what songs
shall we send you on your way? What lips may sing of your
passing? What voice? What words shall express with appropriate grace the great things done for you (Lk 1:49)? Therefore, in place of all others, we shall use these words of you:
'Blessed are you among women' (Lk 1:42), for all generations
(cf. *ibid.* 1:48). Blessed are you in heaven and glorified on
earth. Every tongue shall praise you gratefully, and proclaim
you Mother of Life. All creation is full of your glory (cf. Is
6:3); all things are made holy by your myrrh-like fragrance.
Because of you, sin's aggression is over; the curse of our first
mother has been turned to grace. Because of you, all (angels)
sing with us, 'Glory in heaven, peace on earth' (Lk 2:14). No
tomb can contain you, for corruptible things cannot hide the
body of a queen. Hades has no power to hold you, for the
forces of slavery cannot capture a royal soul.

[9.] "Go, then—go in peace! Depart from your dwelling-
place within creation; be an intercessor with the Lord on behalf of the corporeal reality we share. As long as you dwelt
among the people of this earth, only a small part of the earth
contained you. But since you have been taken from the earth to
your new home, all the universe owns you as its common altar
of cleansing sacrifice. Be magnified beyond Enoch in your
happiness, in your indescribable joy, in your eternal light; you
are in the place of true life, in the kingdom of pure light, in the
incomprehensible dance of the angels. Beyond these blessings, enjoy the beauty of your Son, delight in his inexhaustible

joy and in the beatitude that never grows old. You live by the torrents of eternal delight, in the meadows of incorruptibility, near the spring of life that is always new, near the streams of light that bubble forth from God, near the rivers of that radiance that never dies. There is the goal of all our past and present hopes, the sum of all good things, the revelation of all that is hidden and will only be seen in days to come, the final end, beyond which nothing exists at all. There the Father is worshipped, the Son is glorified, the Holy Spirit is praised in song—all as the unified nature of one God in three Persons."

[10]. Such things as this, I think, those inspired men must have said and sung—and loftier things than these. For I do not know how to say more, being myself earth and dust, wholly corruption, crawling on my belly like the snakes. Yet I have paid the debt of speech sufficiently, I think, within the limits of my powers; nothing relevant to the present celebration has been overlooked. If anyone should wish to add some more exalted word, to round out what we have said, that will only add to the festival. After saying a few words more, then, I will rest my oars in this verbal regatta! For as far as speaking worthily is concerned, all of us fall equally short; as far as wanting to display our powers goes, each is equally eager. But she who gave birth to the Word, I know, will also receive this insignificant word from us, and will give us, in return, not what we ask for, perhaps, but at least what we deserve to receive. For the all-holy one, as giver of many good things, loves to repay little gifts with greater ones. But enough of this! Come, all of you here at this brilliant, illustrious festal gathering: I call you together again to hear the conclusion of my discourse! Come, let us lead on the sacred funeral procession for the Virgin's body; let us sing a song in her memory, and let us crown her, who gave rise to this celebration, with all the honors in our power. And that this may still more splendidly come to pass, let the whole festal company

of heaven and earth join with us today, and complete for me the funeral hymn, which I can only fashion in words like these:

[11.] The camp of God has left, has left the tents of Kedar (cf. Ps 119:5 [LXX]) for the incorporeal tents of a new life. The [true] tabernacle, the archetype of the one in the Law (cf. Hebr 8:5), has received the heavenly ark which the ark in the Law prefigured. "The lintel above the gates has been raised" (Is 6:4; cf. Ps 23:7 [LXX]), that the kingdom may give a royal embrace to that gate of God which reaches above heaven. Receive her, angels robed in white! Sing, O heavens! Give praise, you who are born of earth! Exalt "the city of God, the great King" (Ps 47:3 [LXX]). Clap your hands, O earth! Sing her praise, tell the glorious story of the Virgin—the swaddling-bands of her child-bearing, the miracle of her burial; how she was buried and how she was transported elsewhere; how her tomb was seen to be empty and how it came to be reverenced as a shrine.

Judea, bring your sons together![9] Proclaim the news of the queen who comes from the tribe of Judah—have courage, do not be afraid! Celebrate your festival, Jerusalem; cry out, shout, walk in procession with the mother-city (μητρόπολις) of God! Sing with David's words, and say clearly, "As Israel came forth from Egypt..." (Ps 113:1 [LXX]).[10] Mother Sion, in whom the Lord delights and whom he has chosen, call your daughters together—the Church of the Gentiles. Sing a serious song (cf. Ps 136:4), but nothing tragic; a lament, but not a cry of misery. This present celebration is a happy one, not a day of grief! Gethsemane, receive your new queen; prepare her tomb, begin the burial rites, sprinkle her coffin with unguents. Let her sarcophagus be a treasure-chest for you, to guard her holy body in safety. If that body should remain in its tomb, let it be a common object of reverence for angels and human beings. But if something strange should happen, and that spotless body should be taken away, stay here and proclaim the miracle—tell of that removal to the generations to come. Give the spirit of God's mother to the spirits above, and give the holiness of her body to us, like myrrh flowing from an unfailing spring.

[12.] Let us run, then, all together, to the Mother of God; choirs of fathers and patriarchs, spirits of the prophets and companies of priests, the band of Apostles, the nation of martyrs, the gathering of doctors, the souls of the just, the company of the saints in every age and every rank, kings and potentates, rulers and the ruled. "Lads and maidens, old with the young, praise [her]" (Ps 148:12 [LXX]), beg for her help. Say, say to the Mother of God, "How blessed is the house of David, from whose loins you, O Mother of God, have sprung." Mothers and virgins, praise the one who alone was both mother and always virgin. Brides, go before her who remained an unmarried maiden, the incorrupt one who, uniquely free from the pangs of childbirth, brought forth the incomprehensible one. Childless people and widows, applaud her who "did not know man" (Lk 1:34), but who changed the laws of infertility. Maidens, dance joyfully before the incorruptibility that gave birth to a child. All nations, bless her; all tongues, call her blessed (cf. Lk 1:48); sing to the Mother of God, all tribes of the earth—sing! Begin to sing and sound the cymbals, raise a joyful cry, magnify her, sing her praises! Take up the tambourine, O Miriam—take it up, and lead the virgins on their way! David, play your lyre, lift up your voice, sing to your queen; lead the dance, strike out chords on your harp; call out the young maidens, summon the singers, arrange them in choirs, lead them behind her couch, let them stand before it and on each side of it; let them sing their song all around her tomb!

[13.] Behold, the new ark of God's glory, containing "the golden vase, Aaron's rod that blossomed, and the tablets of the covenant" (Heb 9:4). Behold, the summation of all the things which the oracles of the prophets foretold. Behold, the ladder that Jacob saw in a moment of divine revelation, on which he saw God's angels moving up and down (Gen 28:12; cf. Jn 1:51)—whatever that ascent and descent signified. This is the gate of heaven, of which Jacob said, "How awe-inspiring is this place! It is nothing other than God's dwelling—it is itself the gate of heaven!" (Gen 28:17)

Behold, the altar of expiation in the Holy of Holies, set up in the sanctuary of the tent of God's presence (cf. Ex 40:6). At some times, she is covered over with the Seraphs' wings; at others, she is the place where our sins are expiated through the mystery of Jesus' own initiation. The yoke of slavery to the Law no longer rests on the true Israel, since Christ has written for us a bill of liberation, of free and spiritual worship, using as his parchment[11] the body he took from the Virgin. The priests' yearly procession into the holy place is no longer practiced, for "the great high priest, Christ Jesus, has passed through the heavens" (Heb 4:14), with the flesh he took on and with its rational, intellectual soul, in order to offer his mystical sacrifice in the virgin's sanctuary as in a temple, always interceding for us. He offers sacrifice and is himself offered; bringing his holocaust forward, he becomes the sacrifice; sanctifying himself for our sakes, he sanctifies those who have sacrificed him.

[14.] This, O Mother of God, is the hidden meaning of your supernatural dormition. This is the funeral oration that shall accompany the sacred procession of the tent God raised as his tabernacle; the hymn for your passing, the record of the events both proceeding and following your burial, the memorial ode for that transition that surpasses all knowledge. These are but oblique, blurred images of the divine mysteries, the blessed revelations given us about you. Our mind can go no further, can come no closer to the mark than what we have said; this little discourse, fashioned with all our powers in your honor, is finished—dedicated to you in gratitude and supplication. If it contains anything worthy of your greatness, my thanks are due to you, who gave it to me and who now welcome my eagerness so graciously. If, however, it seems to fall short of your dignity—something most likely to happen to anyone who tries to speak of you—you will surely be understanding, since compassion is your nature, by your very closeness to your son and protector. I am sure, too, that you will accept this as the most beautiful of gifts, even though it is produced by my shabby labors; I had, after all, nothing greater to offer the Mother of the Word, who stands so far above all other creatures, than words of my own: words that simply gush from the plentiful springs of grace within you, the one so blessed by God. As for that awe-inspiring, totally incomprehensible state of divine and ageless beatitude that you now enjoy, let us honor it, as something wholly unknowable and unspeakable, by our silence![12] That is only right; for it is not for us to try and explain what is above us, what is proof against all investigation by being simply beyond our grasp.

[15.] Now, O blessed, thrice-royal Mother of God, we have spelled out—modestly, but as best we could—an account of the hidden truth concerning you that we have learned, in its basic outlines, and which this occasion demands of us. We have been instructed by you, and helped by your prayers, which find such easy access to God. Who shall implant in us a voice adequate to proclaim the height and greatness of the glorious things we know of you? Who shall give us strength to speak? O mistress of all men and women, you who received the living Word who is wisdom in person, the first and original cause of all things! O provider of life, life of the living, part of the cause of our life![13] O holy one, holier than all the saints, supremely holy treasury of all that makes us holy! O woman who as one individual, without division or dissolution, united humanity to God! O kingdom of those formed from earth, drawing your invincible power from the glory on high! O outer bulwark of Christian faith, powerful fighter for those who put their hope in you! Receive from us, who have received the light of truth through you, our solemn utterances formed, as far as we were capable, from murky images pregnant with divine meaning. And give us, who glory in you, Mother of God, this recompense for our little offering: intercede for us with your Son, our Master and King, our God and Lord—a gift more precious and more splendid than all treasures and endless wealth. When we sin, let us be reconciled to God by your prayers, and when we do what is right, let us be confirmed within ourselves still more firmly in goodness. By your prayers, we will look on the arms of savages as if they were children's arrows; by them, the spear, the helmet, the shot of the bow remain ineffectual, fall short of their mark;[14] by them, finally, all good things are obtained for Christians, even likeness to God.

Here, in a word, is the mystery, dear friend; though it falls far short of our hopes, still nothing is missing from our enthusiasm. A more mystical and lofty word you may seek from the Word who, for your sake, emptied himself and took on the cruder fullness of flesh, who united you wholly to himself in his love for humanity. It is no less accurate to say: he became human in order to make you wholly divine in the Spirit, to consume the worse in the better, to raise you up to himself from the earth and to enthrone you among your ancestors. Be drawn up to him, always, in your way of life and in your pure contemplation; live out a pattern of holy words and habits; see God, as far as that is possible, and let him see you. Press on always to see him clearly in flashes of prayerful insight and in the upward climb of virtue, so that you might be mature and solid on both sides—in action, that is, and in contemplation—and that you might come, in the end, "to full manhood, to the full measure of the maturity of Christ" (Eph 4:13). To him be glory and power for ages of ages!

Amen.

1   The phrase "honor by silence" is used with some frequency by the Cappadocian Fathers and later Greek Patristic authors, to suggest the incompatibility of too much analysis with religious reverence, when central Mysteries of faith are being alluded to: see Basil of Caesaraea, *On the Holy Spirit* 18.44 (SCh 17/2, 192.11); Gregory of Nyssa, *Adversus Eunomium* II, 1.105 (GNO I, 257.22); III, 1.105 (GNO II, 39.5); Gregory of Nazianzus, Or. 2.62 (SCh 247, 174.8); Or. 18.10 (PG 35, 996 C5); Or. 28.20 (SCh 250, 140.5); Or. 29.8 (*ibid.* 192.25); Maximus Confessor, *Quaestiones ad Thalassium*, prologue (PG 90, 260 A7-10); *ibid.* Quaest. 43 (PG 90, 412 A4-7).

2   See Gregory Nazianzen, Or. 27.10 (SCh 250.96ff.). In this passage, at the end of his first "theological oration," Gregory includes among subjects safe for theological speculation—and thus not needing to be "honored by silence"—some eschatological themes: the resurrection, the coming judgment, and the retribution of reward or punishment to follow.

3   Here Andrew begins the core of his theological reflection on the celebration of Mary's death and glorification. What is being celebrated is nothing less than the hope of all Christians to triumph over death and to be free of its fear. Mary reveals that hope to us concretely; yet her liberation from death is itself clearly grounded in the death and resurrection of Christ.

4   For a passage somewhat similar in thought and style, although referring to the Incarnation, see Gregory of Nazianzus, Or. 38.13.

5   Andrew here emphasizes that the privileges Christian faith identifies with Mary are rooted in her perfect obedience to God's will, in her acceptance of the vocation that made the Incarnation and the whole history of salvation in Christ possible.

6   In a striking image, Andrew speaks of the body of Mary, as it experiences both death and transformation to life, as being itself a prophetic sign for a troubled humanity.

7   Greek: ἐκκλησία, whose more normal meaning is simply "Church."

8   Andrew now applies to Mary a set of Old Testament images that were already familiar as "types" of Mary's fruitful virginity; for a similar series, see John of Damascus *Homily 2 on the Dormition*.

9   Andrew now heightens the dramatic effect of his words by suggesting that he and his hearers are involved in the events of Mary's burial themselves, and that the outcome of the story is still uncertain.

10 See John of Thessalonica, *Oration on the Dormition of Mary* 13, where Peter begins Mary's funeral procession by intoning this psalm. The reference is doubtless to Mary's own "exodus." Andrew's allusion to the psalm here suggests that his audience may be familiar with this part of the Dormition tradition. It is also possible that this psalm was used in the Byzantine funeral liturgy during this period.

11 I have followed here the suggestion of Combéfis, reading χαρτῇ for the χάριτι of the manuscripts.

12 See above, n. 1.
13 In being the source of Jesus' humanity and thus an integral part of God's way of redemption, Mary is, in Andrew's view, also an integral part of the divine plan for humanity, fulfilled in Christ, that gives meaning to creation. She is thus herself a "part of the cause" of creation's existence, as well as of the redeemed life that fulfills it.
14 Andrew seems to be alluding here to the traditional understanding of Mary in Constantinople as "defender of the city," the one who had saved the imperial capital from barbarian siege in 626. See the account of Theodore Synkellos, *De impiorum Avarum et Persarum incursione* 7, 12, 17-28 (in A. Mai, *Nova patrum bibliotheca* 6/2 [1853] 426f., 429, 431-437); cf. the prologue added to the *Akathistos* hymn in memory of this deliverance, attributed to Patriarch Sergius (ed. G. G. Meersseman, *The Acathistos Hymn* [Fribourg, 1958] 24).

ON THE MOST VENERABLE DORMITION OF THE HOLY MOTHER OF GOD

By Our Holy Father Germanus,
Archbishop of Constantinople

HOMILY I[1]

[1.] A debtor always sings the praises of his benefactor. One who has been saved is not ignorant of his savior's protection. And if one is not rich enough to offer a recompense in real terms, he knows he must at least present his patron with a verbal salutation. Therefore I, too, shall dare to speak out in your praise, O Mother of God, as one who has received marvelous gifts beyond explanation, beyond words or understanding. In my boldness and joy, I speak out to you what your own voice has proclaimed: look on the lowliness of your servant; exalt the mouth of this lowly one; fill me, as I eagerly hunger for words to praise you, with the riches of your good things, that as you guide the steps of my mind with your ready hand, I may not go astray in my praise of you, my mistress. For you rightly said that all generations of men and women would call you blessed—you, whom no one has ever worthily magnified; you, who are always full of compassion for the impulsive poverty, the limitations of spirit, of those who would praise you![2]

What shall I say first, and how shall I continue? Shall I strike up the praises of your life among us in human flesh, or shall I celebrate the glory of your transferral[3] in the Spirit, your falling asleep into life? Both are formidable tasks, each terrifying! But our sermon must eventually reach its conclusion by telling of your triumphs; setting forth, then, from today's theme, let it now begin to praise you, O Mother of God, for your noble and glorious departure from our midst.[4]

[2.] When you moved on from the earthly realm, it is clear that you entered heaven; yet even before that, you had a share of heavenly things, nor did you leave our earth completely when you departed from us—even when you took your place high above both the ranks of heaven and the creatures on earth. For in truth you have become an ornament to heaven, O Mother of God, and a light for all the earth! You are an ornament to heaven, since as soon as the human race came to be, angels were appointed to watch over their life, to lead them on their way, to rule them and protect them in a heart full of unshakable faith in God. As scripture says, "You have established the boundaries of the nations according to the number of the angels of God" (Deut 32:8), and "the angel of the Lord is encamped around those who fear him, and will protect them" (Ps 33:8 [LXX]). But as wretched humanity began, in past times, to live in error and idolatry, and to contaminate the air with the aroma of sacrifices, the angels broke off their companionship with them for good, and God, in turn, took away from them his Holy Spirit. But when you gave birth, at the end of time, to the one who was "in the beginning," the Word of God the Father (Jn 1:1), from that very moment of your labor the angels looked down from heaven and sang the praises of God, now born of you. Crying out that glory had been added to the heights of heaven, they also exclaimed that peace had at last come on earth (cf. Lk 2:14), so that enmity could no longer be called a barrier between angels and human beings, heaven and earth; there was now a reign of harmony, one mutually complementary song of praise sung by both angels and human beings to the God who is one and three.

[3.] The Father of the only-begotten Son, bearing witness to his bodily birth from you without a human father, cries to him, "Today I have begotten you" (Ps 2:7 [LXX]), and again, "From the womb, before the morning star, I have begotten you" (Ps 109:3 [LXX]).[5] O words so revealing of the mystery of God! If before he was begotten of you, his Virgin Mother, this was the only begotten Son of God, how does the Father say to him, "Today I have begotten you"? Clearly the word "today" does not mean that the existence of the Only-begotten's divinity is something new, but it confirms his bodily presence among the human race. And the words, "*I* have begotten you," reveal that the Holy Spirit, who shares the Father's substance, is also—in the Father—the source of divine life and the sharer in his activity. For since the Spirit is not alien to the Father, but dwelt in you, Virgin and Mother, by the Father's good pleasure and commission, the Father makes the activity of the all-holy Spirit his own. That is why, when the Father, along with the Spirit, inaugurates the coming-forth of his Son from you in bodily form, he says to the Son, "Today *I* have begotten you." And the verse, "From the womb, before the morning star, I have begotten you," has the same meaning for our faith: namely, it gives evidence both for the divine substance in the Son, eternally shared with that of the Father before all ages, and also for his taking on natural human flesh, not simply in appearance, from you, the ever-virgin, at the end of history. By "the womb before the morning-star," the Scripture refers to the birth of light which exists before the heavens, but which has now appeared on earth, in order to show that before all creation, visible and invisible, the Only-begotten was brought forth from the Father without beginning, as light is born of light; and "the womb" here signifies your own body, in order to show that the Only-begotten One also came forth from you in flesh. "Before the morning star" also refers to the night before that dawning; for day is fittingly referred to as "the morning star," and since you brought forth light in the night "for those who sit in shadow" (cf. Lk 1:79), Scripture calls the hour of your childbearing "before the morning star." "For shepherds," it says, "were dwelling in the same country, guarding their flocks by night." (Lk 2:8)

[4.] This is the new glory that was bestowed on the citizens of heaven, O Mother of God, because of you. For if it had not been given to them anew, the angels would not have sung out, in praise of what was already glorious, "Glory in highest heavens," at the moment when your ineffable childbirth came to its term. And what light is this that radiates on the inhabitants of the earth? It is that the human person is now made a full citizen of heaven, through your immaculate flesh, and shepherds now mingle with the angels. For the angels <now bend down towards the lowliness of this newborn child, while human beings>⁶ are lifted up towards the glorious dignity of God—that is, they are made wise enough to recognize the common substance of Father and Son as something without beginning, a generation before all ages, but not a creation.

If, then, O holy Mother of God, heaven and—all the more—earth find their beauty in you, how is it possible that you have deprived the human race of all sight of you by departing? Far be it from us to think this! For just as when you led your life in this world, you were no stranger to heavenly ways, so now, after your passing there, you have not been removed in spirit from your associations with men and women. We see you now revealed as a heaven wide enough to hold God most high, in that your bosom was ready to bear him as your child, and we also call you his spiritual earth. As a result, we naturally suppose that when you lived in this world, you were God's neighbor in every way, so now, though you have passed on from human contact, you have never abandoned those who live in the world. Nonetheless, we who are used to offering you faithful veneration continue to prattle on: why have we not been found worthy to encounter you in your body? That is why we call them three-times blessed, who had the privilege of seeing you during the time of your presence on earth, since they could count the Mother of Life as their own contemporary. Yet just as you still walk with us, too, in a certain bodily way, so too the eyes of our souls are being led each day to see you more clearly.

[5.] For as you associated with our forebears in the flesh, so you dwell among us still in the spirit; your great role as our protector is the chief mark of your presence among us. All of us hear your voice, and all of our voices come to your attentive ears. You know us because you care for us, and we know your constant patronage and protection. For there is no barrier, not even that due to the division of soul and body, to the mutual recognition between yourself and your servants. You have never dismissed those whom you saved, nor abandoned those whom you gathered together; your spirit lives always, and your flesh did not undergo the corruption of the tomb. You watch over <us> all, O Mother of God, and your care is for all people; so that even if our eyes may be prevented from seeing you, all-holy one, you love to dwell in the midst of us all, and you show yourself in a variety of ways to those who are worthy of you. For the flesh does not stand in the way of the power and activity of your spirit; your spirit "blows where it will" (cf. Jn 3:8), since it is pure and immaterial, an incorrupt and spotless spirit, a companion of the Holy Spirit, the chosen one of God's only-begotten. "You live in beauty," as Scripture says (Cant 2:13 [LXX]), and your virginal body is all holy, all pure, all the dwelling-place of God. As a result, it is also a stranger to all dissolution into dust. It has been changed, in its humanity, to the highest incorruptible life; it is preserved and supremely glorified. Its life ended, it remains unsleeping, since it was impossible for what was God's vessel, the living temple of the all-holy godhead of the Only-begotten, to be conquered by the lethal confinement of a tomb.

[6.] Truly—truly, I say again, and with thanks—you were not separated from the Christian people when you passed from us; you were not taken far off from this corruptible world, O life of our common incorruption, but you come close to those who call upon you, you are found by those who faithfully seek you. And these things are proof positive of living activity, of a constant spiritual presence, of a body free from decay.[7] For how could fleshly decay turn you back into the dust of the earth, you who have redeemed humanity from death's corruptive power through the Incarnation of your Son? You have moved on from our earthly life, in order that the awful mystery of God's becoming human might be confirmed in more than mere appearance: in order that, as you are separated in this way from temporal things, we might come to believe that the God who was born of you came forth as a complete human being, the son of a real mother who was subject to the laws of natural necessity, [and that this happened] at the command of God's decree and subject to the temporal limitations of our life. You had a body just like one of us, and therefore you could not escape the event of death that is the common destiny of all human beings. In the same way, your Son, even though he is the God of all things, himself "tasted death" (Heb 2:9), as we do, in his flesh, because of the dying human being, if I may put it this way, formed by the whole of our race. Surely he has performed miracles both in his own life-giving tomb and in the life-giving sepulcher where you were laid to rest: both tombs really received bodies, yet neither of them was a workshop of decay. For it was impossible that you, the vessel which bore God, should be dissolved and decomposed into the dust of death. Since he who emptied himself into you was God from the beginning, and life eternal, the Mother of Life had to become a companion of life, had to experience death simply as a falling-asleep; you had to undergo your passage from this world as an awakening to your own reality as Mother of Life. For as a child seeks and yearns for its own mother, and a mother loves to live with her child, it was fitting that you, in your motherly tenderness for your Son and God, should go to him; and it was certainly right that God, holding on to his filial love for you, his mother, should confirm his intimacy with you by making you a sharer in his life.

In this way, when you had suffered the death of your passing nature, your home was changed to the imperishable dwellings of eternity, where God dwells; and becoming yourself his permanent guest, Mother of God, you will not be separated from his company. For you became, in your body, the home where he came to rest, O Mother of God; and by your migration, O woman worthy of all praise, he is himself now the place of your repose. "For this," he says, "is my place of rest for the ages of ages" (Ps 131:14 [LXX]): referring to the flesh which Christ took from you and put on himself, O Mother of God—the very flesh with which he not only appeared in this world and received faith in return, but with which he will also come again in the age to come, and will appear among us to judge the living and the dead. Because you, then, are his eternal place of rest, he has taken you to himself in his incorruption, wanting, one might say, to have you near to his words and near to his heart. So whatever you desire of him, he gives you with a son's affection; and whatever you ask from him, he brings to fulfillment with a God's power—he who is blessed for all ages![8]

[7.] Let the ignorant, raving words of the heretics come to an end! Let their wicked lips be stopped! "Let all who seek you rejoice and be glad," O Mother of God, and let those who rightly love to magnify your name "say always, 'The Lord be magnified!'" (Ps 39:17 [LXX]) For "the mouth" of Christians "will meditate on your righteousness" and your virginity, "and all day long will praise" your holy childbirth (Ps 34:28 [LXX]). "The poor have seen," through you, "the riches of God's goodness" (Ps 68:33 [LXX]; Rom 2:4); they have seen it and said, "The earth is full of the mercy of the Lord" (Ps 32:5 [LXX]). "Sinners have looked for God" through you, "and were saved" (Ps 33:3 [LXX]). And they said, "If the Lord had not come to our aid" by taking flesh from a virgin, "soon our lives would have ended" in Hades, which consumes all things in death (Ps 94:17 [LXX]). For your help is powerful to save us, O Mother of God, and needs no one else to bring our prayers to God. You are the mother of the life that is real and true. You are the yeast of Adam's remaking; you are the one who liberates Eve from all shame. She was the mother of dust, and you of light; her womb harbored corruption, but yours incorruption. She became death's dwelling-place, but you release us from death. She made our eyes downcast, weighted towards the earth, but you are the unsleeping glory of eyes awake. Her children are grief, but your Son is joy for all ages. She, who was earth, came back to earth in the end; but you have given birth to life for us, and you have ascended to life, you are powerful enough to offer life, even after death, to your fellow men and women. We can never have too much of your protection, nor is there any hidden danger for humanity lurking, so to speak, in our sense of your passage into glory through that life-giving sleep. Your patronage, rather, is something living, your intercession gives life, and your protection is without end.

[8.] For if you had not gone before us, no one would ever become perfectly spiritual (πνευματικός), no one would worship God in the Spirit (Jn 4:24).[9] No one is filled with the knowledge of God except through you, all-holy One; no one is saved but through you, Mother of God; no one is free of danger but through you, Virgin Mother; no one is redeemed but through you, Mother of God; no one ever receives mercy gratuitously except through you, who have received God. Who fights on behalf of sinners as much as you do? Who pleads on behalf of those who need correction, and takes their part, as much as you do? For every power that might come to our aid, fearing that the fig-tree of the parable (Lk 13:6ff) might in our case be cut down, hesitated to intercede for us with God, lest when sentence is passed on us for not bearing the promised fruit, his plea might appear to have been spurned. But you, whose power before God is that of a mother, win superabundant forgiveness for those whose sins exceed all bounds. For it is impossible you should be ignored, since God obeys you as his true and immaculate Mother in every way, always, and in all respects. So anyone who is in trouble rightly runs to you for refuge; anyone who is weak clings to you; anyone under attack takes you as his shield against the enemy. You put an end to "anger and wrath and tribulation, and to assaults by the evil angels" (Ps 77:49 [LXX]). You turn away from us [God's] just threat, and his verdict of a painful condemnation, because you love so greatly the people called by the name of your Son. That is why your Christian people, rightly recognizing its own situation, confidently puts into your hands the office of imploring God on its behalf. It unhesitatingly and boldly implores you, all-holy one, because of its past experience of the abundant blessings you have bestowed on us, and it constantly belabors you with petitions.

[9.] Who would not call you blessed (cf. Lk 1:48) because of all these things: your knowledge of God, beyond the understanding of the angels; your human fulfillment, unique among all your peers; your reputation with the Christian people; your much-sought-after role as refuge of sinners; your [memory],[10] constantly in the mouths of Christians? For even if a Christian should be terrified, or if he should "strike his foot against a stone" (Ps 90:12 [LXX]), he calls out your name for help. If some one, after all, should praise you without ceasing, he will not consider <that he is praising you>;[11] he praises you, rather, only if he sets out with the insatiable desire to do so, for it is impossible to sing your praise worthily. He longs to magnify you in every way by continually praising you, finding [in that endless praise] some consolation for his need. For when one who owes you much can repay you nothing, he multiplies his gratitude as you increase your gracious patronage. A supremely valuable gift, after all, which never comes to an end, continues to bring thanks to the benefactor, as it has from the beginning.

Who would not admire you for your unwavering care, your unchanging readiness to offer protection, your unsleeping intercession, your uninterrupted concern to save, your steady help, your unshakable patronage? [Who does not recognize you as] the unconquerable battlement,[12] the treasury of delight, the garden free from reproaches, the citadel of safety, the strong fortification, the mighty tower of help, the harbor of storm-tossed ships, calm for the distraught, a corrective for sinners, a new beginning for those despaired of, welcome for the exiled, return for the outcast, homecoming for the alienated, a good word for the condemned, a blessing for the purified, dew for the soul's dry season, a drop of rain for the parched grass? "For our bones," as Scripture says, "will blossom like the grass, because of you." (Is 66:14 [LXX]) You are mother of the lamb who is the shepherd, the recognized patron of all the good. All your qualities are remarkable, "true, and righteous altogether; all are desirable things, sweeter than honey and the honeycomb. For we, your servants desire them, and in desiring them we find a great reward." (Ps 18:10-12 [LXX]) "Who shall understand your mercies?" (Ps 106:43 [LXX])

[10.] But it is enough praise, O most admirable one, if we simply admit that we have not the resources to praise all your gifts. You have received from God your exalted position, as a cause for triumph; therefore you have formed for him a Christian people from your own flesh, and you have shaped those of a race like your own to be conformed to his divine image and likeness. "For this reason, may your name be blessed for all the ages!" (Ps 71:17 [LXX]) Your light outshines the sun, your honor is above that of all creation, your excellence before that of the angels. "You are higher than heaven" (Job 11:8), and wider than the heaven of heavens—even than that seventh heaven, which a certain holy man, on the basis of Scripture, distinguishes from it.[13] You are greater than the eighth heaven, and than any other heaven beyond it. You are blessed for generations of generations, and "in you all the tribes of the earth will be blessed" (see Gen 12:3; 18:18; etc.). For there is no place where you are not called blessed, no tribe from which fruit has not been borne for God from you. Even the peoples of this world who have not known you will themselves call you blessed, O Virgin, at "an acceptable time" (Is 49:8; cf. 2 Cor 6:2). For when he who was born of you shall come "to judge the world in justice" (Ps 97:9 [LXX]), "they will see and will beat their breasts" (Zach 12:10 [LXX]) who have not already wished to confess you, in good faith, as Mother of God. Then at last they will know of what a treasure they have deprived themselves, through their own evil will.

To us Christians, then, who reverence you in our Christian faith, show the mercy of your unchanging patronage. We rightly consider your falling asleep as [entry into] life, O Mother of God, and we believe you dwell with us still in the spirit. For in times of tribulation you are near, and we find safety in seeking your help; and when it is time to rejoice, you are joy's sponsor. Whenever we find ourselves completely under your maternal care, we cannot help believing that you live among us. Just as the thirsty person hastens to the spring, every faith-filled heart runs towards you, burning to fill himself with your gracious help. And again, just as a breath of air fills a person's nostrils with life, so the breath of every right-believing Christian bears you on his lips. For we do not draw life from breathing the air to the same degree that we draw safety from the protection of your name; so the text of Scripture is fulfilled in Christ and in you, which says, "You are the breath of our nostrils; we shall live in your protection, and in breathing you." (Lam 4:20 [LXX])[14]

[11.] For what race of human beings, except Christians, has been blessed with such glory or is privileged with such a reputation? The angels luxuriate in their heavenly dwellings, but we rejoice to take our leisure in your holy temples.[15] For if the temple of Solomon once represented heaven in an earthly image, will not the temples built in honor of you, who became the living temple of Christ, all the more justly be celebrated as heavens on earth? The stars speak out with tongues of flame in the heavenly firmament; and the material colors of your icons, O Mother of God, dazzle us with the representation of your gifts. The sun and the moon illumine one pole of the sky above and around us; but every house, every city and region, shines with your light, which comes from the light of the Son you bore. For this reason, blessed is the human creature: though a sinner, he has been found to be bound to you by natural ties and to share through you in the nature of God. He is truly "blessed," and it is well with him—or rather, "it shall be well" (Ps 127:2 [LXX]). For you will not abandon those who have been found worthy to enjoy your help until the end.

Far be death from you, Mother of God, for you have brought life to the human race. Far be the grave from you, since you have been made the divine foundation of ineffable exaltation. Far be dust from you, for you are a new creation, since you are now the mistress of those who have decayed into their elementary clay. So we confess, in our faith, that we have you with us as a companion on our journey. For if we did not find consolation in this thought, our spirit would faint in longing for you. "We know by faith that the heavens were formed," as Scripture tells us (Heb 11:3; cf. Gen 1:1); so, too, we believe that we can gaze on you in our midst as our companion, even after your departure from the body. For it is not such torture to the soul to be separated from the flesh as it would be to be deprived of you, O wholly immaculate one. Thus, as it is written, "Even if your body is asleep, your heart is waking." (Cant 5:2 [LXX]); and even if you accepted, as due to your human nature, the inevitable fate of death, your eye that watches over us "neither sleeps nor slumbers" (Ps 120:4 [LXX]).

[12.] Your passing from this world was not without witnesses, nor was your falling asleep a deception. "Heaven tells the glory" (Ps 19:1 [LXX]) of those who then were suddenly brought together on your account; earth guarantees the truth about them, the clouds cry out the honor paid you by them, and the angels proclaim the rich gifts that were then bestowed on you. I am referring to the way that the apostles gathered in Jerusalem at your side, just as the prophet Habakkuk was taken up from the mountainous country and brought, in one hour, by an angel's hand through the clouds, to stand in the pit with Daniel in Persian Babylon (Bel and the Dragon [Dan 12, LXX] 32-39).[16] But just as a drop of water adds nothing when it is cast into the sea, and as a purse given to a poor man does not empty a rich man's treasury, so no one is able to proclaim in human words the exalted beauty and greatness that should make up your praises. You have your own proper praise within yourself, in that you were designated Mother of God. You did not inherit the title, "Mother of God," simply because we "heard this with our own ears" in the explanation of Scripture, and nothing more; nor was it simply that "our fathers pro-

claimed this to us" in a tradition of utter truthfulness (Ps 43:2
[LXX]). Rather, the work you have accomplished in us confirms that your are Mother of God in very fact, literally and
without deceit, not by some verbal self-indulgence but in the
way of true faith. For this reason, it was truly fitting that your
body, which had been the dwelling of God, should not be
bound within the limits of death's mortal decay. Your tomb
had [first] to receive the material proper to it, since that material was human; then, while you passed, at life's conclusion,
from your own life here to that of heaven, your tomb was revealed now as empty of your flesh, while your spirit was found
to be inseparable from human company, thanks to the unseen
activity of Christ our God, whom you, as a virgin, brought
forth into the world. To him be glory for all ages!

Amen.

1   Although it is generally recognized by modern scholars to be a single work, this homily was published in two parts by Combéfis, its original editor—perhaps with the purpose of presenting Germanus's preaching on the Dormition as a trilogy similar to those of Andrew of Crete and John of Damascus.

2   Germanus here paraphrases Mary's own hymn of praise, the Magnificat (Lk 1:47-55).

3   Greek: μετάστασις.

4   Greek: μετάστασις.

5   This passage contains some refined speculation about the inter-related activity of the three persons of the Holy Trinity in accomplishing the incarnation of the Word. According to Luke's account, it is the Holy Spirit's "overshadowing" of Mary which actually makes the Word become flesh; but since the Spirit shares the same substance of the Father and proceeds from the Father as source, Germanus suggests, the Father can also say, in the words of the psalm, "I have begotten you." Germanus thus takes two classic Christological testimonia from the Old Testament—Ps 2:7 and Ps 109:3—as referring to the moment of incarnation rather than to the Word's eternal generation.

6   The Greek text here is obviously deficient; I have followed the supplement suggested by Germanus' first editor, François Combéfis.

7   Here Germanus expresses the main point of this first homily most clearly: the glorified Mary still makes her presence felt in the Church, through her intercession and care for her devoted people, and this continued activity is itself an indication of the fullness of salvation she has attained.

8   The text from here to the end is published by Combéfis and in Migne as a separate sermon.

9   In this paragraph, Germanus develops to a degree unparalleled in Patristic Marian literature the idea of Mary's role as chief intercessor with God for sinful humanity.

10   Some word like memory (μνήμην) seems to be missing from the Greek text.

11   Again, a word (δοξάζειν) seems to be missing from the Greek by haplography. Germanus is cleverly playing on the two meanings of this verb: "to consider" and "to praise".

12   Here Germanus begins another of the litany-like series of metaphors for Mary's role in the life of the Church, which abound in Marian homilies in the early Church.

13   See Basil, *In Hexaemeron* Hom. 3.3. The idea of eight heavens appears in Jewish apocalyptic literature: e.g., *Test. Levi* 3:3.

14   Gerard Manley Hopkins develops this same conceit at greater length in his poem of 1883, "The Blessed Virgin Compared to the Air We Breathe." There is no evidence, however, that he was familiar with this homily of Germanus, although it is certainly not impossible.

15 Germanus may be referring here especially to the Church of the Blachernai in Constantinople, built in honor of Mary about 450 by the Empress Pulcheria, where the liturgy of the feast of the Dormition was celebrated by the imperial court, with great solemnity, since the reign of the Emperor Maurice (582-602).

16 This story of the Prophet Habakkuk and Daniel, from the story of Bel and the Dragon appended to Daniel 12 in the Septuagint, does not mention the prophet's mountain origin. This may have been suggested, however, by the last words of the "prayer of Habakkuk" (Hab 3:19f. [LXX]): "The Lord God is my strength; he will place my feet in order at the end, he will make me walk on the high places..." Cf. Hab 3:3, 6 and 10 for other references to mountains as places of God's activity.

An Encomium on the Holy and Venerable Dormition of Our Most Glorious Lady, the Mother of God and Ever-Virgin Mary

By Our Father St. Germanus,
Archbishop of Constantinople

HOMILY II[1]

[1]. "A good, upright reputation puts flesh on the bones," we read in Scripture (Prov 15:30). And the story of the bodily sleep of the Mother of Life, Mary ever virgin—of her who is the divine breath, the fragrance of the supremely holy flesh of Christ—brings a blessing to those who call that flesh blessed. For when her human bones were once transformed, by the mercy of God, in the depths of the earth, the immaculate body of the Mother of God again put flesh on them, though they had become hard and shrivelled in decay;[2] indeed, they grew "softer than oil" (Ps 54:22 [LXX]) in their incorruptibility, because of the resurrection of him who was born of her. Let us, then, recall a little of her passage into glory, which is always worthy of memory; for hearing a story such as this is truly a source of joy.

When Christ, our God, wished to bring his Mother, the bearer of life, to himself, he indicated to her again, through an angel with whom she was familiar, that the time of her falling asleep was at hand, so that death should not come upon her suddenly, as it does for the rest of humanity, or cause disturbance in her as she parted from this life. Normally, the separation of body from soul depresses the spirit, even in the greatest men and women. In order, then, that she should not also be disturbed by the natural characteristics of her flesh in depart-

169

ing this life unexpectedly, without foreseeing her own
end—she who had borne as her child the God who knows all
things—an angel was sent to her to comfort and strengthen
her, with these words from Christ himself:

[2.] "It is time, my Mother," says the Lord, "to take you to
myself. Just as you have filled the earth and all who dwell in it
with joy, O you who enjoy such grace, come, make the heavens joyful once again.[3] Make my Father's dwelling-place radiant; be a spiritual guide for the souls of the saints. For when
they see your glorious passage here to my side, escorted by angels, they will be convinced in their faith that their own place,
too, through you, will be to dwell here in my light.[4] Come,
then, in exultation; rejoice now, as you rejoiced at the angel's
greeting. In every way you now have the dignity of your title,
'full of grace.' As when you were about to conceive me you
were invited to rejoice, so rejoice again in my desire to take
you to myself. Do not be disturbed at leaving behind the corruptible world, with all its desires. Forget about its power of
corruption. For you will not leave those who live in the world
bereft of your protection; but just as I, who am not of the
world, watch over those who live in it and take care of them, so
your patronage will not be taken away from those who live in
the world, until its consummation.

"The extravagant demands of the flesh will no longer dis-
turb you. You are ascending to a fuller life, to joyful rest, to
unconquerable peace, to an existence untroubled by cares, to
delights free of passion, to permanent freedom from distrac-
tion, to unending enjoyment, to a light that never fades, to a
day without evening—to me, the creator of all that is, including you. Where I am, there is eternal life, incomparable joy, a
dwelling-place without parallel, an indestructible city. Where
I am, then, you will be also: a mother inseparably one with her
undivided Son.[5] Where God is, there is all goodness of heart,

all delight, all brilliance. No one who knows my glory wants to abandon it. No one who comes to my rest seeks again the things of the corruptible world. Ask Peter if there was any comparison or likeness between the world and Mount Tabor, when he gazed for a short time there on my glory.

"When you lived in the world of corruptible things, I revealed my power to you in visions; now that you are passing from that life, I will show myself to you face to face. Give the earth what belongs to it, without anxiety. Your body belongs to me, and since the ends of the earth are in my hand, no one can take anything from me. Entrust your body to me, just as I placed my divinity trustingly in your womb. Your soul, full of divine power, will see the glory of my Father. Your immaculate body will see the glory of his only Son. Your pure spirit will see the glory of the all-holy Spirit.[6]

[3.] "Death shall make no boast at your expense, for you have given birth to life. You are my vessel; the mortal cracks caused by the fall shall not break you apart. The overshadowing gloom shall not rob you of sight. Come eagerly to the one whom you brought into the world. I want to make you happy, as a son should do—to pay you the pension due a mother's womb, to recompense you for feeding me milk, to reward you for your nurture, to give your maternal love its full return. You begot me, Mother, as your only Son; now make the choice to come and live with me, for I know your heart is not divided by love for another child. I revealed you as my virgin mother; now I will make you a mother who rejoices in her Son. I will show the world now to be your debtor, and when you come to me I will glorify your name still more. I shall build you into the wall of the universe, into a bridge for those who are awash in the waves, an ark of salvation, a staff for the disabled, an advocate for sinners, a ladder to heaven strong enough to bear the weight of all humanity as it climbs.

"Come, then, with joy! Open up Paradise, which your ancestor Eve, your natural sister, had locked. Enter into the joy of your Son. Let go of the Jerusalem that is below, and hasten up to the heavenly city; for the Jerusalem below, 'lamentation will soon be multiplied,' as Scripture has it, 'like the lamentation for the pomegranate grove cut down in the plain' (Zach 12:11 [LXX]). Lie down to rest, if only in appearance, in Gethsemane, the place of your tomb. I will not leave you alone there for long. I will come to you very quickly, when you have been buried in the sepulchre—not to dwell in you again by being conceived, as once I was, but rather to take you now to dwell with me. Rest your body confidently in Gethsemane, as once I rested my knees there in human prayer, before my passion. I gave you an image of your own death, bending on that very ground the knees I took from your body. As I came forth willingly, then, after that prostration, to a death on the cross that was the source of life, you, too, will pass immediately into life when your remains have been laid in the earth.

"Behold, my disciples are coming to receive you; they, my spiritual sons who are filled with my light, will bury you in all reverence and piety. I have bestowed on them the grace of adoption as sons, as you yourself can testify (see Jn 19:26f). So when you are laid by them in the tomb, consider that it is my hands which are caring for you; for it is not fitting that you should be laid to rest by anyone else but my apostles, in whom the Holy Spirit makes his home and who represent my own person. Only they can do honor to your passing, O all-immaculate one!"

[4.] When she heard this message, the Mother of God rejoiced greatly, taking but little account of this passing human life; lighting great lamps throughout her house, she invited her relatives and neighbors, swept her room and decked her bed with flowers, as if it were all a virgin's bridal-chamber—that bed which until then she had flooded every night with prayerful tears, in her longing for Christ her Son. "On my bed," as Scripture says, "I have sought him whom my soul loves." (Cant 3:1 [LXX]) Eagerly, she prepared all that was needed for her departure. She announced she was about to pass on, made public what had been revealed to her by the angel. And she showed everyone the baton that had been given to her: a palm branch,[7] the symbol of victory over death and the token of unfading life. This was to assure her, at her moment of departure, that she would utterly overcome decay, just as Christ, whom she brought forth into the world, had triumphed over the realm of death. It was the same kind of palm branch that the devout young Hebrews waved in acclamation for Christ, when he approached his passion as one who would be victorious over death, crying "Hosanna in the highest!"—that is, "Save us, you who dwell on high!" for "Hosanna," in Hebrew means "Save us." Just as palm branches then indicated, by a symbolic figure, that Christ's death would be a victory, so this baton of palm, given to the Mother of God, was meant as an assurance of victory over mortal decay.

[5.] The women who had been invited began to weep; those gathered around her wailed in lament, flooding the house, so to speak, with rivers of tears. They begged her not to leave them alone. But she said, "Let the will of my Son, my God, be accomplished in me. 'For he is my God, and I will praise him; my Father's God, and I will exalt him.' (Ex 15:2) He became my Son in the flesh, but he is himself Father and Creator and God to his own Mother. If you, then, who are parents of mortal children, through a sordid kind of union, cannot bear to be separated from them for an instant, how shall I, who have borne God the Son, not be overcome even more than you by maternal affection? For I offered him a womb that was whole, conceived him as a pure virgin, without help of a husband. You are consoled by each other for the loss of your children; but since I have been privileged to have this Christ as both my God and my only son, how can I fail to rejoice at going to him, who lives forever and gives life to all?"

[6.] When she had said this, there was suddenly a mighty clap of thunder, and a rush of wind from a cloud that hung low over the earth; like drops of rain, the disciples of Christ appeared from its midst, gathered together to stand as one before the Virgin's house. When they saw her, they bowed before her reverently, and after learning the reason for their arrival from her, they spoke as follows: "For the very reason that we have you as our neighbor in the the city of this world, O Mother of God, and that we are encouraged by the sight of you as if we were gazing on Christ himself, we must reflect deeply on your departure. But since you have been summoned to go on to God—partly by divine power, partly through a Son's human affection for his mother—we rejoice at what is fittingly being done for you, and at what will surely turn out for all our good. For in you we, too, receive a promise of eternal life, and we will have in you a mediator with God. It is not appropriate, after all, that the Mother of God should go on living in the midst of 'a crooked and perverse generation' (Phil 2:15); you should move on to the tents of heaven, to incorruptible dwellings."

All the while they said this, they wept inconsolably. But she said to them, "Greetings, spiritual sons of my son! Remember his words, how he ordered us at the time of his passion not to turn the world's joy into mourning (Jn 16:20); today, as I take my departure to him, do not turn my delight into sadness. All of you must lay my body to rest, just as I arrange it on my bed. For I will seem to be buried by the very hands of my Son, if I am reverently laid to rest by you who are his disciples."

[7.] As she was saying this, the apostle Paul arrived, summoned from afar by the news. He knocked at the door of the house, and the master of the house, John the Apostle, opened for him with joy; a virgin himself, he had "received" the Virgin "into his household" (Jn 19:27) from the household of Christ, as if she were his mother. The apostles saw Paul and took heart, and made him sit in a raised seat of honor. The Virgin received him with joy, and Paul threw himself at her feet, feet that once supported God; when he learned why he, too, had been brought there, he opened his mouth—ever ready to teach—with a great and tearful cry, and praised the Virgin lavishly. These are a few of the things he said:

"Hail, Mother of life, the content of my preaching! Hail, fulness of my consolation! For even if I have not seen Christ in the flesh, by seeing you in bodily form I am persuaded that I see Christ, since you gave the bodiless one that body in which he clothed himself. I have fulfilled my longing to see Christ by looking at your face. Until yesterday, I have preached to the Gentiles that you have given birth to God in the flesh; from now on, I shall also teach that you have been allowed to pass over into his presence, so that the Gentiles may realize that their own salvation is confirmed by your intercession, so that they, too, might have a permanent patron before God."[8]

[8.] After Paul had said many other things—so far as we can ascertain—by way of offering praise to the Mother of God, the Virgin took her leave of them all. She lay back on the pallet which she had herself arranged, composed her immaculate body as she wished, and gave up her spirit as if she were falling asleep. Or I should say, she left her flesh behind while fully awake, departing from it in a way free of all corruption. And when she had entrusted her blameless spirit, in the hearing of all, to Christ, her God and her own bodily Son, Peter urged his fellow chief apostle Paul to formulate the customary prayer over the Virgin's remains. But Paul declined, saying it was fitting for Peter, as chief shepherd, to do this. Peter encouraged him, yielding modestly to Paul with the excuse that he was weary from the heavy burden of his preaching; but Paul was not at all to be persuaded, insisting that Christ had conferred a leadership on Peter that could not be set aside for new arrangements. So Peter spoke the prayer; the rest of the apostles lifted the bier onto their shoulders, and with hymns and lighted lamps they reverently and solemnly carried the Virgin's body out to its tomb.

[9.] An uncountable throng joined in the funeral of the Mother of Life. They were at her sudden passing, and they also marvelled at the Apostles' arrival, through the air, from distant parts of the world. For the report went out about them in all Jerusalem, that a thunderstorm had overshadowed the city a moment before, and that a whirlwind had brought them there like drops of rain, falling before the Virgin's house. A certain foolish member of the unbelieving Jewish people—for they are a "vanity of vanities" (Eccl 1:2), always giving offense and always ready for a quarrelsome argument—reached out his lawless hand (for Scripture says, "In these hands there is always iniquity" [Ps 25:2 (LXX)]), and shook the pallet that served as her bier, daring to molest the body of the immaculate one and not fearing even to throw to the ground the fleshly throne of the Most High. Immediately his hands were cut off, and he became a dreadful example to the Jews, who are always so aggressive against Christ. Her body was now near the sarcophagus. The Apostles shrank back, in godly reverence and fear, from touching the Virgin's body. And this hesitation the disciples showed about touching her body was praiseworthy: they knew how much honor it deserved, since the pure one's body was God's vessel. But the faithful people tried to take from her some part of her burial wrappings, to bring them a blessing. No one, however, laid hands directly on her, since they had before their very eyes the example of the Jew who had acted so rashly.

But at the common decision and urging of the Apostles, Peter and Paul picked up the ends of the shroud that hung down loosely on either side of the bier, and by handling only the shroud, and not attempting to touch her body with their hands, the worthy and reverent Apostles placed her body in the tomb. So through their longing for God these two men revealed their reverence for him, exalted like the heavenly hills by their very humility. In their self-effacing service, they won honor for themselves, and in their love for Christ they earned distinction. For they showed reverence then to the Son through his Mother, and to the Mother—in an outstanding degree—because of the Son; because God had become flesh, they showed genuine honor to his Mother, the one who endowed him with that flesh. And it was from their hands, as all looked on, that the Virgin's pure body was taken away.[9] Who took it, no one could see—for God is invisible! But the shroud was then gently taken up into the air from the Apostles' hands in a light cloud—in what the words of the prophet had spoken of, in a fleshly sense, as a "light cloud" (Is 19:1)—and disappeared.

[10.] The disciples realized that Christ had come, with his angels, to meet his Mother, and trusting that she had been taken to heaven by him, they glorified God with joyful voices, speaking to the people in these words: "People of Israel, you should now know what has been revealed to all of you concerning Mary, the fleshly Mother of Christ: that having been carried dead, by us and by you, to her tomb here, she has been lifted up out of our hands. Let no one show himself slow to believe what has happened in our midst. Let no one falsely accuse us of stealing her body, too, as they did for the body of Christ! But if anyone should hear such an accusation from the governor or from your priests, pay attention to the truth, not to lies. Be witnesses of what you have seen! Go forth from this tomb today yourselves, as new, fleshly messengers of heaven.

Give your tongues wings to proclaim the truth. Say for yourselves, 'Behold, here is the place where the Virgin was buried.
Mary, the Mother of Life, has been taken up to heaven.
Look—here is the shroud without the one who was wrapped in
it, lacking its burden; it once was wrapped around her as a lifeless corpse, and now it yearns to be a carpet for her in her new
life. You, too, must become the 'myrrh-bearing women' for
the one who has gone to heaven.[10] Run, tell of her passage
from the tomb that enclosed life!

"Blessed are you, too, region of Gethsemane! You are renowned because of the Garden of Joseph (of Arimathea),
which is near; there Peter and John ran to find the burial cloth
and napkin, and believed that Christ is risen.[11] In you, Gethes-
mane, all of us have seen the ever-virgin Mary buried in her
tomb and taken up to heaven—we disciples, and also this
crowd, which gathered in such numbers for her funeral. She
was taken from our view here, beyond any dispute, before her
tomb was sealed with a stone, so that no one might find an easy
opportunity, in the absence of seals and guards, to convince
unbelievers of a theft. But see: with hymns of praise she was
brought to this tomb, and then left the tomb empty; now she
fills paradise with her glory, and she shares the refreshment of
the life of heaven. Now she lives on, as a participant in the delights of God." These were the words of the Apostles about the
Mother of God.

[11.] But I, too, have gone far enough, my immaculate
Lady, in this rash torrent of words; an age, after all, would not
be enough time for those who dare to speak your praises! Here,
then, I bring my hymn to a close. Remember your Christian
servants; present the prayers and the hopes of us all [to the
Lord]. Confirm our faith, unite the Churches, give victory to
the Empire and fight with our army;[12] give peace to the world,
save us all from danger and trials, and beg that for each of us

the day of judgment may not be a day of condemnation. To whom else shall we go? You have the words of life (Jn 6:68)—the petitions you make to God on our behalf. For you are the one who has always done great things among us, and who never ceases to do them; holy is your name (see Lk 1:49),[13] which is blessed by angels and human beings from generation to generation (*ibid.* 48, 50), now and to the ages of ages.

Amen.

1   This sermon appears as Sermon III in the original edition of Combéfis
    and in Migne.
2   This statement that Mary's body had already corrupted in the tomb be-
    fore it was taken up into the presence of God is unusual in early litera-
    ture on the Dormition.
3   Germanus here plays on the words χάρις, "grace," and χαρά, "joy," in
    his echo of the angel's greeting in Luke 1:28.
4   This is one of the clearest statements in these ancient homilies of the sig-
    nificance of Mary's glorification as a promise of resurrection for all the
    faithful.
5   This reference to Christ as "undivided" seems to be a condensed allu-
    sion to the affirmation of the Council of Chalcedon that in him two dis-
    tinct natures are united in a single hypostasis or individual, "without
    change, without confusion, without separation, without division".
6   This is a curious allocation of the eschatological vision of God to three dif-
    ferent aspects of Mary's person, each made to correspond with one of the
    persons of the Holy Trinity. The division of the human person into "body,
    soul, and spirit" was traditional in early Christian literature, inspired by
    Paul in 1 Thess 5:23. For the background of this conception in Greek phi-
    losophy, see A.-M. Festugière, "La trichotomie de 1 Thess 5:23 et la phi-
    losophie grecque," *Recherches de science religieuse* 20 (1930) 385-415.
7   This detail of the palm branch links Germanus's account of the death of
    Mary to one family of the *Transitus* apocrypha, represented in Greek by
    the dormition narrative of Ps.-John and the homily of John of Thessa-
    lonica, as well as a number of other works.
8   Germanus here emphasizes the importance of the doctrine of Mary's
    entry into the glorious presence of God by allowing Paul to proclaim it
    as parallel to the doctrine of the virginal conception of Jesus; the real
    significance and providential purpose of her glorification, in his view,
    seems again to be to establish her as permanent intercessor for human-
    ity, alongside the risen Christ.
9   At this point in his narrative, Germanus clearly presents Mary's bodily
    assumption into heaven as taking place during her funeral rites and be-
    fore her actual burial, even though earlier in the sermon he has followed
    the usual sequence of placing it after she had been sealed in the tomb,
    and so as after she had dwelt in the "realm of the dead" for a short time.
10 Conceiving of Mary's assumption into heaven as parallel to the resur-
    rection of Jesus, Germanus has the Apostles call on the faithful of Jeru-
    salem to be witnesses of this event, as the holy women had been wit-
    nesses of Jesus' empty tomb on Easter morning. The emphasis on
    Mary's empty shroud probably reflects the veneration of this relic in
    Constantinople in Germanus's time.
11 Germanus seems here to confuse the site of Jesus' tomb, traditionally
    located next to Calvary, with the site of Gethsemane and Mary's tomb in
    the valley of the Cedron, at the foot of the Mount of Olives.

12 Germanus here alludes to the conception of Mary as "defender of the city" of Constantinople which appears in other works of the period: see Andrew of Crete, Oration II on the Dormition, n. 14.

13 Germanus rather daringly applies to Mary, as intercessor and patron, both the disciples' words of confidence in Jesus at the end of Jn 6, and Mary's own words of praise to the God of Israel in Lk 1:49. Even the normal closing Trinitarian doxology is replaced here by a similar formula of praise addressed to Mary.

ON THE DORMITION OF THE HOLY MOTHER OF GOD

By John, Lowly Monk and Sinner, Servant of the
Servants of Our Lord Jesus Christ, of the Old Lavra

HOMILY I

1."The just are remembered with praise," says the wise Solomon (Prov 10:7). "Precious in the sight of the Lord is the death of his saints," proclaims God's ancestor David (Ps 115:6 [LXX]). If, then, all the just are remembered with praise, who will not give praise to the source of justice, the treasury of holiness—not in order to glorify her, but in order to win eternal glory for oneself? The tabernacle of the Lord's glory, after all, is in no need of glory from us; [she is] the city of God, of whom "glorious things are spoken," as holy David says to her: "Glorious things are spoken of you, City of God!" (Ps 86:3 [LXX]) For what other city shall we understand for the invisible and uncircumscribed God, who contains all in his own hand, but her who alone truly welcomed the super-essential Word of God, in a way beyond all nature and essence—who received the God who exists in a way beyond all limitation? Glorious things were spoken of her by the Lord himself; for what could be more glorious than to receive the true and original will of God (cf. Is 25:1)?

2. Neither the human tongue nor the mind of the angels that live beyond this universe can give worthy praise to her, through whom it has been granted to us to gaze clearly on the glory of the Lord. What, then—shall we keep silent, cowering in fear, because we cannot praise her worthily? Not at all! Or shall we stretch out our foot over the boundary, as they say, and ignore our own limitations? Shall we shake off the reins of

fear, and boldly reach out to the untouchable? Never! Mingling, instead, fear with longing and weaving from them both a single wreath, let us, in holy reverence, with trembling hand and yearning soul, pay gratefully the humble first-fruits of our minds, as we must, to the Queen Mother, the benefactress of all nature!

The story[1] is told that some farmers once were ploughing the earth behind their oxen, when they saw a king pass by, majestically clad in purple and resplendent in his shining crown, and surrounded by an enormous crowd of bodyguards. Since there was nothing at hand for them to present to their ruler, one of them immediately scooped up some water in his hands—for there was abundant water flowing nearby—and brought it to the king as a gift. The king said to him, "What is this you bring me, my son?" And the peasant boldly replied, "I bring what I have, since I thought it best not to let my poverty hide my eagerness to give. You have no need of our possessions, nor do you desire anything from us but good will. But for us, giving you a gift is both a duty and a praiseworthy gesture; for glory has a way of coming to those who show themselves grateful." The king was filled with wonder, and praised the man's wisdom; he received the farmer's act of kindness graciously, and bestowed on him many generous gifts in return. If, then, that haughty tyrant preferred good will to abundant wealth, will not this truly good lady, the Mother of the God who alone is good (see Mk 10:18), whose graciousness is without limit and who judged two farthings more valuable than great contributions (Mk 12:42)—will she not receive us, too, by judging our intention rather than our ability? Yes, surely she *will* accept this act of praise, for we offer it as our duty, and she will repay us with incomparable blessings.

Since, then, it is wholly necessary for us to speak, in order to perform our simple duty, let us address her now as follows:

3. What shall we call you, O Lady? With what titles shall we address you? With what words of praise shall we crown your holy and glorious head—you who are the giver of good things, the source of our wealth, the ornament of the human race, the boast of all creation, the one through whom creation itself is truly called blessed? Through you, it has come to hold what it never held before; [through you] it gazes "with unveiled face" (2 Cor 5:18) at him whom it lacked the strength to look on before.

Open our stammering mouths, O Word of God! Give us graceful words as you open our lips! Breathe in us the grace of the Spirit, through which fishermen become orators and illiterate people speak a wisdom that is above human powers! Let us, who are so weak of voice, find a way to utter, if only indistinctly, the great news about your dear Mother. For she was chosen from generations of old by the providential will and pleasure of God the Father, who begot you outside of time without alteration and without passion; she gave you birth, made flesh from herself at the end of the ages, to be our propitiation and salvation, our righteousness and our redemption—you who are "life from life and light from light, true God from true God."[2] If her childbearing was remarkable, if her conceiving was beyond all nature and understanding and of saving worth for the world, surely her falling asleep was glorious, too—truly sacred and wholly worthy of praise.

The Father predestined her, and the prophets spoke of her through the Holy Spirit. The sanctifying power of the Spirit reposed on her, cleansed her and made her holy; in a certain sense, he fertilized her in advance. Then you, the Father's self-defining Word, dwelt in her without being limited, summoning the farthest reaches of our nature up to the endless heights of your incomprehensible divinity. Taking the first-fruits [of our nature] from the holy, spotless and utterly pure blood of the holy Virgin, you built around yourself a structure of flesh, livened by a rational and intelligent soul; you gave it individual existence in yourself, and became a complete human being without ceasing to be completely God, of the same essence as your Father. Taking on our weakness, rather, in your unutterable mercy, you came forth from her a single Christ, a single Lord, one and the same who is both Son of God and Son of Man, at once completely God and completely human, the whole God and a whole human being, one composite individual [formed] from two complete natures, divinity and humanity, and [subsisting] in two complete natures, divinity and humanity.[3] You are not simply God or merely human, but one who is both Son of God and God enfleshed, God and human at the same time; you have not undergone confusion or endured division, but you bear in yourself the natural qualities of two natures essentially distinct, yet united without confusion and without division in your concrete existence: the created and the uncreated, the mortal and the immortal, the visible and the invisible, the circumscribed and the uncircumscribed, divine will and human will, divine activity no less than human activity; two self-determining realities, divine and human at the same time; divine miracles and human passions—I refer to natural and blameless passions[4] For you assumed the first Adam entire, Lord, in the mercy of your heart; [you assumed him] free from sin, as he was before his transgression, with body, soul, mind and all their natural characteristics, that you might bestow salvation on the whole of me—for truly "what is not assumed is not healed"[5] So you became "the mediator between God and humanity" (1 Tim 2:5); you put our alienation to an end, and led the apostates back to your Father; you restored what had gone astray, you gave light to what was in darkness, you renewed what was worn away, you transformed what was corruptible into incorruption. You freed creation from the error of worshipping many gods; you made human beings children of God, and revealed disgraced men and women to be sharers in your divine glory. The one who was condemned to the lowest parts of the earth you raised "above every principality and power" (Eph 1:21); the one who was sentenced to return to earth and to dwell in the underworld you seated—in your own person—on a royal throne[6] Who, then, served as the place where these boundless blessings, [these gifts] beyond all mind and understanding, became real? Was it not the everlasting Virgin, the one who gave you birth?

4. Do you see, my fathers and brothers who are friends of God, the grace of this present day? Do you see the lofty and venerable standing of her whom now we praise? Are not the mysteries of her being awe-inspiring? Are they not full of wonder? Blessed are they who can see what is, above all things, worth seeing! Blessed are they who have acquired spiritual senses![7] What bolts of lightning light up this present night! What companies of angelic guards glorify the falling-asleep of the mother who gave us life! What inspired utterances come from the Apostles, pronouncing blessings at the burial of that body that bore God! See how the Word of God, who deigned in his tender mercy to be her son, has cared for this holy and godly mother of his with his lordly hands, and has received her sacred soul to himself! O benign lawgiver! Not subject to the law, he fulfilled the law which he himself had imposed; for he commanded that children do their duty towards those who begot them, when he said, "Honor thy father and thy mother." (Ex 20:12) That he has done this will be evident to anyone who is even slightly initiated into the divine words of the holy Scriptures. For if, as divine Scripture says, "The souls of the just are in the hand of the Lord" (Wis 3:1), will not she, all the more, have commended her soul into the hands of her son and her God? The argument is true beyond all contradiction!

If you wish, however, [let us consider] who she is, where she came from, and how she has been allowed to grace this life of ours—this gift at once more exalted and more dear to us than all the other things God has given us. Let us consider, as far as we can, how she spent this life of ours, and what mysteries she was allowed to share in. For the pagans honor the departed with funeral orations, and eagerly work into them whatever details they consider attractive, so that the words of praise will be both a fitting tribute for the one being eulogized and an encouragement and an invitation to virtue for those left behind. Most of the time they weave such a speech out of legends and impossible inventions, since those being celebrated have, on their own, so little that is worthy of praise. How, then, shall we fail to seem wholly ridiculous if we shroud in deep silence what is radically true and worthy of veneration, what really obtains for all people blessing and salvation? Will we not receive the same sentence as he who hid the talent (Mt 25:25)? Let us begin our eulogy, then, being careful to keep our discourse brief, lest it have the same negative effect on your hearing that too much food has on the human body.

5. Her parents were called Joachim and Anna. Joachim, being the shepherd of a flock, was no less careful of his thoughts than of his sheep, and led them both as well as he could, wherever he wished. For since he had been watched over like a sheep himself by the Lord God, he lacked none of the choicest gifts. Let no one think that I mean by "the choicest gifts" the things that are to most people's liking—the things greedy minds always long for, but which do not last, nor are capable of making their possessor a better person. Such are the pleasant things of the present life, which cannot attain to lasting power, but "collapse around themselves"[8] and immediately perish, even if people possess them in superfluity. No indeed, it is not for us to admire such things, nor is this the portion of

those who fear the Lord! Rather, we admire the gifts that are really attractive and lovely to those whose thoughts are true, goods that remain forever: things that please God and that produce ripe fruit in those who have acquired them (see Ps 1:3). I mean the virtues, which give their fruit in due season—give the fruit, that is, of eternal life in the coming age for those who have labored worthily and have invested the results of their exertions there, as far as possible. Labor, after all, comes before the virtues, and eternal blessedness follows them!

Joachim, then, habitually shepherded his inner thoughts "in green pastures" (Ps 22:2 [LXX]), abiding in the contemplation of holy Scripture; he enjoyed the "refreshing water" (*ibid.*) of divine grace, turning away from immoral things and walking on "the paths of righteousness" (*ibid.*). And Anna, whose name means "grace," was one with her husband in heart as well as home; yet although she abounded in all good qualities, she was, for some mysterious reason, affected by the complaint of sterility. For grace was truly sterile [then], unable to bear fruit in human souls. Therefore "all people were in a state of decline and frustration"; no one "had understanding, no one sought after God" (Ps 13:3, 2 [LXX]). Then the good God looked down and had pity on the creatures of his own hand; willing to save his creation, he put an end to the sterile period of grace—I mean the sterility of Anna, whose thoughts were turned to God. She bore a child, one such as never before had been, and never again will be. And the healing of her sterility revealed most clearly that the world's sterility in goodness was also about to be healed, and that its bare trunk was about to bear the fruit of indescribable blessedness.

6. Then the Mother of God came forth, according to the promise. An angel announced the conception of her who was to be born. For in this respect, too, it was right that she who was to be the bearer, in flesh, of the sole and truly perfect God

should not be lacking anything, or take second place. She was later consecrated in the holy temple of God and lived there, displaying a better and purer ideal and way of life than others, free from all contact with immoral men and women. But when the bloom of her maturity came upon her, and the law forbade her to remain within the sacred precincts, she was betrothed to a suitor who was to be, properly speaking, the guardian of her virginity: Joseph, from the ranks of the priests, who until his old age had kept the law without compromise, far better than his peers. This holy and spotless maiden now lived with him, remaining at home and knowing nothing of what transpired outside her doors.

7. "When the fullness of time came," as the divine Apostle says (Gal 4:4), the angel Gabriel was sent by God to this woman who was truly a child of God; he said to her, "Hail, full of grace, the Lord is with you!" (Lk 1:28) The word of the angel, to her who is higher than an angel, is lovely: it brings joy to the whole world. But "she was troubled by his word" (Lk 1:29), having no experience of contact with men—she had chosen rather to keep her virginity intact. So "she wondered within herself what this greeting might mean." (Lk 1:29) And the archangel said to her, "Do not be afraid, Mary, for you have found grace with God." (Lk 1:30) She had truly found grace, who was worthy of grace. She had found grace, who had labored much in the field of grace and had reaped grace's abundant harvest. She had found the depths of grace, who had kept safe the vessel of a twofold virginity—for she preserved the virginity of her soul no less than that of her body, and thus her bodily virginity was also preserved.

"And you shall bear a son," he said, "and shall call his name Jesus." (Lk 1:31) "Jesus" means "savior": "for he will save his people from their transgressions." (Lk 1:34) What did the treasury of true wisdom reply to this? She did not imitate

Eve, her mother, but rather made good Eve's lack of caution, using nature as her protection; so she spoke out thus in response to the angel's word: "How shall this happen to me, since I do not know a man?" (Lk 1:35) "You are speaking of the impossible," she tells him. "Your words break the boundaries of nature, which he who formed nature established. I will not let myself act as a second Eve and overturn the will of the Creator. If you are not speaking godless things, tell me the manner of this conception, and put an end to my difficulty." And the messenger of truth replied, "The Holy Spirit will come upon you, and the power of the Most High will overshadow you. Therefore the holy one to be born of you shall be called Son of God (Lk 1:36). What is now being achieved is not subject to the laws of nature, for the Creator is also lord of nature, and it is in his power to change nature's boundaries." And she, hearing with holy reverence the name she always yearned for and revered, uttered her obedient answer in words full of fear and joy: "Behold the handmaid of the Lord; be it done to me according to your word" (Lk 1:38).

8. "O depth of the riches and wisdom and knowledge of God," I, too, wish now to say with the Apostle; "how incomprehensible his judgments, and how unsearchable his ways!" (Rom 10.33f.) O boundless goodness of God! O love that has no explanation! He who calls what is not into being (cf. Rom 4:17), who fills heaven and earth (cf. Jer 23:24), for whom heaven is a throne and earth a footstool (cf. Is 66:1), has made the womb of his own servant his ample dwelling-place, and accomplishes in her the mystery newer than all that is new. Being God, he becomes a human being; in a supernatural way, he is brought into the world at the time of his birth, and opens the womb without damaging the closed portal of virginity. He, "the shining-forth of the Father's glory, the stamped impression of his reality, who sets all things in motion by the word of

his mouth" (Heb 1:3), is carried as an infant in earthly arms. O truly divine wonders! O mysteries above nature and under-standing! O virginal boasts that outstrip the human condition!

What is this great mystery about you, O holy mother and virgin? "Blessed are you among women, and blessed is the fruit of your womb." (Lk 1:28 [var.], 42) Blessed are you for generations of generations; you alone are worthy to be called blessed. Behold, all generations do call you blessed, as you have said (Lk 1:48). The daughters of Jerusalem (Cant 6:8)—that is, the Church's daughters—saw you, and the royal princesses—the souls of the just—proclaimed you blessed and will praise you for all ages.

You are the royal throne, around which angels stand (cf. Is 6:1), to see their Lord and creator seated upon it.[9] You are called the spiritual Eden, holier and more divine than that of old; for in the former Eden the earthly Adam dwelt, but in you the Lord from heaven. The ark prefigured you (cf. Gen 6:14), in that it guarded the seeds of a second world; for you gave birth to Christ, the world's salvation, who overwhelmed <the flood of> sin and calmed its waves. The burning bush was a portrait of you in advance (cf. Ex 3:2); the tablets written by God described you (cf. Ex 32:15f.); the ark of the law told your story (cf. Ex 25:10); the golden urn (cf. Ex 16:33) and candela-brum and table (cf. Ex 25:23, 31), the rod of Aaron that had blossomed (cf. Num 17:23)—all clearly were foreshadowings [of you]. For from you issued the flame of divinity, the self-definition and Word of the Father, the sweet heavenly manna, the nameless "name that is above every name" (Phil 2:9), the eternal and inaccessible light, the heavenly "bread of life" (Jn 6:48), the uncultivated fruit that grew bodily to maturity from you. Did not the furnace point to you, whose fire was at once dew and flame (cf. Dan 3:49f.), a type of the divine fire that dwelt within you? The tent of Abraham, too, quite obviously signified you (cf. Gen 18:6); for human nature brought to God the Word, still dwelling in the tent of your womb, its own first-fruits taken from your pure blood, as bread hidden in the ashes: bread shaped and baked by the divine fire, [humanity] existing within its own divine individuality and finally reaching the true existence of a body animated by a reasonable and an intelligent soul. And I almost forgot Jacob's ladder (cf. Gen 28:12)! What, then? Is it not obvious to everyone that it too is an anticipation and a type of you? Just as [Jacob] saw that ladder joining heaven and earth by its [two] ends, so that angels could go up and down on it, and just as he saw the strong and unconquerable one symbolically struggling with him, so you, too, are an intermediary; you have joined distant extremes together, and have become the ladder for God's descent to us—the God who has taken up our weak material and has woven it into a unity with himself, making the human person a mind that sees God (cf. Gen 32:31).[10] Therefore angels came down to [Christ], worshipping their God and master; and human beings have taken on the angelic way of life, in order to lay hold of heaven.

9. Where shall I put the testimony of the prophets? Do they not refer to you, if we wish to show their true meaning? What, after all, was that fleece of David (cf. Ps 71:6 [LXX]; Jg 6:36-40), on which the Son of that God who is king over all things came down like rain—the Son who is also without beginning and who reigns with the one who begot him? Was it not you, most obviously? Who was the virgin whom Isaiah, in his vision of the future, predicted would conceive in her womb, and bear as a son, the one who is "God with us" (Is 7:14): that is, the one who would remain God after becoming human? What was Daniel's mountain, from which Christ, the cornerstone, was cut without the use of a human instrument (cf. Dan 2:34, 45)? Was it not you, who gave birth without human seed, and continued to remain a virgin? Let the divine Ezekiel come for-

ward and show us the locked gate, passable to the Lord but never opened, which he proclaimed in prophecy (cf. Ezek 44:1f.). Let him point to the fulfillment of his words. Surely he will point to you, through whom came the God who is above all—a gate of virginity he did not open when he took flesh. For truly the seal remains eternally unbroken!

The prophets, then, proclaim you. The angels serve you, the apostles revere you, the virginal mouthpiece of God[11] takes care of the ever-virgin who was Mother of God.[12] Today the angels minister to you as you go home to your Son, joined by the souls of the just, of patriarchs and prophets. The Apostles are your escort, with a countless throng of inspired Fathers gathered from the ends of the earth as in a cloud, by your Son's divine command, in this holy and sacred city, Jerusalem. In their godly enthusiasm, they sing holy hymns to you, the source of the Lord's body that is for us a stream of life:

10. "Oh, see how the source of life is carried over into life, through the midst of death! See how the one who overcame the defining limits of nature in her childbearing now gives way to those same limits, and submits her unsullied body to death! It was only right for that body to 'lay aside what is mortal and put on immortality' (1 Cor 15:53), since the Lord of nature himself did not refuse the test of death. He died in the flesh, and by that death destroyed death, bestowed incorruptibility on corrupt nature, and made death the source of resurrection. See how the maker of all things receives into his own hands her holy soul, now separated from that tabernacle that received God.[13] He rightly honors her who was by nature his handmaid, but whom by his saving plan he made to be his mother, in the unfathomable ocean of his love for humanity. For he truly became flesh, and did not feign his incarnation!"

They [i.e., the Apostles] saw, we are told, the ranks of angels awaiting your departure from this world of human life. O lovely emigration, which was for you a migration to God! For even if this is granted by God to all who are inspired to serve him—and it *is* granted to them all, we believe—still there is an infinite difference between God's servants and his mother.[14] What, then, shall we call this mystery concerning you? Death? But even though your holy and blessed soul was separated from your privileged, immaculate body, and your body was committed to burial, as custom demanded, still it did not remain in death, nor was it dissolved by corruption. For she whose virginity remained undamaged in childbirth also kept her body undamaged in her passage through death. She was brought over to "a better and more divine tent" (cf. Heb 9:11) that is not cut down by death, but endures always, for endless ages of ages. For just as the all-bright, ever-shining sun, when it is hidden for a while by the body of the moon, seems in a way to fail and to be covered in darkness, accepting shadow in place of light, yet nonetheless never ceases to produce its own light—for it has welling up within itself an ever-flowing fountain of light, or rather *is* itself an inexhaustible fountain of light, as the God who created it has ordained—so you, too, the ever-flowing fountain of true light, the inexhaustible treasure of life itself, the abundant spring of blessing, the cause and sponsor for us of all good things, even if your body is hidden for a short space of time in death, still you pour forth light for us in a generous and endless stream: immortal life, unceasing, pure and inexhaustible waves of true blessedness, rivers of grace, springs of healing, blessings without end. "You are like an apple tree growing in the midst of the deep woods" (Cant 2:7), and your fruit is sweet in the mouths of the faithful. Therefore I will not call your holy passing [from this world] a death, but rather a falling-asleep, a parting, or—more properly speaking—a homecoming. For when you parted from the things of the body, you went to make your dwelling among greater things.

11. The angels and archangels carried you there. The unclean spirits of mid-air trembled at your departure. The air was blessed by your passing through it, the aether of the upper regions was sanctified. Heaven received your soul with joy. The powers [of heaven] met you with holy hymns and splendid ceremony, crying out words such as these: "'Who is this who ascends, robed all in white' (Cant 8:5), 'spreading over us like the dawn, beautiful as the moon, singular as the sun' (Cant 6:10)? How beautiful you are, how sweet! 'You are the flower of the plain, like a lily among thorns' (Cant 2:1f.)! 'Therefore the young maidens love you—we rush towards the fragrance of your myrrh' (Cant 1:3f.). 'The king bears you into his chamber' (*ibid.*), where the powers accompany you in procession, the principalities sing your blessings, the thrones praise you, the cherubim are struck dumb with joy, the seraphim praise you, for you are called, by nature and by God's own plan, the mother of their Lord. You have not simply gone up into the heavens like Elijah (see 2 Kg 2:11 [LXX]), nor have you simply been transported, like Paul, to the third heaven (see 2 Cor 12:2). You have gone on to the very royal throne of your Son, where you see him with your own eyes and rejoice; you stand beside him in great, indescribable freedom (cf. Ps 44:10 [LXX]; Heb 4:16; 9:12; 10:19-35). For the angels and for all the powers that exist above this world, you are ineffable gladness; for the patriarchs, endless happiness; for the just, unutterable joy; for the prophets, continual exaltation. You are a blessing for the world, sanctification for all things, rest for the weary, consolation for the grieving, healing for the sick, a harbor for the storm-tossed, forgiveness for sinners, friendly encouragement for the sorrowing, ready help for all who call on you."

12. O wonder truly above nature! O amazing event! Death, long seen as revolting and hateful, is now praised and called blessed. Long known as the bearer of sadness and depression,

of tears and melancholy, it is now revealed as the cause of joy and celebration. So it is, if for all God's servants, whose death is now called blessed, the ends of their lives give sure proof that they have found God's favor—if their death is called blessed for this reason! Death brings them to fulfillment and shows them to be blessed by making their goodness unchanging; as the proverb puts it, "Do not call a person blessed before his death" (Sir 11:28).

But we do not understand this as applying to you. Blessedness was yours—not death! Your passing was not your arrival at perfection, nor did your departure bestow security on you. For to you[15] the beginning, middle and end of all the good things that are beyond our minds, their security and true confirmation, was your conceiving without male seed, God's dwelling in you, your childbearing without damage [to your virginity][16] So you truly predicted that you would be called blessed by all generations, not from the moment of death but from the very moment of that conception (Lk 1:48). Therefore death has not made you blessed, but you have yourself made death glorious; you have destroyed its horror and shown death to be a joy.

And so your holy, spotless body is committed to a reverent burial, as angels go before you and stand around you and follow after, doing all the things by which it is fitting to serve the mother of their Lord. The Apostles, too, are there, and all the full membership of the Church, crying out divine hymns to the music of the harp of the Spirit, and singing: "We shall be filled with the riches of your house; holy is your temple, wonderful because of [God's] salvation" (Ps 64:5 [LXX]); and again, "The Most High has made his tabernacle holy" (Ps 45:5 [LXX]), and "God's mountain is a mountain of plenty, the mountain where God is pleased to dwell" (Ps 67:16f. [LXX]). The company of Apostles lift you up on their shoulders, the true ark of the Lord God, as once the priests lifted up the typological ark that pointed the way to you; placing you in the tomb, they carry you, as through another Jordan (cf. Jos 3:15), into the true land of promise—to the "Jerusalem which is above, the mother of all the faithful" (Heb 11:10), whose builder and craftsman is God. For your "soul did not go down into the underworld, nor did your flesh see corruption" (Ps 15:10). Your immaculate, completely spotless body was not left on earth, but you have been transported to the royal dwelling-place of heaven as queen, as lady, as mistress, as Mother of God, as the one who truly gave God birth.[17]

13. Oh, how could heaven receive one who is called "wider than the heavens"? How could a grave contain the one who contained God? Yet surely it did receive her, surely it did make room for her; for that body was not "wider than heaven" in any spatial sense. How, after all, can something three cubits long,[18] something that grows more frail each day, be compared with the breadth and length of heaven? But in grace, surely, she surpassed the measure of every height and depth; for nothing can be compared with what is divine. O sacred, wonderful, august and adorable monument! Angels come to venerate it, standing by in much reverence and holy fear; the demons tremble; human beings come forward in faith, showing it honor and worship, venerating it with eyes and lips and yearning of soul, and drinking deep of its inexhaustible store of blessings.

Just as if one should store up costly ointment in his clothes or in some other place, and later remove it, some trace of the fragrance would remain when the ointment is gone, so now, too, that holy, sacred and spotless body, full of divine fragrance, that boundless spring of grace, even though it was first placed in the tomb and then taken away again to a better, higher place, still did not leave that tomb without honor: it gave it a share of divine fragrance and grace, and left it as a source of healing and of all good gifts for those who approach it in faith.

14. We, too, have sat in attendance upon you today, O Lady—Lady, and once again, Lady—Mother of God who knew not man! We have fastened our souls on you as our hope, letting ourselves hang on you—mind, soul and body—as on a strong and unbreakable anchor. We have given you honor, as far as we could, with "psalms and hymns and spiritual songs" (Eph 5:19; Col 3:16), though we can never honor you worthily. For if, as a holy writer has taught, honor towards our fellow servants demonstrates respect for our common Lord,[19] how can we neglect to honor you, who gave your Lord birth? How shall we be less than eager to do it? Shall we not count you more precious than breath itself, necessary though that is, and more valuable to us than life? For so we may express even more fully reverence for our own Lord. But why do I even speak of reverence for the Lord? The precious gift of recalling you, surely, is reward enough to those who commemorate you devoutly, an excess of joy that will never be taken away. What pleasure does not fill such a person? What blessings [does he lack] who makes his mind the storehouse of your holy memory?

This is our sacrifice of thanks to you, the first-fruits of our words, a dedicatory offering of our impoverished intelligence, moved by its longing for you to forget its own weakness. Receive our desires kindly, since you know they exceed our power. And you, good Lady, bearer of our good Lord, watch over us; lead and guide our lives where you will; put the urges of our most shameful passions to rest, calm the tossing of their waves, lead us to the safe harbor of God's will, make us worthy of the blessedness to come, the sweet light of his own face, who is God the Word, made flesh from you. With him, may there be to the Father glory, honor and majesty, with his holy, good and life-giving Spirit, now and always and unto ages of ages!

Amen.

1   This anecdote, probably familiar to John from his rhetorical training, is
     told by Plutarch, *Artaxerxes* 5 (108.18-22), and by Aelian, *Varia His-
     torica* 1.32 (13.28-15.2).

2   John here incorporates the familiar phrase about the generation of the
     Word from the Niceno-Constantinopolitan creed into his evocation of
     the birth of the Word in time.

3   With characteristic balance and precision, John here digresses slightly
     from his theme to summarize the orthodox understanding of the person
     of Christ, as it was formulated at the great early councils of the Church,
     particularly at Chalcedon (451) and at the Second Council of Constan-
     tinople (553).

4   Following the thought of Gregory of Nyssa (*Catechetical Oration* 16),
     John here implies a distinction between the "passions" (πάθη) or pas-
     sivities that naturally belong to vulnerable, finite human nature and that
     are in no sense sinful, such as mortality and the need for food and sleep,
     and the unhealthy drives or "passions" of an embodied soul, which in-
     cline it towards self-seeking. Christ shared fully in the first kind of
     human passion, but his moral freedom and vision of the good remained
     undiminished.

5   Gregory of Nazianzus, Ep. 101 (To Cledonius I).

6   See Gregory of Nazianzus, Or. 40.36.

7   For the beginnings of this doctrine of "spiritual senses," by which the
     reverent and learned reader becomes aware of the deeper and more
     authentic meaning of Scripture and the Christian Mysteries, see Origen,
     De principiis I, 1.9; II, 11.6f.; IV, 4.10; *Dialogue with Heracleides*
     15-24. See also Karl Rahner, "Le début d'une doctrine des cinq sens
     spirituels chez Origène," *Revue d'ascétique et de mystique* 13 (1932)
     113-145 (and in an abridged English translation: "The 'Spiritual
     Senses' according to Origen," *Theological Investigations* 16 [New
     York, 1979] 81-103).

8   Cf. Demosthenes, II Olynthiac 10.

9   To explain the dimensions of "the mystery of Mary," John here and in
     section 9 applies to her a long series of familiar objects and events from
     the Old Testament. The practice is familiar in Marian homilies since the
     fifth century (see above: Introduction, pp. 2-3; Andrew of Crete, Or. II,
     n. 8), and may well have its roots in the liturgical and spiritual poetry of
     the Syriac tradition.

10   The most common etymological interpretation of Jacob's epithet "Is-
     rael," in the Greek Fathers, is "one who sees God"; see, e.g., Clement of
     Alexandria, *Paedagogos* I,9; Origen, *De principiis* IV, 3.12; Cyril of
     Alexandria, *Glaphyra in Genesim* 2.—This passage, applying to Mary
     the figure of Jacob's ladder, implies that she, too, plays an important
     mediatorial role between God and humanity.

11   Greek, θεόλογος: literally, "one who speaks of God," the common epi-
     thet for the Evangelist John in the early Greek tradition.

12 Greek: θεοτόκος.
13 Like Andrew of Crete and Ps.-Modestus, John here clearly follows the tradition represented by the *Transitus* account of John of Thessalonica, according to which Mary's soul was actually separated from her body in death for a period of time before her bodily resurrection. Another tradition, represented in Germanus's second homily, depicts Christ taking her body into glory almost immediately after her death, before it was laid in the tomb.
14 With characteristic clarity, John here sums up both the unique dignity and the universal significance of Mary's entry into glory. What Christians believe has already happened to her, because of her unique role as Mother of the Incarnate Word, is promised to all people at the end of history as the fulfillment of the salvation achieved by her Son.
15 Reading, with manuscripts E, J, Sc and with Voulet, σοί rather than σύ.
16 John makes it clear that the source of Mary's dignity, and the ultimate explanation for her being taken directly into the fullness of glory at death, is her relation to Christ, her role as Mother of God.
17 Literally, "as the true Theotokos".
18 It seems to have been part of the ancient tradition on Mary's life and death that she was only three cubits (about four and a half feet) tall; see also John of Damascus, *Homily II on the Dormition* 17; Andrew of Crete, *Homily III on the Dormition* [2]. This may be connected with the Jerusalem tradition of the liturgical veneration of her tomb, even with the dimensions of the site itself.
19 Basil of Caesaraea, *On the Holy Forty Martyrs* 1 (*PG* 31.508 B 2-4).

ON THE HOLY AND GLORIOUS DORMITION AND TRANSFORMATION OF OUR LADY MARY, MOTHER OF GOD AND EVER-VIRGIN

By Our Holy Father John, Monk of Damascus and Son of Mansour

HOMILY II

1. No human being can worthily praise the holy passing of the Mother of God—not if he had ten thousand tongues and as many mouths! Even if all the tongues of the world's scattered inhabitants came together, they could not approach a praise that was fitting. It simply lies beyond the realm of oratory.[1] But since God loves what we offer, out of longing and eagerness and good intentions, as best we know how, and since what pleases her Son is also dear and delightful to God's Mother, come, let us again grope for words of praise. So we shall obey your orders, O excellent shepherds so beloved of God,[2] as we invoke the help of the Word who became flesh from her, who fills every mouth that is open towards him (Ps 81:11 [LXX]), and who is her only ornament, her perfect commendation. We know that when we begin to praise her, we are only paying what we owe, and that once we have offered this honor we become debtors again, so that our debt [of praise] always remains new, even when it has been discharged.

May she whom we celebrate be gracious to us—she who is above all creatures and reigns over all God's works as Mother of God, the God who created and shaped and rules over all things. And I ask for your understanding towards me, too, O company so eager to hear God's word; accept my good intentions, applaud my desires, be compassionate towards the weakness of my words. Imagine a king, given the governing authority over his fellow men and women by God himself, whose table is always abundantly furnished and crowded with food of every kind, whose palace enchants us with the fragrance of costly ointments. If one should bring him, out of season, a violet as purple as the sea, or a fragrant rose blooming amid its thorns, emerging mottled from its green calyx and gradually developing its color to full blush, or perhaps some honey-sweet fruit of autumn, he would notice not the slight value of the gift but its rarity at that time; and being a man of judgment and discernment, he would marvel at how unexpected it is, and would bestow on the peasant, in return, generous and elegant gifts. So we, too, bring this flower to the Queen in our wintertime of words; we arm an aging tongue for a contest of praise, and sharpen our mind with yearning as we might sharpen iron with a stone. And so, too, crushing words out of our mind like unripe grapes, we offer to you, connoisseurs of language and lovers of good oratory, this dim spark, this unfermented wine. May we be received still more favorably than that peasant![3]

What should we offer the Mother of the Word but words? Like always rejoices in like, because it recognizes it as its own. Let us, then, open the starting-gates of speech, let us loosen the reins a little, and spur this discourse on as if we were riding a race-horse. And you, O Word of God—ride with me as my helper; give words to my stammering mind, make the track smooth for my speech, and lead my course straight towards your good pleasure, the goal of a wise person's every word and thought.

2. Today the holy, incomparable virgin enters the heavenly sanctuary that lies above the universe. She so longed for virginity that she was transformed into it, as if consumed by the purest fire. Every virgin, after all, loses her virginity in giving birth; but she, who was a virgin before giving birth, remained

so during her labors and even after them.[4] Today the holy, living ark of the living God, the one who carried her own maker within herself, comes to her rest in the temple of the Lord not made by hands. David—her ancestor and God's—leaps for joy (2 Sam 6:4; 1 Chr 15:25); the angels join in the dance, the archangels applaud, the virtues give praise, the principalities rejoice with them, the powers exult, the dominations delight, the thrones make festival, the cherubim sing their hymn, and the seraphim glorify God.[5] They glorify him in no negligible way, when they give glory to the Mother of glory.

Today the sacred dove, the pure and innocent soul who was also purified by the Holy Spirit, has flown from the ark—I mean from that body which received God and is the source of our life; and she has found "a place of rest for her feet" (Gen 8:9), flying up to the intelligible world and pitching her tent in the spotless land of our heritage on high.

Today the Eden of the new Adam welcomes the spiritual Paradise where our condemnation has been cancelled, where the tree of life is planted, where our nakedness is clothed again. For we are no longer naked and exposed, lacking the radiance of the divine image and stripped of the abundant grace of the Spirit; we need no longer tell the story of that tragic, ancient nakedness, saying, "I have taken off my tunic, and how shall I put it on again?" (Cant 5:3) For in this Paradise, the serpent has no means of entry—that serpent whose false promise of divinization led us to a covetousness that made us the equal only of irrational beasts. The only Son of God, who is God and of the same substance as the Father, formed himself into a human being from this virgin, from this pure soil; and so I, who am human, am made divine—I, who am mortal, have now become immortal, and have stripped off my tunic of skin. For I have taken off corruption, and put on the robe of divinity.

Today the immaculate Virgin, who never involved herself

in earthly passions but was nourished on heavenly thoughts, did not return to earth (cf. Gen 3:19); being truly a living heaven, she now dwells in the tents of heaven. For who could err in calling her heaven, unless one were to say—and say rightly—that she has been lifted even above heaven in her incomparable privileges? For the maker and preserver of heaven and of everything in and beyond this universe, the craftsman of all that has been made, visible and invisible—he who has no place, because he *is* the place of all other beings (if, indeed, place is defined as what contains the things within it): he has created a child in her, of his own power and without human seed, and has revealed her as the spacious treasure-house of that divinity that fills all things, alone and uncircumscribed. He has gathered himself up completely in her, without suffering diminution, yet he remains wholly beyond her, abiding in himself as his incomprehensible home.

Today the treasury of life, the abyss of grace (I do not know how I can say these things with my bold, fearless lips!) is wrapped in a death that brings life. Undaunted, she draws near to death, having given birth to death's destroyer—if one may call her departure from the world, so full of holiness and life, a death at all. For how could she, who brimmed over with true life for all, ever become subject to death's power? Still, she yields to the law established by her own Son, and as a daughter of the old Adam she undergoes the ancestral trial, since even her Son, life itself, did not refuse it. But as Mother of the living God, it is also right that she should be brought into his presence. For if God was concerned "lest the first human being reach out his hand and take from the tree of life and eat, and live forever..." (Gen 3:21), how can she, who has received the life that knows no beginning or ending, the life free from the boundaries of both birth and death, not live herself for endless ages?

3. Long ago, the Lord God punished the ancestors of this

mortal race, who had gorged themselves on the strong drink of disobedience and had made the eyes of their heart drowsy with the wine of sin, weighing down their eyelids with sinful self-indulgence until they fell asleep in death; he banished them from the garden of Eden and drove them away. But now Mary has shaken off all the assaults of passion, and has planted again the shoot of obedience to God our Father, introducing life anew for all her race. Shall not Paradise receive her? Shall not heaven open its gates wide with joy? Surely it will! Eve once lent her ear to the message of the serpent, and allowed herself to hear the Enemy's advice; her senses all enchanted by the deceiving charms of counterfeit pleasure, she received the sentence of grief and sorrow, undergoing the pangs of childbirth, the judgment—with Adam—of death, and imprisonment in the depths of Hades. But Mary, the truly all-blessed one, lent her ear to the Word of God, and was filled with the energy of the Spirit. She bore the Father's good pleasure in her womb, at the angel's word, and without sensual passion or contact conceived the very person of God the Word, who fills all things. She brought him into the world without suffering the pains that adhere to our nature, for she was wholly united with God. How shall death consume her? How shall the realm of death receive her? How shall corruption dare to assault that body once filled with life? These things do not belong to her; they are all foreign to both the soul and the body of the one who bore God.

Death saw her and was afraid. For he had assaulted her Son, but learned from his defeat and grew wise from the experience![6] For her the gloomy path down to the underworld remains untrodden; a straight, gentle, easy path to heaven is opened for her. For if Christ, who is life and truth, has said, "Where I am, there will my servant be also" (Jn 12:26), is it not even more certain that his Mother will abide with him? She bore him before she knew suffering; her passing from life, too, must be free from suffering. "The death of sinners is burdensome" (Ps 34:22 [LXX]); but since in her "the sting of death, which is sin" (1 Cor 15:56), was quelled, shall we say that the end of life was anything but the beginning of a better life, one that will know no end? "Precious," truly, "is the death of the saints" of the Lord God of hosts (Ps 116:15 [LXX]); and precious above all the rest is the passing of the Mother of God!

"Let the heavens rejoice now," and the angels applaud; "let the earth be glad" now (Ps 96:11; 97:1 [LXX]), and all men and women leap for joy! Let the air ring out now with happy song, and let the black night lay aside its gloomy, unbecoming cloak of darkness, to imitate the bright radiance of day in sparkles of flame.[7] For the living city of the Lord God of hosts is lifted up, and kings bring a priceless gift from the temple of the Lord, the wonder of Sion (cf. Ps 68:30 [LXX]), to the Jerusalem on high who is free and is their mother (Gal 4:26): those who were appointed by Christ as rulers of all the earth—the Apostles—escort to heaven the ever-virgin Mother of God!

4. It does not seem to me out of place to describe now, in what words I can—to sketch out in at least a few scenes and images—the marvels that came to pass at the death of this holy woman, the Mother of God, as we have learned of them in summary form from ancient times, as we say, at our mothers' knees.

I can see in my mind this woman, holier than all things holy, sacred and venerable above all others—the sweet vessel of the manna, or rather its true source—lying on a pallet in the celebrated Holy City of David: on Sion,[8] that prominent and glorious mountain, where the law of the letter was fulfilled and the law of the Spirit proclaimed; where Christ, the lawgiver, brought to completion the symbolic Pasch and where the God of the Old and the New Covenant gave us the true Pasch; where the "lamb of God, who takes away the sins of the world" (Jn 1:29), initiated his disciples into the mystical banquet, immolated himself for them like the "fatted calf," and trod out the grape of the "true vine" (cf. Lk 15:23, 27; Jn 15:1); where Christ was seen by the Apostles when he rose from the dead, and proved to Thomas—and through him to all the world—that he is God and Lord, possessing two natures even after he had come back from the dead, and with them two ways of acting and two autonomous wills, which shall remain in operation for endless ages.[9] This city is the citadel of the Churches; she is the refuge of the disciples. Here the all-Holy Spirit was poured forth on the Apostles in the form of fire, making a great sound and communicating in many tongues. Here John the Theologian received the Mother of God into his care, and ministered to her needs. It was this city, the Mother of all the world's Churches, which played home to the Mother of God, after her Son's return from the dead. In this city, then, the Blessed Virgin lay, on a bed one can only call thrice blessed.

5. Having come to this point in my discourse, I am—if I may express my inner feelings—on fire with hot and restless yearning, I am seized with a thrill of awe and bathed in joyous tears, imagining that I could embrace that blessed and beloved bed, so filled with wonders. This bed has received the tabernacle from which came life itself; by its very nearness it has come to have a share in her sanctity. And this holy temple—truly holy, truly worthy of God—I seemed for a moment to embrace with my own arms! I pressed my eyes, my lips, my forehead, my neck, my cheeks to her limbs, rejoicing in these sensations as if her body were present and I could touch it, even though I knew full well that I cannot see the one I long for with these eyes. How can one touch what has been lifted up into the heavenly sanctuary? But enough of this!

6. What honors, then, were paid her by the one who has commanded us in the Law to honor our parents?

The Apostles were scattered everywhere on this earth,

fishing for men and women with the varied and sonorous
tongues of the Spirit, seeking to capture people in the net of
their preaching and to save them from the pit of error by bringing them in to the spiritual, heavenly table at that mystic feast,
that sacred banquet, that spiritual wedding of the heavenly
Bridegroom—the banquet which the Father has spread, most
royally and splendidly, for the Son who is his equal in power
and who shares his nature. But by a divine command, a cloud
swept the Apostles to Jerusalem from the ends of the earth as if
it were itself a net, gathering eagles and drawing them in. For
"where the body is," said Christ the Truth, "there the eagles
will gather" (Mt 24:28). If this saying, after all, refers to the
second coming of the one who spoke these words, to his second great and manifest arrival from heaven to dwell with us,
still it is not inappropriate if we borrow it here, too, to season
our discourse. The eye-witnesses, then, the servants of the
Word, were there, ministering also to his Mother as they were
bound to do and hoping to claim from her a blessing, as something valuable beyond price. For who can doubt the suggestion
that she is the source of blessing and the fountain of all good
gifts? The companions and successors of the Apostles were
with them, too, to share in both their service and her blessing;
for those who share in the labor will share proportionately in
its rewards. And the holy community, God's chosen ones from
Jerusalem, were also standing by.

It was fitting that the most outstanding saints and prophets
of old were with them, too, sharing in this holy guard of honor:
those, namely, who had proclaimed beforehand that God's
Word would be born in flesh from her, for our sakes, out of
love for us. Nor was the company of the angels excluded. For
every creature who remained obedient to the King's desire,
and who therefore was worthy of such an honored position,
had to be part of the escort for his fleshly Mother—that truly

fortunate and blessed woman, honored before "all generations" and all creation (Ps 103:20f. [LXX]; Dan 7:9f; Lk 1:48).
All of them stood near her, as she was bathed in the beacon-
light of the Spirit and illuminated them in turn with brilliant radiance, while each of them fixed the pure eyes of his spirit on
her, in reverence and awe and unwavering affection. For there
is not one being to whom this office does not fall—at least, no
more than One alone; for no creature has received from on
high supreme and incomparable Being, which, when it descended, would be capable of doing all things and accept no
obligation to offer worship[10]

7. Then there must have been inspired speech, words that
spoke of God! Then there must have been heavenly singing,
celebrating her departure from this world! For it was right
then, too, to sing the praises of the superabundant goodness of
God, his greatness beyond all greatness and his power beyond
power's bounds, his self-restraint towards us beyond all height
and magnitude, the richness beyond all riches of his unimagin-
able kindness, the inexhaustible abyss of his love. It was right
to celebrate how [the Son], without abandoning his own greatness, came down and emptied himself in the way that led to his
exaltation (cf. Phil 2:6-10), supported by the good pleasure of
the Father and the Spirit. It was right to sing of how the One
who is above all substance took on substance in the womb of a
woman, in a way above all substantial explanation,[11] of how
he is God, yet became human—remaining both, yet the same
person; of how he did not leave behind the divine essence, yet
"shared like us in flesh and blood" (Heb 2:14); of how he who
"fills all things" (Eph 3:19; 4:10) and "carries the universe with
the word of his mouth" (Heb 1:3), came to dwell in a narrow
place; of how the body of this celebrated woman, material and
fragile as grass (cf. Is 40.6), received the consuming fire of the
Godhead (Deut 4:24; Is 33:14; Heb 12:29), yet remained un-

consumed, like purest gold. All these things came to pass by
the will of God; for if God wills it, all things are possible, but
nothing can be achieved against his will.

All this story became the subject of a great contest of
words: not so that one might outdo the others—that kind of
competition, after all, belongs to vainglorious minds that are
far from pleasing God—but so that nothing might be lacking
from their eagerness and force of expression, as they sang
God's praises and honored the Mother of God.[12]

8. It was then, indeed, that Adam and Eve, the ancestors of
our race, cried out piercingly, with joyful lips: "Blessed are
you, our daughter, for canceling the punishment of our transgression! You inherited from us a corruptible body, but you
bore in your womb, for our sakes, the garment of incorruptibility. You took your being from our loins, but you restored to us
our well-being. You put an end to our travail, and broke
through the swaddling-bands of death. You made available to
us again our ancient home: we were the ones who locked Paradise, you the one who opened the way to the tree of life.
Through our actions, sad times overtook good; but through
yours, yet better times have come again out of sadness. How,
then, shall you, the immaculate one, taste death? For you,
death will be the bridge to life, the stairway to heaven, the ford
to the banks of immortality. Truly you are blessed, O most
blessed one! For who has been offered in sacrifice but the
Word himself, suffering all that we have learned he did?"[13]

All the chorus of the saints[14] joined in the applause: "You
have fulfilled the prophecies! You bring us the joy we have
been waiting for! Through you, we have been released from
the bonds of death! Come to us, holy and life-giving
treasure—come to us who long for you, for you have brought
our longing to its end!"

But the throng of holy ones, still living in the body, who

stood by, took up a contrasting strain with equal emphasis: "Stay with us," they said, "our consolation, the only comfort we have on earth! Do not leave us orphans, O Mother, as we face danger in order to share the sufferings of your Son. Let us keep you among us, as rest in our labors and respite in our trials. If you wish to stay, it will surely be possible, and if you prefer to go, nothing will stand in your way. But if you go away, O tabernacle of God, then let us go with you, we who are called your people because of your Son! In you, we have the only consolation left to us on earth; to live and die in your company is the lot of the blessed! But how can we speak of your dying? For you, even death is life—and better than life, for it exceeds this life to an incomparable degree. But for us, how will life be livable, if we do not have you for a companion?"

9. This, it seems to me, is what the Apostles must have said to the Blessed Virgin, along with the whole assembly of the Church. But when they saw that the Mother of God was hastening towards the end of her life, even eager for it, they turned their minds towards hymns for the departing; for they were moved by divine grace, and lent their mouths to the Spirit, borne beyond flesh and yearning to leave this world with the departing Mother of God, even hastening ahead of her, in a way, in the intensity of their desire (cf. 2 Cor 5:1-8). And when all of them had brought to completion what desire and duty led them to do, when they had woven a colorful and abundant garland of sacred song, they received her blessing, as if it were some God-given treasure, and spoke their final words, fitting for the moment of death. They said, I imagine, words recalling how fleeting and insecure this present life is, and revealing the hidden mysteries of the good things to come.

10. Just then, it would seem to me, something must have happened that fit these circumstances and that would naturally

follow them.[15] I mean that the King must have come to the one who gave him birth, to receive her soul into his pure and holy hands, her soul so upright and spotless. And it seems likely that she would have spoken thus: "'Into your hands, my Son, I confide my spirit!' (Ps 30:6 [LXX]; Lk 23:46; Acts 7:59) Receive the soul that is so dear to you, which you have preserved blameless. Yours is my body, too; I do not give it to the earth! Keep it safe, since you were pleased to dwell in it, and to preserve its virginity as you were being born. Bring me close to you, so that where you are, the fruit of my womb, I too may be, and may share your home. I am hastening towards you, who came to dwell so immediately in me. And you must console my dear children, whom you have been pleased to call your brothers and sisters, when I go away from them; add a blessing to the blessing I shall now give them by laying on my hands."

Then, having spoken these words, she would have raised her hands, I imagine, and would have blessed those gathered there; and she would have heard, "Come, my blessed Mother, 'into the place of my rest' (Ps 132:8 [LXX]; cf. Ps 95:11 [LXX]). 'Arise, come, my dear one,' beautiful among all women; 'for behold, winter has passed, and the time of pruning has come' (Cant 2:10-12). 'My dear one is beautiful, and there is no blemish in you' (Cant 4:7). 'The odor of your ointments surpasses all fragrance' (Cant 1:3; cf. 4:10)." And having heard these words,[16] the holy woman would have committed her soul to the hands of her Son.

11. And what happened next? I imagine that the elements of nature were stirred up and altered, that there were sounds, crashes, rumblings, as well as remarkable hymns from angels who flew before her, providing her with an escort and with companions on the way. Some of them would have acted as a guard of honor for her spotless, holy soul, and would have ascended with it on its way to heaven, until they had brought the

Queen to her royal throne (cf. Ps 44:10 [LXX]); others would
have surrounded her holy, sacred body, singing the songs that
only angels can sing in honor of the Mother of God. And what
of those [humans] who stood around that holy, sacred body?
They would have woven a tissue of reverent love, of joyful
tears, around that holy, blessed temple; they would have embraced and kissed each limb belonging to that body, and that
very contact would have been for them a sanctification and a
blessing. Then sickness would have melted away; the cohorts
of demons would have fled, rushing every which-way to their
dens beneath the earth. The air, the fiery ether, the sky would
have been made holy by the ascent of her spirit, as earth was
sanctified by the deposition of her body. Even water had its
share in the blessing: for she was washed in pure water, which
did not so much cleanse her as it was itself consecrated.[17] Then
the deaf received perfect hearing again, the feet of the lame
had their power to walk restored; sight was renewed in the
blind, and the writ of condemnation was torn up for sinners
who approached in faith (cf. Is 35:5f.; Mt 11:5; Lk 7:21f.; Acts
3:7; Col 2:14).

And what happened then? Her pure body would have been
wrapped in fresh cloths, and the Queen placed again on her
couch. Then lamps would have been brought, ointments applied, funeral hymns sung; the angels would have chanted, in
their own tongue, a song most fitting for them, while the Apostles and holy ancestors would have sung sacred canticles, inspired by the Spirit.

12. And then, then, the ark of the Lord would have departed from Mount Sion; borne on the glorious shoulders of
the Apostles, it would have been brought, by way of a tomb, to
its heavenly precincts.[18] But first it is carried through the midst
of the City, like a beautiful bride adorned with the unapproachable splendor of the Spirit; so its makes its way to the

sacred enclosure of Gethsemane, with angels before and beside it, covering it with their wings, and in the full assembly of the Church.

King Solomon, when he wanted to deposit the ark in the temple of the Lord, which he had built, called together "all the elders of Israel to Sion, to bear the ark of the covenant of the Lord up from the city of David, which is Sion... And the priests lifted up the ark and the tent of witness, and the priests and Levites brought it up. And the King and the whole people went in front of the ark, sacrificing bulls and sheep without number. And the priests brought the ark of the covenant of the Lord into its place, in the innermost chamber of the Temple, to the holy of holies, under the wings of the cherubim." (1 Kg 8:1-6 [LXX]) So now, to bring to its place the spiritual ark, not of the Lord's covenant but of the very person[19] of God the Word, the new Solomon himself, King of Peace[20] and master-builder of the universe, called together on this day the sublime ranks of heavenly spirits, and the leaders of the new covenant—I mean the Apostles—with all the holy people then in Jerusalem. And he solemnly led her soul, accompanied by angels, into the real and original Holy of Holies in heaven (see Heb 9:12; 10:20), resting on the very wings of the four "living creatures" (Ezek 1:6); he seated her next to his own throne, within the veil where Christ himself, our forerunner, has gone in his own body (cf. Heb 9:12; 10:20). But her body was carried by the hands of the Apostles, the King of Kings overshadowing it with the radiance of his invisible divinity, while the whole community of the saints ran before her, crying out holy acclamations and offering "a sacrifice of praise" (Ps 106:22 [LXX]), until the body was laid in the tomb as in her bridal chamber, and through it was given to the delights of Eden and the tabernacle of heaven.

13. It happened that Jews were present as well—those, at least, who were not wholly without good sense. And it might

not be a bad idea to add to our account, like a bit of spice in a cooked dish, what is reported on the lips of many people.[21] They say that when those bearing the blessed body of the Mother of God came to the steep descent of the mountain, a certain Jewish man, enslaved by sin and committed to error, imitated the servant of Caiaphas who slapped the divine, majestic face of Christ, our God; becoming an instrument of the devil, carried forward by a bold, irrational whim, he rushed with demonic impulse towards that holiest of vessels, which even the angels approached with fear, and wildly seized the bier with both his hands, insanely trying to wrest it down to the ground. This attack, too, had its origin in the envy of the Prince of Evil. But the fruits came before the labors were ended, and the man reaped bitter grapes, worthy of his own foul purpose! For they say that his hands failed him,[22] and it was possible suddenly to see the perpetrator of this dreadful deed, caught not only red-handed but completely handless, until he changed his mind and began to believe, and was converted. Immediately the pallbearers stood still; the wretched man placed both his arms on that dwelling-place of life, that bearer of miracles, and was brought in an instant from being mutilated to having healthy hands again. So a crisis can often be the mother of decisions that are for our good.[23] But let us return to the subject of our discourse.

14. From there, her body was carried to that holy place, Gethsemane. Again there were kisses and embraces, again words of praise, hymns and invocations and tears; they were bathed in streams of sweat from their anguish and affectionate grief. So that holy body was placed in its glorious, peerless monument; and from there it was lifted up to its heavenly home on the third day.

For it was fitting[24] that this worthy dwelling-place of God—the spring of the water of forgiveness, which no human ever dug; the wheatfield of the bread of heaven, which no human ever ploughed; the vine of the grape of immortality, which no human ever watered; the ever-blooming, richly fruitful olive-tree of the Father's mercy—should not be confined within the hollows of earth. But rather, as the holy, spotless body which came from her, and which had its concrete existence in God the Word, rose on the third day from the tomb, so indeed it was right that she, his Mother, should be taken out of her grave and joined with her Son; and just as he had come down to her, so she, his first love, should be taken up to that "greater and more perfect tabernacle, ...to heaven itself." (Heb 9:11, 24)

It was fitting that she, who gave refuge to God the Word in her womb, should dwell in the tent of her own son; and as the Lord said that he must be in his own Father's house (Lk 2:49), so it was right that his mother should make her home in her son's palace, "in the house of the Lord, the courts of the house of our God" (Ps 134:1; 135:2). For if "the home of all who rejoice is in him" (Ps 87:7), where else should we find the cause of our joy?

It was fitting that she, who preserved her virginity undamaged by childbirth, should have her body preserved from corruption even in death. It was fitting that she, who held the creator in her lap as a baby, should rest in the tabernacle of God. It was fitting that the bride, whom the Father took for his own, should dwell in the bridal-chamber of heaven. It was fitting that she, who gazed at her own son on the cross, and who [there] received in her heart the sword of pain that she escaped at childbirth, should look on him enthroned with his Father. It was fitting that the Mother of God should receive the blessings of her son, and be reverenced by all creation as Mother and servant of God.[25] For a heritage always passes from parents to children; but now, as a wise man has said, the streams of the sacred rivers flow upwards! For the Son has subjected all creation to his mother!

15. Come, then, let us celebrate today ourselves a funeral feast[26] for the Mother of God! We do not bring flutes and revelers, or join in revels like those that are said to be celebrated for the mother of the so-called gods[27]—the one whom, the myth-makers say, had many children, while the truth is she had none. These are but spirits, shadowy apparitions, bravely pretending to be what they are not, and they find their support in the foolishness of those they deceive. For how can one produce a bodiless being by sexual relations? How are they united to each other? And how can that be a *god*, which first did not exist, and is later brought into being? That the race of spirits is bodiless is surely clear to everyone, even to those whose intellectual eyes are blind. For Homer said, somewhere in his works, when describing the condition of those he considered gods,

> They eat no bread, nor drink the fiery wine;
> Therefore they lack blood, and are called immortal.[28]

They do not eat bread, he says, and do not drink the wine that warms us; for this reason they are bloodless, they have no blood—yet they are called immortal! How rightly he says that "they are *called*" this! For they are called immortal, but *are* not what they are called; they have already died the death of wickedness.

But we, for whom God is the object of worship—God, who has not come from non-existence into being, but who always and from all eternity is, beyond cause and explanation, beyond any notion of time or nature: *we* honor and venerate the Mother of God! We do not mean to suggest that the timeless birth of his divinity was from her—for the begetting of God's Word lies outside time, of equal eternity with the Father—but we confess his second birth, a freely-chosen birth in the flesh, and we know and proclaim the cause of this birth. For he who without beginning exists without a body became flesh "for us and for our salvation,"[29] that like might be wholly saved by its like; and taking flesh from her, the holy virgin, without the union of human parenting, he was born, while remaining wholly God. Becoming wholly human, he is himself the whole God with his flesh, and a whole human being with his supremely transcendent divinity. So we, who recognize this virgin as Mother of God, now celebrate the feast of her dormition. We do not call her a goddess—we will have none of such pedantic classical fabling[30]—for we proclaim her death. But we recognize her as Mother of the God who became flesh.

16. Let us praise her, then, today with sacred songs, we who are privileged to be called and to be the people of Christ. Let us honor her with an all-night assembly.[31] Let us delight in her holiness of soul and body; after all, she is truly, after God, the holiest of all beings, for like always delights in like! Let us do her homage by our mercy and our compassion for the poor. For if God is honored by nothing so much as by mercy, who can deny that his mother is glorified, too, by the same thing? She has opened up to us the unspeakable depth of God's love for us!

Through her, our age-old war against our creator has come to an end. Through her, our reconciliation with him has been forged, peace and grace have been bestowed on us, human beings join with the chorus of angels, and we who were once without honor have now been made children of God. From her, we have plucked the grape of life; from her we have harvested the flower of incorruptibility. She has become the mediator of all good things for us. In her, God has become human and the human being God!

What could be more paradoxical than this? What could be more blessed? My head spins with reverent fear at what I have just said! Let us dance to the sound of tambourines, O you who are young at heart, with Miriam the prophetess (Ex 15:20), putting to death "our earthly members" (Col 3:5)—for that is the mystic significance of the tambourine.[32] Let us shout in our hearts the cry of victory for the ark of the Lord God, and the walls of Jericho will fall—I mean those grim fortifications of the hostile powers (Jos 6:20). With David, let us dance in the Spirit: for today the ark of the Lord comes to its rest. With Gabriel, the chief of the angels, let us cry out, "Hail, full of grace, the Lord is with you!" (Lk 1:28) Hail, inexhaustible ocean of grace! Hail, our only salve for sorrow! Hail, medicine that banishes pain from every heart! Hail, you through whom death has been banished, and life made welcome!

17. And you, most holy of holy tombs, after the tomb of the Lord, which is the source of our life, the spring of the resurrection—I speak to you now as if you were alive[33]: where is that unadulterated gold, which the hands of the Apostles confided to your keeping? Where is that inexhaustible wealth? Where is the treasure that received God? Where is the living tablet, where is the new book, in which God's Word was ineffably written, without a hand? Where is the depth of grace? Where is the ocean of healing? Where is the life-giving spring? Where is the body of the Mother of God, that body we so love and long for?

<The tomb replies:> "Why do you seek in a tomb one who has been taken up to the tabernacle of heaven? (cf. Lk 24:5) Why do you exact a reckoning from me about her disappearance? I have no power to resist the divine command. Her holy, sacred body left its wrapping cloth behind, and after sharing with me her holiness, after filling me with the fragrance of ointments and making of me a holy shrine, she was raised up and departed, escorted by angels and archangels and all the heavenly powers. Now angels take care of me; now divine grace dwells in me. I have been revealed as a source of healing, a remedy for pain. I am a constant spring of health; I put demons to flight. I have become a city of refuge for those who flee to me (cf. Ex 21:13f; Num 35:9-34). Come to me in faith, you peoples, and draw from my river of blessings; keep your

faith above reproach (James 1:6), and come! 'You who thirst, come to the water,' Isaiah urges, 'and you who have no money, come, buy without price.' (Is 55:1) I have cried out to all, as the Gospel does: if anyone thirsts for the healing of illness, for release from the soul's passions, for the cancellation of sin, for freedom from all kinds of assaults, for the repose of the Kingdom of Heaven, let him come to me in faith and draw from the stream of grace, so full of power and goodness (cf. Jn 7:37-39). Just as the action of water, which like that of earth and air and the all-enlightening sun is simple and single, still adapts itself in a different way to each creature who shares in it, according to its nature, becoming wine in a grape and oil in an olive, so grace, which is simple and single, works for the good of those who share in it in various parallel ways, according to the need of each (cf. 1 Pet 4:10). I do not possess grace of my own nature. Every tomb is full of bad odors, a source of sadness, the enemy of joy; but I have been given precious ointment, I have shared in its fragrance—an ointment so fragrant and powerful that even a tiny touch of it bestows a share in a gift that can never be lost. Truly, 'God does not repent of his graces' (Rom 11:29). For I have received into myself the spring of happiness, and I have been enriched with an ever-flowing well of joy."

18. You see, dear fathers and brothers, what this illustrious tomb has to say to us.[34]

19. And what shall we answer to the tomb ourselves? Your grace is unceasing, ever-flowing; yet God's power is not limited to places, nor are the gracious actions of the Mother of God. If they were restricted to her sepulcher, after all, God's gift would inspire very few people! But in fact, it is given without measure in all corners of the world. Let us, then, make our own remembrance of her into a rich monument for the Mother of God.[35]

How shall we do this?[36] She is herself a virgin, and a lover of virgins; she is herself pure, and a lover of the pure. If we consecrate her memory along with our own bodies, we will receive her grace to dwell within us. She avoids all impurity, and turns away from the morass of our passions. She loathes gluttony, and is the foe of our base drive of sexual self-indulgence; she flees from our impure thoughts like a "brood of vipers" (Mt 3:7; 12:34; etc.); she shuns wicked and frivolous talk and singing, and will have no contact with seductive perfumes. She hates the swellings of pride, and will not accept inhumane behavior or quarreling. She rejects vainglory, that exerts itself to no purpose. She opposes puffed-up arrogance as a bitter enemy. She loathes an unforgiving mind, as the enemy of salvation. She considers all vice as a deadly poison, but she rejoices in their opposites: for opposites are the cure for what they oppose! She delights in fasting, in self-control, in the singing of psalms; she rejoices in the presence of purity, of virginity, of temperance. She bestows on these things unfailing peace, welcomes them with affection. She embraces the peaceful and gentle heart, she takes love and mercy and humility into her arms as her own children. To put it briefly, she is horrified and angered by any kind of wickedness, but rejoices in all goodness as if it were a gift bestowed on herself.

If, then, we bravely avoid the evils of our old way of life, and earnestly love the virtues and make friends with them, she will often come to visit her own servants, leading along with her the whole assembly of the just.[37] And she will also bring with her Christ her Son, the King and Lord of all things, to dwell in our hearts. To him be glory, honor, power, majesty and splendor, with the eternal Father and the Holy Spirit, now and always and for ages of ages.

Amen.

APPENDIX I:

Excerpt from the "Euthymiac History"
(see above, c. 18 and n. 34)

And that all this is true is confirmed by the third book of the
Euthymiac History, chapter 40, where we read, in so many
words: "It was said above that Saint Pulcheria erected many
churches for Christ in Constantinople. One of these is the
church in Blachernai, built at the beginning of the reign of the
divinely-appointed Emperor Marcian [who acceded to throne
August, 450]. When the two of them built a worthy house there
for the all-glorious and all-holy Mother of God, the ever-virgin
Mary, and adorned it with every sort of decoration, they hoped
to find her holy body, which had been the dwelling-place of
God. And summoning Juvenal, the archbishop of Jerusalem,
and those bishops from Palestine who were staying in the capital because of the synod then being held at Chalcedon [Octo-
ber, 451], they said to them: 'We have heard that the first and
most outstanding church of the all-holy Mother of God, the
ever-virgin Mary, is in Jerusalem, in the place called Gethsemane, where her life-giving body was put in a coffin. We now
wish to bring this relic here, to protect this royal city.'

"Juvenal answered, on behalf of them all: 'There is nothing
in the holy, inspired Scripture about the death of Mary, the
holy Mother of God; but we know from ancient and wholly reliable tradition that at the time she so gloriously fell asleep, all
the holy Apostles, who were traveling the world for the salvation of the peoples, were lifted up in a single instant of time
and were gathered at Jerusalem; and as they stood by her, they
saw a vision of angels, and heard the divine chanting of the
higher powers. So it was that she gave her soul, in an ineffable
way, into God's hands, surrounded by the glory of God and all

heaven. Her body, which had been God's dwelling place, was brought for burial amidst the singing of the angels and the Apostles, and laid to rest in a coffin in Gethsemane; and the angelic dancing and singing continued without pause in that place for three days. But after three days, the song of the angels ceased; the Apostles were there, and since one of them—Thomas—had not been present [for her burial] and came at the end of three days, and wished to reverence that body which had housed God, they opened the coffin. And they could not find her body, which had been the object of such praise; all that they found were her burial wrappings. And being overcome by the ineffable fragrance that came out of the wrappings, they closed the coffin again. Amazed by this miraculous discovery, they could only draw a single conclusion: the one who had deigned to become flesh in her own person, and to take his humanity from her, the one who willed to be born in human flesh as God the Word, the Lord of glory, and who had preserved her virginity intact even after childbirth, now chose, after her departure from this world, to honor her immaculate and pure body with the gift of incorruptibility, and with a change of state even before the common, universal resurrection.

"'The excellent Apostle Timothy, the first bishop of Ephesus, was present there with the [other] Apostles, and also Dionysius the Areopagite, as the great Dionysius himself tells us in his elaborate remarks about the blessed Hierotheos—who also was present then—which are addressed to Timothy. Dionysius writes: "Once we, as you know, and he and many of our holy brethren had come together, along with our inspired hierarchs, to see the body that had been our source of life; James, brother of God, was there, and Peter, the chief and senior leader of those who spoke of God. After we had seen it, all the hierarchs resolved to sing the praise, as each was able, of the infinitely powerful goodness of the divine strength. After the witnesses of God, as you know, he [Hiero-theos] far surpassed all the other initiates in the holy Mys-tery—completely enraptured, completely transcending himself, experiencing a real communion with the things of which they sang. And he was judged by all who heard and saw and recognized him—though he did not recognize them—to be inspired, a singer of divine song. But why do I tell you about the holy oracles that were spoken then? For if I am not completely forgetful, I know that I often heard parts of those inspired canticles from you.'" [Ps.-Dionysius, *On the Divine Names* 3.2; cf. also the commentary of Maximus Confessor (PG 4.236 C), which identifies the incident in the passage as that of the death and glorification of Mary.]

"When the imperial couple heard this, they asked the arch-bishop Juvenal to send them the holy coffin, properly sealed, with the funeral garments in it of the glorious, all-holy Mary, Mother of God. And when he had sent it, they placed it in the church of the holy Mother of God that had been built at Blachernai."

So far this account.

1   Stressing the impossibility of praising one's subject adequately is a *topos* in classical epideictic oratory, especially at the beginning of the oration: see Menander (ed. Bursian 95, 2; 96, 6; 142, 8).

2   John is apparently addressing bishops or abbots here, who have commissioned him to give these festal orations and who are presiding at the vigil or liturgy at which he is preaching.

3   In this passage, John not only makes use of the conventional rhetorical device of emphasizing his own limitations, often used at the beginning of orations, but also makes it clear that this sermon is expected to be a literary display-piece. His reference to his "aging tongue" suggests at least that he was no longer a young man; the fact that he has been invited to preach at such a brilliant occasion suggests he was already widely known as an orator, theologian and poet.

4   John here clearly enunciates what has been, since the fourth century, the general belief of both the Eastern and the Western Churches about Mary's continuing virginity.

5   John here adopts the classification of the nine "choirs" of angelic beings worked out by Ps.-Dionysius the Areopagite on the basis of scriptural references. See *On the Celestial Hierarchy* 7.1; cf. 1 Sam 4:4; Is 6:2; Eph 1:21; Col 1:16; etc.

6   John refers here to the familiar Greek Patristic notion that Satan had been deceived by the apparent ordinariness of Jesus' humanity and had consumed him in death as his prize, only to discover that he was God and therefore immortal, and that his presence in the realm of the dead meant their liberation from his power. Cf., for instance, Gregory of Nyssa, *Catechetical Oration* 22-26. Even though Mary also truly died, in John's view she did not go down to the underworld as Jesus did, or even remain as long as he did in death's power, because of the victory of her Son.

7   John may be alluding here to the singing of the psalms and canticles, and to the candle-lit gathering before him, at the vigil liturgy. In the next sentences, however, he begins to describe the events of Mary's burial and glorification as if they were taking place before his hearers' eyes, thus moving their attention from the liturgical celebration to the drama of their imagination.

8   John here develops his reference to Mount Sion by mentioning all the significance the Temple Mount, especially the Western spur identified in late antiquity as "Sion," bears for Christian faith: as the traditional site of the "upper room," where Jesus ate the Last Supper with his disciples and appeared to them after his resurrection, and where the Holy Spirit descended at Pentecost; and as the place of Mary's residence in the final years of her life.

9   John includes in his evocation of the role of Sion a brief summary of orthodox Christological faith, as it had developed by the end of the seventh century; so he explicitly mentions, in the context of Jesus' resur-

rection appearances, his two complete natures and the two complete and operational wills they include.

10 This last sentence is very obscure in the Greek; the text, as contained in the manuscript tradition, may be defective here. My translation presupposes a reading of μηδενί at 732 D2. For the vocabulary of "descent" (κατιέναι) and "supreme being" (ὑπερεῖναι) in the works of Ps.-Dionysius—whose style seems clearly echoed here—see *De div. nom.* 5.5 (PG 3.820 B5), 5.8 (824 B4), 7.1 (865 B4), 11.6 (953 C8), 13.3 (981 A8); *Myst. theol.* 2 (PG 3. 1025 B7), 3 (1033 C2).

    Another hypothetical interpretation, represented by Michel Lequien's Latin translation in the *Patrologia Graeca*, might run as follows: "For there is not one being who did not join in this with a single accord—not even one of those beings who surpass all others and can be compared with none: all of them descended, and in descending they did as the others, and did not refuse to join in their activity." This seems, however, to do less justice to the Greek as it stands.

11 Once again John meditatively summarizes, in Dionysian language, the central paradoxes of Christian faith in the Incarnation, as the foundation of the honor given by the Church—and, in his view, by all creation—to Mary.

12 In the paragraphs that follow, John develops his dramatic depiction of the scene of Mary's death by composing speeches that might have been spoken by various groups of famous onlookers—a time-honored rhetorical exercise.

13 Here again the Greek is obscure and perhaps corrupt.

14 John is referring here to the saints of the Old Testament.

15 Note here John's caution in narrating his version of the apocryphal story of Mary's burial and glorification. He makes it clear to his hearers that the story is an imaginative projection of what "might" or "must have happened," given the understanding which faith has of Mary's importance in the whole economy of salvation. In the version he presents, Mary's soul first enters the glory of heaven by itself, and her body is "lifted up" from its sepulcher "on the third day" (see below, par. 14).

16 It is worth noticing that John does not presume to put words into the mouth of Jesus; what Mary "hears"—from an unspecified source—in response to her own words are all quotations from the Old Testament, appropriate to her inner and outer holiness.

17 John sees in Mary's entry into glory an event that sanctifies the whole of material creation; thus the four "elements" traditionally recognized by ancient physics—air, earth, fire and water—are all singled out here as made holy by her ascent, as is even Aristotle's hypothetical "fifth element," the fiery "ether" of which the heavenly bodies are composed.

18 John here presents Mary's entry into the "sanctuary" of heaven by a narrative reversing the Old Testament narrative of the ascent of the ark of God to its "resting place" on Mt. Sion (2 Sam 6:1-18; 1 Kg 8:1-6; Ps

132). Now Mary, the typological fulfillment of the ark, is carried down from the place of her death on Sion to her tomb at the foot of the Mount of Olives; it is from there that her real "ascent" to heaven begins.

19 Greek: ὑπόστασις.

20 John here plays on Solomon's name, which in Hebrew means "peace".

21 John shows extra diffidence here in recounting the story of the Jewish man who tried to obstruct Mary's funeral procession and who lost his hand in the process—a "spicy" detail included in all the apocryphal *Transitus Mariae* literature. John seems to regard it as at best intriguing gossip.

22 Literally, "abandoned him" (Greek: ἐκλελοιπέναι). Other accounts of the incident, as well as the later iconographic tradition, clearly suggest that the man's hands were severed from his body and adhered to the bier, but John seems to prefer to leave the picture somewhat vague.

23 John deftly draws a moral lesson from this rather lurid part of the narrative tradition.

24 In this section, John elaborates the Church's belief in Mary's immediate glorification at death by giving the only possible explanation: "it was fitting..."

25 This paragraph, up to the end of this sentence, was quoted by Pope Pius XII in *Munificentissimus Deus* (1950), the proclamation of Mary's glorification as a dogma of Christian faith.

26 Greek: ἑορτὴν ἐξόδιον.

27 John refers here to the orgiastic rites celebrated by Hellenistic Greeks and Romans, originally in Asia Minor and later throughout the Mediterranean world, in honor of Cybele, the "great mother of the gods". His purpose is to contrast pagan ritual and myth with this celebration in honor of the true Mother of God.

28 Iliad 5.341f.

29 John here alludes to the Niceno-Constantinopolitan creed, as once again he stresses the Mystery of Christ that is the foundation for celebrating Mary's glorification.

30 Having alluded to Greek cult and to Homer's view of the gods, and having followed the classical principles of rhetoric for religious hymns and celebratory discourses throughout his sermon, John is at pains here to underline the distinctively Christian character of the mystery he is commemorating.

31 Here John refers directly to the liturgical context of his three orations: apparently an all-night vigil service (πάννυχος στάσις) preceding the great celebration of August 15th.

32 John alludes here to a tradition going back to Philo (*De agricultura* 80; *De vita contemplativa* 87), which saw in the figure of Miriam a symbol of the prophetic power of virginity and ascetical purification. For a number of early Christian writers, Miriam's tambourine—making music out of dead and preserved skin—was itself a symbol of the effect

of purification: see Origen, *Hom. in Exod.* 6.1 (GCS Origen 6, 192.3-5);
Gregory of Nazianzus, Or. 4.12 (SCh 309, 102.6); Gregory of Nyssa, *De
virginitate* 19 (SCh 119, 484-488). For further details, see the note of
Michel Aubineau to this last-mentioned passage (SCh 119, 486f., n. 1);
J. Doignon, "Miryam et son tambourin dans la prédication et l'archéolo-
gie occidentales au IVe siècle," *Studia patristica* 4 (TU 79) 71-77.

33 By this somewhat unusual device of addressing Mary's tomb, John fo-
cuses his listeners' attention on the site at which her burial was venerated in Jerusalem—perhaps the site at which he was preaching—near
the Garden of Gethsemane. He also uses it to remind them of the absence
of relics of her body, one of the main pieces of evidence for her assumption into heaven. The tomb itself is thus allowed here to be the principal
witness for Mary's being taken up into glory.

34 At this point, all the manuscripts add, as the remainder of chapter 18, an
account of the bringing of Mary's funeral shroud as a relic to Church of
Blachernai in Constantinople in the fifth century—a narrative which
purports to be an excerpt from an otherwise unknown work called the
Euthymiac History. Another Greek version of the passage, in a Sinai
manuscript (Sin. 496, ff. 246v-251v) from the eighth or ninth century,
has been identified by Antoine Wenger, *L'assomption de la T. S. Vierge*
136-139. Michel van Esbroeck has also found and edited an Arabic
translation of the passage, from another Sinai manuscript: "Un témoin
indirect de l'Histoire Euthymiaque dans une lecture arabe pour l'Assomption," *Paroles d'Orient* 6-7 (1975-76) 479-481. The passage
seems to be part of a legendary anonymous life of the monastic founder,
St. Euthymius, the rest of which is now lost. In any case, all critics agree
that it is not part of John Damascene's sermon, but that it was apparently
added to his text within a century and a half of its composition (since the
oldest manuscript of the sermon, dated 890—Par. gr. 1470—already
contains it). The passage is translated below in Appendix I.

35 Here John deftly connects the Jerusalem tradition of pilgrimage to the
site of Mary's tomb—the place, presumably, where he is preaching—with the universal celebration of the feast, suggesting that the very
universality of the liturgical festival makes the grace experienced by
pilgrims at her tomb universally available.

36 Returning to the rhetorical genre of epideictic oratory, John concludes
his sermon with a moral exhortation. Mary is presented here as showing
the same concern for the behavior of all Christians that any mother
might display towards her grown children.

37 John expresses in a concrete way here the Church's faith in the "communion of saints": Mary is seen as personally present still in the community of the faithful, especially by her patronage of those who struggle
to live up to their faith and its moral demands.

A DISCOURSE ON THE DORMITION OF OUR LADY, THE MOTHER OF GOD

By John of Damascus, Monk and Presbyter

HOMILY III

1. It is the way of those who are consumed with love for something to have it always on their tongue, to have an image of it in their mind night and day. Let no one pass judgment on me, then, if I have composed this third eulogy in honor of the Mother of my God, a kind of funeral gift, in addition to the two that have gone before. It is no great favor to her, but for myself and for you who are gathered here before me, O holy and sacred assembly, I mean to serve a nourishing meal for the soul's health, appropriate for this holy night, and to provide spiritual joy for your hearts. We are usually faced with a dearth of nourishment, as you realize; so I am improvising a full-course banquet, and even if it is not very rich, or worthy of the invited company, at least it will have to be enough to satisfy our hunger. She, after all, stands in no need of our speeches of praise, but we do stand in need of the glory that comes from her (cf. Rom 3:23). How shall what is already glorious be glorified further? How shall the source of light be illumined? By what we do here, we weave a crown rather for ourselves. "For I live," says the Lord, "and I shall glorify those who glorify me." (2 Sam 2:30)

Wine is truly sweet to drink, and bread is a nourishing food. The one gladdens, the other strengthens the human heart (cf. Ps 104:15). But what is sweeter than the Mother of my God? She has captivated my mind; she has kidnapped my tongue! I gaze on her in my thoughts, waking or sleeping. She, who is the mother of the Word, has become the patron also of

231

my words; the offspring of a barren woman is the one who makes barren souls fruitful. Today we celebrate the sacred event of this woman's holy departure for heaven!

Come, then, let us approach the mystical mountain. Passing beyond the images of living, material things and into the holy darkness of incomprehensible realities,[1] let us enter the divine light and sing the praise of the power beyond all power. How has he, who came down from his super-essential, immaterial height, beyond all things, into a virgin's womb, without ever leaving the Father's heart; who was conceived and made flesh and who willingly walked the way of suffering to death; who has returned again to the Father with a body whose origin is from this earth, winning imperishability by perishing himself—how has he drawn his fleshly mother up to his own Father, and raised to the land of heaven the one who is called "heaven on earth"?

2. Today the spiritual, living ladder, by which the Most High has appeared on earth to "walk among human beings" (Bar 3.37), has herself climbed the ladder of death, and gone up from earth to heaven.

Today the earthly table, which without marital experience bore the heavenly bread of life, the coal of divinity, was lifted up from earth to heaven; for her, God's "gate towards the East" (Ezek 44:1f.; cf. Ps 24:7, 9), the gates of heaven are opened.

Today the living city of God is transported from the earthly Jerusalem to "the Jerusalem which is on high" (Heb 12:22); she who has brought forth, as her own first-born, "the first-born of all creation" (Col 1:15), the only-begotten of the Father (cf. Jn 1:14), now dwells in the "assembly of the first-born" (Heb 12:23). The living, spiritual ark of the Lord has "gone up to the resting-place" of her Son (Ps 131:8 [LXX]).

The gates of Paradise are opened, and welcome the field that bore God, where the tree of eternal life has grown, to put an end to the disobedience of Eve and the death imposed on Adam. This Christ, the cause of life for all people, welcomes the cave that has <not> been hollowed out[2]—the unquarried mountain, from whom, without help of human hands, that stone has been cut, which fills the universe (Dan 2:35, 45 [LXX]).

The bridal chamber of the Word's holy Incarnation has come to rest in her glorious tomb, as in her mansion; when she ascended to the shrine of her heavenly nuptials, to reign in public splendor with her Son and her God, she left her tomb as a bridal chamber for those who live on earth.[3] A tomb as a bridal chamber? Yes, and one much more splendid than every other bridal chamber, for it is radiant not with flickering gold or shining silver or brilliant gems, not with silken threads or cloth of gold and spun purple, but with the divine glory of the Holy Spirit. It offers not bodily contact for earthly lovers, but to those linked by bonds of the Spirit it offers the life of holy souls—a state better and sweeter in God's sight than any other.

This tomb is more lovely than Eden. I need not tell again what happened there—the "kindness" of our worst enemy, his "friendly advice" (if I may call it so!), his envy, his deceit, Eve's weakness, his persuasiveness, the sweet but bitter bait by which her mind was captivated and she captivated her husband's, their disobedience, their banishment, their death: if I tell the whole story, I shall turn our festival into a depressing occasion! But this tomb sent a mortal body from earth to heaven, while Eden brought the mother of our race down to the earth from on high. For was it not there that the one who had been made in God's image heard the sentence, "You are earth, and to earth you shall return" (Gen 3:19)?

This tomb is more precious than the tabernacle of old, for it contained the radiant, living lampstand, the table spread with life—holding not the showbread but the bread of heaven, not earthly fire but the immaterial fire of God.

This tomb is more richly endowed than the ark of Moses, for its treasure was not shadows and types, but truth itself. For it has displayed to us the vessel of purest gold, which bore the heavenly manna (Ex 16:33; Heb 9:4); the living table of stone, written on by the all-powerful finger of the Spirit, which received God's Word made flesh—the Word in his own substance; and the golden censer, which gave birth to the divine coal, spreading his fragrance through all creation.

3. Let the demons flee; let the thrice-wretched Nestorians cry out in pain as the Egyptians did of old, and with them their leader, the new Pharaoh, the cruel scourge, the tyrant! For they are buried in the depths of blasphemy. But we, who have been saved with our feet dry, who have walked across the salty sea of impiety—let us sing our song of Exodus to the Mother of God! Let the Church, as Miriam, raise the tambourine in her hands and begin the festal hymn! And let the young maidens of the spiritual Israel cry out loudly "with tambourines and choral songs" (Ex 15:20)!

Let the "kings of the earth, the judges and rulers, the lads and maidens, the old with the young" (Ps 148:11-12), all sing in praise of the Mother of God! Let there be gatherings and speeches of all kinds, let the diverse tongues of the nations and peoples strike up "a new song" (Ps 40:4; 149:1). Let the air resound with the reeds and trumpets of the Spirit, and inaugurate the day of salvation with flashes of fire! Rejoice, O Heavens (Ps 95:11), and "let the heavens rain down rejoicing"(Is 45:8)!

Leap, O rams of God's chosen flock, you holy Apostles, lifted like lofty mountain-tops by your sublime vision; and you, too, lambs of God, his holy people nourished by the Church and reaching up, in your desire, like foothills towards the mountains (cf. Ps 113:4, 6 [LXX])!

What a remarkable story! The source of life is dead, the mother of my Lord; for it was right that she who was formed of earth should go home to the earth again, and so rise from there to heaven, taking from the earth the pure life entrusted to it when her body was laid there to rest. It was right that her flesh should rise from the tomb, pure and incorruptible, having cast off the earthy, lusterless mass of mortality like gold in the crucible of death, and that she should shine with the brilliance of incorruption.

4. Today she receives the beginning of a new existence from the one who gave her the beginning of her former existence—she who gave the beginning of a second existence, in a body, to him who had no temporal beginning to his previous, eternal existence, even though he has the Father as the beginning and cause of his own divine being.

Rejoice, O Sion, holy mountain of God, where the living mountain of God dwelt: the new Bethel, where the stone of human nature was anointed by the oil of the divinity (cf. Gen 28:18). From you, she has been taken to the heights, as her Son went up from the Mount of Olives (Acts 1:9-12).[4] Let a cloud be made ready, to cover and embrace the whole world, and let the wings of the wind bring the Apostles from the ends of the earth to Sion. "Who are these, who fly like clouds" (Is 60:8) and eagles towards the corpse (cf. Mt 24:28) which, above all others, deserves to rise again? Who are these who come to venerate the Mother of God? "Who is this who goes up, as white as a flower," "all beautiful," resplendent "as the sun"? (Cant 8:5; 4.7; 6:10) Let the lyres of the Spirit sing—the tongues of the Apostles! Let the cymbals shout—the ringing bearers of God's word! Let the chosen vessel Hierotheos,[5] made holy by the Holy Spirit, who experienced and learned holy things by being united with the Holy One himself, be totally withdrawn from his own body in ecstasy; let him be wholly transported in his devotion, and strike up the festal hymns! "Let all the nations clap their hands" (Ps 47:2), let all sing the praise of the Mother of God! Let the angels bow in veneration before this mortal body! Daughters of Jerusalem, walk in procession behind the queen; virgins, young in the Spirit, come near her and be drawn with her towards the bridal chamber (cf. Ps 45:15), to place her "at the right hand of her Lord" (*ibid*. 10).

Come down, come down, O Lord, and pay your mother the debt you owe her, the return she deserves for having nourished you. Open your divine arms; receive your mother's soul, you who on the cross entrusted your own spirit into your Father's hands. Call to her in a gentle whisper, "Come, my beautiful one, my dear one (Cant 2:10; 4:7), you who in your virginity are more radiant than the sun. You gave me a share in what was yours; come, enjoy what is mine! Mother, come to your Son! Come, reign with him who became poor with you by being born from you!" (cf. 2 Cor 8:9) Go, mistress, go! Do not first go up, as Moses did, and then die (Deut 32:49f.), but die, and so go up! Place your soul in the hands of your own Son! Give what is made of earth to the earth, since that, too, will be raised up with you.

Lift up your eyes, O people of God—lift them up! Look! The ark of the Lord God of hosts is in Sion, and the Apostles stand bodily around her, paying final respects to the body that is our source of life, the vessel of God. Angels watch round her, too, in reverent fear, incorporeal, invisible, as servants assisting the Mother of their Lord. The Lord himself is there: he is present everywhere, he fills all things and watches over the universe, although no place is simply his, for all things are in him, as the cause who made and sustains them all. Behold the virgin, the daughter of Adam and Mother of God: because of Adam she commits her body to the earth, but because of her Son she gives her body to the heavenly tabernacle above. Let the holy city be blessed! Let it enjoy blessing upon blessing forever! Let the angels go before the holy tent as it passes on; let them prepare her tomb carefully! Let the radiance of the Spirit beautify it! Let perfumes be made ready, to anoint that wholly spotless, wholly fragrant body. Let a pure wave come and bathe it in blessings from the pure spring of blessing. "Let the earth rejoice" (Ps 96:11), as her body is laid to rest; let the air leap as her spirit ascends! Let the breezes blow, filled with grace as soft as dew! Let all creation celebrate the ascent of the Mother of God! Let choirs of youths cry out, let the tongues of orators flow with lyric praises, let the hearts of the wise reflect on the meaning of this wonder, let the elders—revered for age's white hairs—peacefully profit from what they have seen! Let every creature make its contribution to this festival, for even all of them together will not achieve a tiny fraction of the praise that is her due.

5. Come, let us all go forth from the world with her in spirit as she departs![6] Come, let us go down into the tomb with her, in the love of our hearts! Let us, too, surround that holy bier! Let us raise holy songs, in words such as these: "Hail, full of grace! The Lord is with you!" (Lk 1:28) Hail, you who were predestined to be Mother of God![7] Hail, you who were chosen before all ages by God's will, most holy shoot of the earth, vessel of the divine fire, sacred image of the Holy Spirit, spring of the water of life, paradise for the tree of life, living branch of the holy vine that flows with nectar and ambrosia, river filled with the perfumes of the Spirit, field of divine wheat, rose glowing with virginity and breathing the fragrance of grace, lily robed like a queen, ewe who gave birth to the Lamb of God who takes away the sin of the world, workshop of our salvation, higher than the angelic powers, servant and mother!

Come, let us surround that spotless tomb and let us drink of God's grace. Come, let us carry her ever-virgin body in the arms of our spirit, and let us, too, go within the sepulcher; let us die with her, leaving behind the weaknesses of our bodies and living a pure and passionless life with her. Let us listen to those divine hymns, coming forth from the immaterial lips of angels. Let us bow low and enter that tomb, and let us recognize the wonder of this mystery: she has been raised, she has been lifted up, she has been taken to heaven, she stands by her Son, above all the ranks of angels.[8] For there is nothing between mother and Son!

I have now finished a third funeral oration for you, as well as the first two, O Mother of God, in reverence and love of the Trinity which you served, when through the Father's pleasure and the Spirit's power you received the Word without beginning, the wisdom and power of God which can do all things. Receive my good will, then, which far surpasses my powers, and grant me salvation, freedom from my soul's weaknesses and relief from my body's ills, a solution to my crises, a peaceful state of life, and the enlightenment of the Spirit. Enkindle our love for your Son, make our lives pleasing to him, so that we may come to share in that blessedness on high, and may see you, radiant in the glory of your Son, and raise our holy songs in eternal rejoicing, in the assembly of those who keep a festival worthy of the Spirit for him who wrought our salvation through you: Christ, the Son of God and our God, to whom be glory and power, with the Father and the Holy Spirit, now and always and for ages of ages!

Amen.

1   John seems here to be alluding to the image of mystical knowledge of God as entering the darkness at the top of Mount Sinai, developed most fully by St. Gregory of Nyssa in his *Life of Moses*: see esp. *Vita Moysis* I, 46; 56; II, 152, 162-166, 169, 315.

2   The manuscripts omit a negative particle here which the context seems to require.

3   John now proceeds to develop a picturesque meditation on the religious significance of Mary's tomb, with the help of a number of familiar Old Testament images. His stress on her tomb, in this and the previous oration, suggests strongly that these sermons were originally delivered in the Church built on the site where it was venerated.

4   Here Mary's entry into heavenly glory is put in parallel with the Ascension of Jesus, just as it has been compared with his resurrection in the preceding paragraph. It is significant, perhaps, that the site venerated as the place of Jesus' ascension, near the top of the Mount of Olives, was only a short distance above that of Mary's death and glorification at the foot of the Mount.

5   See Ps.-Dionysius, *De div. nom.* 3.2, which seems to refer to the story of Mary's death as an already-established tradition. John here plays on the name "Hierotheos," which means "holy one of God".

6   As he reaches the conclusion of this third oration, John skillfully invites his hearers to see in their own liturgical celebration a re-enactment of Mary's obsequies, as narrated in the apocryphal accounts.

7   John inserts here a brief set of *chairetismoi* or festal acclamations, which again articulate a litany of bold poetic images for Mary, mainly drawn from the Song of Songs.

8   With carefully chosen words, John here makes it clear that the feast of the Dormition really is a celebration of Mary's resurrection from the dead; yet her role, like the verbs he uses, is wholly passive: her resurrection is a participation in the resurrection of Jesus.

CANON FOR THE DORMITION OF THE
MOTHER OF GOD
(*Tone IV*)

By John of Damascus

Ode 1[1]

I open my lips today:
Fill them, O Spirit, with energy
To utter this hymn to the Mother who governs us,
To cry out among the throng of those who praise her,
And join them in singing the wonders we celebrate!

Come, maidens and choristers,
Join with the prophetess Miriam
And raise up your voice in the song of her exodus;
For this virgin now, God's Mother, who is peerless,
Has come to the goal of her heavenward pilgrimage.

As heaven made womanly,
Heaven itself now has welcomed you
And leads you, most holy one, into its sanctuary;
There you stand beside the King in robes of splendor,
God's bride, without wrinkle or spot, for all ages.

Ode 3[2]

All those, Mother of God, who would acclaim you,
O living, undying spring of life,
You strengthen charismatically:
Give them the power to celebrate,
Crowning their minds with glory by
The holy touch of your memory.

Descended from mortals like your brethren,
You showed us an exodus from death,
A pathway supernatural;
Mother of Christ, the source of life,
You have now crossed death's barrier
To life divine, in reality.

Apostles, evangelists were gathered
Along with the angels from on high
To Sion's mount, your dwelling-place:
Brought at the nod of Providence—
Rightly, my Queen, and fittingly,
To join the rites of your funeral.

Ode 4[3]

Lord of highest heaven, your mysterious will
Stood before the ages: to come to us
Born of a virgin;
Holy Habakkuk exclaimed,
Full of prophetic clarity,
"Glory to your power and your goodness, Lord!"[4]

Shaken with amazement to see on the earth,
Raging through the valleys like animals,
Whirlwinds from heaven,
Living creatures of the King,
He cried, "How great your handiwork!"[5]
Glory to your power and your goodness, Lord!"

Taking you to heaven, O Mother of God,
Covering your holy and receptive, God-
Welcoming body
With their many-splendored wings,
Angelic hosts surrounded you,
Shielding you with radiant modesty.

Once her very offspring, mysterious God—
He of whom the heavens gave prophecy—
Died and was buried,
Sharing willingly our lot;
She, too, must share the sepulcher,
She who had conceived him in purity!

Ode 5[6]

The world is revivified,
Seeing your holy majesty;

You, unmarried mother, holy virgin,
Rise now above us, into your heavenly home,
Ascending to life without an end:
Grant to all who sing to you
Everlasting vitality.

Evangelists, waken us,
Sounding your trumpets joyfully!
Tongues of many nations, sing her praises,
Tell of her glory; let there be joy in the air,
And let it be radiant with light;
Angels, sing the mystery
Of the death of God's holy one.

O vessel of Providence,
Truly such praise is justified;
All of your virginity has risen,
Homeward to heaven, completely radiant with God:
For us, you are a source of holy light,
Holding and revealing God
As his mother most glorious.

Ode 6[7]

Come here, good friends, let us celebrate,
With all of God's own faithful and holy ones,
Mary's great festival;
Come, sing to Christ, who was born of her,
Clapping our hands to praise him:
Glory to both of them!

From you the flower of life sprang forth,
Not bursting the gates of your virginity;
Source of vitality,
How could your temple immaculate
Ever be made to share in
Death's dissolution?

You sheltered life as its sanctuary;
Now life without end is your inheritance,

Life is your dwelling-place.
Crossing this river mortality,
You who call life your offspring,
Share his eternity.

Ode 7[8]

When commanded not to adore him who created them,
Three sons of Israel
Chose, in their courage, to defy even furnaces,
Braving the fire, as they sang exultantly,
"Praised be the God of Abraham; may the Lord be
      blessed forever!"

Come, young men and gentle maidens, join the festival;
Honor that maiden, the
Mother of God today; come, elders and emperors,
Masters and magistrates, join our canticle:
"Praised be the God of Abraham; may the Lord be
      blessed forever!"

Let the mountains, in the Spirit, blow a trumpet-call,
Fanfares and flourishes;
Joyously dancing like the hills,[9] let the Apostles now
Leap in their revelry; let our banqueting,
Sacred to Mary's memory, fill this day with consolation.

For the wonderful transition of your Mother, the
Holy and spotless one,
Calls to our revelry heaven's company:
Angels and archangels join our festival,
Singing with us the canticle: "May our God be blessed
      forever!"

Ode 8[10]

The lads who were cast into the furnace
Were rescued by Mary's Son, who guides the universe—
Then by a prefiguring, now becoming flesh in her,
Waking the world to victory, inspiring anthems of praise;

O come, acclaim the works of the Savior,
And call him blessed forever and forever!

Your name, too, O spotless, holy Virgin,
The powers and principalities now celebrate,
Angels with the archangels, thrones and dominions all,
Cherubim, too, and seraphim, aglow with awe-struck,
    burning acclaim;
So we, mere men and women, dare praise you
And call you blessed forever and forever!

The one who mysteriously has entered
Within you, to take his flesh from your virginity,
He it is who welcomes you, taking your immaculate
Soul in his hands, embracing you—a loving, dutiful Son.
How justly we exalt you, holy Virgin,
And call you blessed forever and forever!

O marvel of marvels past all knowing:
God's mother and yet a virgin, you are wonderful!
Entering your sepulcher, you leave it as a paradise!
All who today are privileged to gaze in joy at that tomb
Acclaim her, and acclaim him who made her,
And call them blessed forever and forever!

Ode 9[11]

Come now, bring a torch, come join the festivity,
Sons of mortality;
Dance in exultation now, O race of spirits free of our
    history,
Acclaim the great transition of her who is Mother of God.
Let us greet her: "Hail to you, most holy One,
Virgin Mother of God for eternity!"

Come now to this shrine, this mountain of holiness,
Sion all-glorious;
Today let us celebrate, our faces shining with Mary's
    radiance!
For to a greater sanctuary, and to a holier tent

Christ now brings his tabernacle glorious—
To the temple in heaven's Jerusalem.

Come, people of God, draw near to this sepulcher
Filled with her memory;
Show it veneration with the lips, the eyes, the heart of
        fidelity,
And in sincere humility, let us now draw from this spring
Of God's healing, spiritual probity—
Let us drink of God's gifts at his mother's tomb.

Take from our hands this solemn processional,
Mother of mysteries!
Keep us in the shade of your protecting hand, from
        shadows deliver us;
And to our king give victory, to all your people give
        peace,
To us sinners, pardon and deliverance:
Bring us all to that bliss which we celebrate!

APPENDIX II:

*Metrical Pattern of John of Damascus,
Canon for the Dormition of the Mother of God*

Ode 1

```
  x / x x / x x
  / x x / x x / x x
x / x x / x x / x x / x x
x x / x x x / x x x / x
x / x x / x x / x x / x x
```

Ode 3

```
x / x x / x x x / x
x / x x / x x x /
x / x x x / x x
/ x x / x / x x
/ x x / x / x x
x / x / x x / x x
```

Ode 4

```
/ x x x / x x / x x /
/ x x x / x x / x x
  / x x / x
  x x / x x x /
  x x x / x / x x
/ x x x / x x / x x
```

Ode 5

```
  x / x x / x x
  / x x / x / x x
  / x x x / x x x / x
/ x x / x x x x / x x /
  x / x x / x x x /
  / x x x / x x
  x x / x x / x x
```

Ode 6

```
  x / x / x x / x x
  x / x x / x x x / x x
    / x x / x x
  / x x / x x / x x
  / x x / x / x
  / x x / x x
```

Ode 7

```
x x / x x x / x x x / x x
    / x x / x x
/ x x / x x x / x x / x x
/ x x / x x x x / x x
x x x / x / x x x x / x x x / x
```

Ode 8

```
  x / x x / x x x / x
  x / x x x x / x x x / x x
/ x x x / x x / x x x / x x
/ x x / x / x x x / x / x x /
  x / x x x / x x / x
  x x / x x / x x x / x
```

Ode 9

```
/ x x x / x / x x / x x
    / x x / x x
/ x x x / x x x / x / x / x x / x x
x x x / x / x x x x x / x x (/)
  x x / x / x x x / x x
  x x / x x / x x / x x
```

1 Traditionally, the first Ode of the night office in the Orthodox liturgy is the song of triumph sung by Moses and all Israel in Exodus 15:1-9. Thus John alludes here, in the second strophe, to Miriam's song.

2 Since the second ode of the office, Deut 32:1-43, was considered to have a penitential character, it was usually omitted outside of Great Lent. Thus most festal canons have no corresponding ode, but retain the numbering of those that follow. Ode 3 is the canticle of Anna, the mother of the prophet Samuel, in 1 Kg (1 Sam) 2:1-10.

3 This ode corresponds to the canticle of Habakkuk in Hab 3:2-19. The image of a storm in strophe 2 may be an allusion to Hab 3:6-10.

4 There is no exact equivalent to this phrase in the prophecy of Habakkuk; its nearest parallel is Hab 3:18f.: "I shall rejoice in God my savior; the Lord God is my power..."

5 Cf. Hab 3:2.

6 The Biblical ode corresponding to this section is Isaiah 26:9-20. Reference there, in vv. 14 and 19, to the reawakening of Israel's dead may be the inspiration for John's emphasis here on the universal hope of resurrection implied in Mary's entry into glory.

7 The corresponding Biblical ode is Jonah 2:3-10. The theme of that text, the rescue of the prophet from the depths of death itself, is echoed here.

8 The corresponding Biblical ode is the prayer of Azariah in Daniel 3:26-45 (LXX). John seems to conflate it with the Song of the Three Young Men, which follows both in the Septuagint version of Daniel and in the office.

9 The language here echoes Ps 113:4, 6 (LXX): "Then the mountains skipped like rams, the hills like lambs."

10 The corresponding Biblical ode is the Song of the Three Young Men in Daniel 3:52-88 (LXX).

11 The corresponding Biblical ode is a combination of the canticles of Mary and Zachary, the *Magnificat* and *Benedictus*, in Luke 1:46-55 and 68-79.

ENCOMIUM ON THE DORMITION OF OUR HOLY LADY, THE MOTHER OF GOD

By St. Theodore the Studite

1. To do justice to the holy celebrations proclaimed for today, my friends, our words call for the sound of the trumpet, for the voice of the horn sounding out more loudly and echoing to the ends of the earth; yet I fear they must be borne by the weak instrument of our own voices. Still, the queen and mistress of the world cares little for honor, and may well accept our short, poor discourse, offered here in her service, as graciously as the long and splendid works of great orators. For she is moved by the prayers of those who have asked me to speak, since she values true goodness, after all, and looks only at our intentions.

But come, gather around me, everyone under heaven—all you hierarchs and priests, monks and people of the world, kings and rulers, men and women, young men and maidens, of all nations and tongues, of every race and every people—change your clothes for the robes of virtue, wrap yourselves in them as in "bright garments fringed with gold" (Ps 44:13 [LXX]), and come with hearts rejoicing to celebrate the festival of the burial and the passing [into glory] of Mary, the Mother of the Lord. For she has gone away from here and draws near the eternal mountains, she who is the true Mt. Sion, where God was pleased to dwell, as the Psalmist's lyre sings (Ps 131:14 [LXX]). Today she who was heaven on earth is wrapped in a cloak of incorruptibility; she has moved to a better, more blessed dwelling-place. Today the spiritual moon, shining with the light of God, has come into heavenly conjunction with the "sun of righteousness," eclipsing her temporary home in this present life; rising anew in his home, she is radiant with the dignity of immortality. Today that ark of holiness, wrought with gold and divinely furnished, has been lifted up from her tabernacle on earth and is borne towards the Jerusalem above, to unending rest; and David, the ancestor of God, poet as he is, strikes up a song for us and cries, "Virgins"—meaning souls—"will be led to the King"—to you, O God—"behind her" (Ps 44:14 [LXX]).

2. Now the Mother of God shuts her material eyes, and opens her spiritual eyes towards us like great shining stars that will never set, to watch over us and to intercede before the face of God for the world's protection. Now those lips, moved by God's grace to articulate sounds, grow silent, but she opens her [spiritual] mouth to intercede eternally for all of her race. Now she lowers those bodily hands that once bore God, only to raise them, in incorruptible form, in prayer to the Lord on behalf of all creation. At this moment her natural form, radiant as the sun, is hidden; yet her light shines through her painted image, and she offers it to the people for the life-giving kiss of relative veneration,[1] even if the heretics are unwilling. The holy dove has flown to her home above, yet she does not cease to protect those below; departing from her body, she is with us in spirit; gathered up to heaven, she banishes demons by her intercession with the Lord.

Long ago, death took charge of the world through our ancestor Eve; but now it has engaged in combat with her blessed daughter and been beaten away, conquered by the very source from whom it had received its power. Let the race of women rejoice, then, for it has received glory in place of shame! Let Eve be glad, for she is under a curse no more, having produced in Mary a child of blessing. Let the whole of creation jump for joy, drinking the mystical flood of incorruption from that virgin spring and putting an end to its mortal thirst. These are the things we celebrate today, this is the subject of our solemn song: Mary provides it for us—the root of Jesse who bore the flower Christ; the rod of Aaron with its sacred bud; the spiritual Paradise containing the tree of life; the meadow alive with the fragrance of virginity; the blooming vine, cultivated by God, which became the ripe grape flowing with life; the high, exalted cherubim-throne of the universal king; the home full of the glory of the Lord; the sacred veil of Christ; the bright land of sunrise. She has fallen asleep in peace and righteousness—fallen asleep, I say, but she is not dead! She has passed on from us, yet she does not cease to protect her people.

With what language should we speak of your mystery? We are incapable of conceiving it, too weak to describe it, too stunned to write of it; it is strange, sublime, above all human thoughts! For it is not as if it could be included or compared with other events, so that we could make easy explanations, drawing from our own experience; but receiving reverently from above what we have learned about you, we ascribe to you alone privileges beyond what is human! By that ineffable act of generation, you have transformed nature; for who has ever heard of a virgin conceiving without seed? O wonder! See, now: the mother giving birth is also still an incorrupt virgin, because God was the cause of her conceiving! So in your life-giving sleep, since you are different from all the rest, you alone have rightly found incorruption for both [body and soul].

3. Let Sion, then relate the miraculous events of this day. The measure of her life was finished; the hour of her dissolution had come. Because she was Mother of God, the holy one knew in advance the course of her passing—friends of Christ, in comparison with any other seer who serves the Lord, could one not ascribe this knowledge all the more to the Mother of God and chief of prophets? And since she perceived and knew this, what may our minds imagine that she said? "The day of my Exodus has come, the time of my journey to you. Let those

who will celebrate my burial come, O Lord; let the ministers who will carry out my funeral stand at my side. 'Into your hands I commend my spirit' (Ps 30:5 [LXX]), but into the hands of your disciples I commit my unsullied body, God's vessel, from which you came forth as the rising sun of immortality. Let those who are scattered to the earth's ends, the heralds and servants of your Gospel, come near to console me. And if it was your good pleasure to transfer the just Enoch (to heaven), while still alive, in his time of need (see Gen 5:24), or to raise up Elijah the Tishbite in a fiery chariot from this visible world to a place unseen (2 Kg 3:11), where both of them await the time of your awful and splendid second coming; if you worked the miracle of transporting the prophet Habakkuk from Jerusalem to Babylon in an instant because of the needs of Daniel, and then back again ("Bel and the Dragon" [Dan 12] 33-39)—what can be impossible to the mere act of your will?"

When the celebrated one had said such things, the apostolic band of Twelve appeared, borne from every direction on the wings of the Spirit, like clouds rushing towards the cloud of light, and coming to rest near her. What did she say then, that woman whose names are so many, so great and so divine? As she lay in her bed, she raised her eyes and looked around, and seeing those she had sought for, she said: "My soul rejoices in the Lord, and this will be a title of rejoicing for me, a cause of praise and exultation among all nations of the earth: for he has gathered the pillars of the Church around me here, he has brought together for me the rulers of the universe, as the wondrous ministers of my funeral. O great and marvelous sign! O proof of a mother's sanctification! O gift of a Son's devotion! Heaven has been revealed as my home, for it contains in itself all the bright lights of earth; the Lord's temple above us has appeared, presenting to me these holy celebrants, these priests of the sacred rites. The Jewish establishment will no longer plan violence against me; the council of their priests will no longer prepare armed assaults against me, hoping to kill me. For according to their scheme, those bloodthirsty people would have destroyed the Mother with the Son long ago, but they failed in their plan because Providence prevented them from on high. Now I go from here to a safe dwelling-place, to a place of security, peace and rest, where the enemy will no longer lay his snares, where I will see the delights of the Lord and where I, who am myself his radiant temple, will gaze upon his temple [in heaven]."

4. But this is what the blessed Apostles answered to her, either speaking on their own or quoting the words of the prophets:[2]

(1) "Hail," one said, "ladder set up from earth to heaven, on which the Lord came down to us and returned to heaven again, as in the vision of the great patriarch Jacob (Gen 28:12)!

(2) "Hail, miraculous bush where the angel of the Lord appeared in flames of fire, where the flame burned without consuming, as Moses realized, who alone saw God face to face (Ex 3:2)!

(3) "Hail, fleece moistened by God, from which a basinful of heavenly dew flowed forth, according to Gideon, that worker of wonders (Jg 6:37-8)!

(4) "Hail, city of the great king, which all the admiring sovereigns praised, according to David the psalmist (Ps 47:2,5 [LXX])!

(5) "Hail, spiritual Bethlehem, house of Ephratha, 'from whom the glorious king came forth who was to become ruler of Israel, and whose goings-forth were from the beginning, from eternal days,' according to the divine Micah (Mic 5:2)!

(6) "Hail, shady mountain of virgins, from which the holy one of Israel appeared, according to Habakkuk, whose proclamation was divine (Hab 3:3)!

(7) "Hail, shining golden lamp radiating light, from which

the inaccessible light of God has shone out on those in darkness and the shadow of death, according to the inspired Zechariah (Zech 4:2; Lk 1:79)!

(8) "Hail, altar of purification for all mortal creatures, through which 'the Lord's name is glorified among the pagans from the rising of the sun to its setting,' and where 'a sacrifice is offered to his name in every place,' according to the holy Malachi (Mal 1:11)!

(9) "Hail, 'light cloud where the Lord dwells,' according to Isaiah, who spoke the most sacred things (Is 19:1)!

(10) "Hail, holy book of the Lord's commands, newly-written law of love, through which we can know what pleases God, according to the mournful Jeremiah (Jer 25:13; 38:33 [LXX])!

(11) "Hail, locked gate, through which the Lord God of Israel comes in and out, according to Ezekiel, who gazed on God (Ezek 44:2)!

(12) "Hail, unquarried mountain-peak, higher than human hands, from which that rock was cut which became the corner-stone, according to Daniel, that great teacher about God (Dan 2:45; Ps 117:22)!"

5. What mind can receive, what speech can do justice to what those teachers of divine truth sang and said, and to how they blessed God? But when they performed all the appropriate sacred rites in a sacred way, when they had completed the holy ceremonies in holy fashion, suddenly the Lord was there among them in all his glory, with all the hosts of heaven. The bodiless spirits celebrated their invisible liturgy, while the Apostles used their bodily voices to sing the praises of God's greatness. The heavenly rejoicing mingled with the earthly feast, my brothers and sisters (and let no one be shocked by our attempt to describe these divine mysteries): angels, archangels, dominations, thrones, principalities, powers, virtues,

cherubim and seraphim, apostles, martyrs, holy men and women, some walking ahead, some coming to meet them, some leading or acting as advance guard, some following or walking alongside, all crying out in one joyful voice, "Sing to the Lord, praise the Lord! Blessed be the Lord on his righteous and holy mountain (see Ps 47:1 [LXX])! Let heaven be raised on high!" Who has ever heard, from all eternity, such a funeral hymn, O friends of Christ? Who has ever seen such a burial procession? Who has ever witnessed such a passing as this, which was accorded to the "Mother of my Lord" (Lk 1:43)? And it is not undeserved, since no one has ever been judged higher than she, who is greater than all others.

My spirit trembles when it reflects on the greatness of your passing, O Virgin; my mind is struck dumb with amazement as it considers the wonder of your falling-asleep. My tongue is held fast, when it tries to recount the mystery of your return to life. For who is the person who can worthily express your praise, who can narrate all your wonders? What mind can find words lofty enough to speak in your honor? What tongue can utter words grand enough, can speak of your goodness, can make your deeds come alive, can do justice to your life in human speech or approach your wonders in sacramental mysteries, celebrations, feasts, narrative or festal oratory? So, too, in this present festival our words are weak, lifeless, inaccurate, obviously off the mark. For you are beyond us, you exceed our powers; you incomparably surpass in height and greatness the summit of heaven, in holy brilliance the light of the sun, in the full realization of freedom the ranks of angels and all the immaterial, spiritual race of intellectual powers.

6. O, what a radiant, brilliant festival! It is only joy that lets me speak at all! O great sign of your passing, moving us to wonder! O burial of the bearer of light, life and the gift of endless incorruption! As you rise through the clouds on your way

to heaven, as you enter the holy of holies with cries of joy and praise, O Mother of God, remember to bless the bounds of this earth. By your intercession temper the air, give us rain in due season, rule over the winds, make the earth fruitful, give peace to the Church, strengthen orthodox faith, defend the Empire, ward off the barbarian tribes, protect the whole Christian people. And have pity, too, on my rashness; for it is but the fulfillment of your word, O Mother of God, of your prophetic incantation, that "henceforth," as you said, "all generations will call me blessed" (Lk 1:48). Since your inspired word cannot have been spoken in vain, receive the words that I, your unworthy servant, have uttered as best I can. And "give me the joy of your salvation" (Ps 50:14), support me with the strength of your intercession, along with my excellent Father[3] here and with this, the flock under his care, in Christ Jesus our Lord, to whom be glory and honor and power, with the almighty Father and the life-giving Spirit now and always and for the ages of ages.

Amen

1   Theodore is clearly alluding to the veneration by the faithful, in the place where he is preaching, of an icon depicting Mary's Dormition. "Relative veneration" (σχετικὴ προσκύνησις) is a term used elsewhere by Theodore and his contemporaries for the kind of veneration properly due to icons, as opposed to the adoration (λατρεία) due God alone: see Theodore the Studite, Epist. 2.85 (PG 99.1329A); *Antirrhetikos* 1.20 (PG 99.349C); cf. *ibid.* 1.12 (344C), on the "relative" identity of the icon with its subject.

2   Theodore now presents, as coming from the assembled Apostles, a series of acclamations (χαιρετισμοί) to Mary, which apply to her twelve familiar images from the Old Testament—a poetic technique familiar from the earlier *Akathistos* hymn in praise of the Mother of God.

3   Theodore seems to be preaching in the presence of a major bishop, perhaps even of the Patriarch of Constantinople. During an important period in Theodore's time as hegumen of the monastery of Studios, this was St. Nikephorus I (806-815).

Index

A

Adam, 61, 160, 186, 207, 212, 233, 237

Alexandrian theology, 11

Anastasius, Patriarch of Constantinople, 19

Andrew of Crete, Saint, 16-19, 21, 28f., 30, 32

angel(s), 50, 93, 112, 245; announces news of coming death to Mary, 49f., 169f.; carry her to heaven, 196, 215, 242; at death and burial of Mary, 85, 92, 97, 195, 211, 236f., 254

Anna, mother of Mary, 72, 105, 188f.

anti-Chalcedonian Christology, 10

Antiochene theology, 11

aphthartists, 10

apocrypha of Dormition, 7f., 22, 30, 48

apokatastasis (universal salvation), 19

Apollo, Sminthiac, hymn to, 34

Apostles: gathering for Mary's death, 48, 55, 57, 92f., 130, 165, 172, 174, 194, 197f., 210, 235f., 242, 252, 254; John, 53, 56, 175, 178; at Mary's funeral, 94-97, 137-145, 174, 194, 197f., 212f., 215; Paul, 55, 175f., 196; Peter, 55f., 58, 61, 65f., 171, 176, 178, 225; speeches and oratory, 34, 58, 211f., 234; Thomas, 209

Assumption of Mary, bodily, 14, 31, 74, 76, 114, 177, 195, 218, 237, 242f., 255; entry of soul into heaven, 109f., 170, 187, 196, 198, 206, 216; fittingness of, 23, 31, 158, 206, 218f.; honor of Son to Mother, 187, 194; rejoicing of angels and saints, 208, 255; repayment by Christ of his debt to her, 171; resurrection from grave, 100, 110, 169, 235; reunion of Mother and Son, 174; terminology, 27f.; vision of Son and Holy Spirit, 171

B

Basil of Seleucia, 3

beauty: of Christ, 144; of festival, 111; of heaven, 120; of Mary, 30, 157; of Mystery of Dormition, 106

Benedictus, 123

Bethlehem, 4, 253

bier of Mary, 64, 66, 99, 113, 133, 138, 176, 208

Blachernai,Church of, 37, 224, 226

body of Mary, 66, 133, 138, 146, 176, 199

Breviarius de Hierosolyma, 40

burial of Mary, 67, 75, 98, 143, 146, 197-199, 217, 236, 242. *See also* death of Mary

C

canon for Dormition (John of Damascus), 241-246; metrical pattern, 247

canon (liturgical hymn), 16, 24

Chalcedon, Council of, 4, 6f., 11, 224; definition of, 112, 186

Christ: death of, 194; descent into Hades, 119; person of, 11f., 15, 91, 96, 112, 186, 209, 220; took flesh from Mary, 159; victor over death and Hades, 101, 117f.

Chrysippus of Jerusalem, 3

Church, the, 87, 108

Church of Constantinople, 20

Churches in honor of Mary, 4, 37, 41

Index of Scriptural References

POPULAR PATRISTICS SERIES

ST VLADIMIR'S SEMINARY PRESS
1-800-204-2665 • www.svspress.com